Women
in Green

Voices of Sustainable Design

KIRA GOULD & LANCE HOSEY

ECO*tone* ᴸᴸᶜ
publishing company

ECOtone LLC

www.ecotonedesign.com

Ecotone LLC

3187 Point White Drive NE

Bainbridge Island, WA 98110

Authors: Kira Gould and Lance Hosey

Book Design: Erin Gehle

Edited by: Fred McLennan

Library of Congress Control Number: 2007922859

Library of Congress Cataloging-in Publication Data

ISBN 978-0-9749033-7-8

1. Architecture   2. Environment   3. Women's Studies

First Edition

Printed in Canada on Rolland Enviro 100 – 100 percent Post-Consumer Waste Fiber, Processed Chlorine-Free, using Soy-Based Ink.

for Rachel Carson (1907-1964) and Jane Jacobs (1916-2006)

ECOTONE AND *WOMEN in GREEN*

Ecotone Publishing is dedicated to seeking out and publishing works on important subjects that are vital to the present and future of sustainable design. To this end, we commissioned Kira Gould and Lance Hosey to explore the connections between gender and sustainability. Throughout their months of research and writing they demonstrated a thoughtfulness and a passion for the subject that honors the inspirational work and the pervading spirit of the people in *Women in Green*. It was our pleasure to work with these two talented writers and dedicated professionals in the creation of this important and timely book. The profound ideas and wisdom they have documented should serve as inspiration for us all. Ecotone is proud to present *Women in Green*.

COLOPHON

Reflecting the environmental ethos of Ecotone, we selected environmentally-responsible materials for the production of this book. Rolland Enviro 100 paper is manufactured from 100 percent Post-Consumer Waste Fiber (PCW), is Processed Chlorine Free (PCF) and uses biogas energy in its production in order to reduce emissions that lead to the depletion of the ozone layer. Rolland Enviro 100 saves the harvesting of mature trees, reduces solid waste from entering landfill sites, uses 80 percent less water than conventional paper manufacturing, and helps to reduce air and water pollution. Ecotone also chose soy-based black ink to complement the paper selection. Compared to petroleum inks, soy-based inks release less than 20 percent of the mass of volatile organic chemicals and are more readily recycled.

For more information on Ecotone Publishing, please visit www.ecotonedesign.com or call 250.274.4444

The challenge is to give
back to our children a
world of beauty and wonder.

WANGARI MAATHAI

Another world is not only
possible, she is on her way.
I can hear her breathing.

ARUNDHATI ROY

TABLE OF CONTENTS

ACKNOWLEDGEMENTS

We asked architect Gail Lindsey what she thought this book might offer. "The energy of all these people," she told us. "What a gift!" While writing this book, we received the gifts of many great people, and we are grateful to all of them for their time and energy. In particular:

Mark Rylander, for introducing us
Jason F. McLennan, for asking us
Tammi Wright, for assisting us
Marc L'Italien and Tess Taylor, for giving us feedback
Erin Gehle, for giving us shape
Mary Rowe, for challenging us
Sally Helgesen, for educating us
Dianne Dillon-Ridgley, for embracing us
and Janine Benyus, for inspiring us

LANCE: To my family and to Michelle Amt, Amy Ogden, Dana Bourland, Sydney Hamilton, Jill Salisbury, Heidi Hackford, and especially Tatjana Vichnevsky, I owe heartfelt thanks. You all made a big difference. To Kira, I owe my awe. You are a force of nature. "Slime mold is cool!" And to my late mother, Anna, I owe anything worthwhile I might have to say. I miss you, Mom.

KIRA: To my family and my friends, I owe my thanks for your time and tolerance. My debt is greatest to Michael Ebeid, who lived this book so intimately, as it changed his wife and life. To Lance, I owe gratitude for your willingness to take a chance on this wondrous journey—of mind, heart, and body—and for the friendship that resulted. And to all the people whose names I do not know who are living, learning, and working toward a sustainable tomorrow, you have my respect and thanks.

IT'S TIME
BY DIANNE DILLON-RIDGLEY

It was one of those debilitating snow storms that are infrequent but can really wallop Washington, DC. By switching airlines a few times, I had made it from Raleigh/ Durham on what turned out to be the last flight to land at Washington National. It was a Saturday night. I eventually completed the usually forty minute drive to my friends' home after almost three hours of inching along well-known but deeply snow-covered roads whose lights were dark from the storm. I was almost to the driveway before sliding off the road—my car was stuck in a muddy bank of snow. The next day, after this cold welcome to Washington, I met Kira and Lance for the first time. Almost everything was closed, but we decided to try anyway. Adjustments, changes, detours, a tow, some brief sunlight, two or three darkened restaurants; we finally sat down to talk for an hour or so. Five hours later, we had covered a good part of the sustainability universe.

I see our meeting as a good metaphor for the path of sustainability. We are mostly female (two of three), mostly young (two of three). We encounter obstacles and some sudden roadblocks, but we go on creating solutions, making adjustments, charting a new path. We are determined, despite all the deterrents—a stubborn lot, because we must be.

So, why women and sustainability? Look throughout history and mythology. It relates to being a mother with a sick child—vomiting, diarrhea, the works—it's not glamorous. The mess won't go away and clean itself. You take a deep breath and get busy caring for your child. It's not that fathers cannot or do not. Many do. But the world over, for centuries, caring is what mothers and all women have done. And this is true of the women leading change now. The mess is there. We are the mothers and midwives of this twenty-first century effort to care for our world. As we said in 1991, when more than 1,500 women and "non-women" from eighty-three countries gathered in Miami at the World Women's Congress for a Healthy Planet: "It's time to mother earth."

If we look historically at the early voices, bold and often scorned, we see true "*she*roes." For so many of us it was Rachel Carson, whose clarity, poetry, and chilling imagery informed and inspired us—and continues to today. There are others who would be pleased with this book but impatient with our pace of progress. They are gone, too soon—Dana Meadows, Jean Sindab, and especially for me, Bella Abzug. A former Congresswoman, Bella turned her attention again and again to women's issues worldwide. Working on the Rio Earth Summit (1992), she realized the absence and exclusion of women's voices had resulted in impoverished programs. And five years earlier it was Gro Harlem Brundtland, then Prime Minister of Norway, who chaired the commission that bears her name and coined the concept of sustainable development. Fast forward a dozen years and we have what may be the pinnacle of *she*roes tending earth—Wangari Maathai receiving the 2004 Nobel Peace Prize for founding Africa's Green Belt Movement. How moving it was to be there with my friend in Oslo forty years after Martin Luther King accepted the same award. It was historic to witness the Nobel Committee recognizing the connection between peace and environmental sustainability.

These pages tell many stories of those who, like me, are blessed to labor in these fields—to be friends and colleagues with so many incredible women and men working for the future, not only of my children, Karima and Dasal, but also for my grandchildren yet unborn and for so many generations to come; that they may have a world to enjoy even more beautiful, abundant, vibrant, and healthy than the one into which I was born half a century ago.

PREFACE

WHY WOMEN?

We began research for this book with little more than an instinct about how to answer that question. While we didn't yet understand all the important connections between women and sustainability, we were convinced that those connections exist. Still, there was the vague worry that this subject was either too broad to address effectively or too narrow to contribute to a wider dialogue about sustainable design. So we started asking questions. A lot of questions.

Some people told us the topic was passé. "Who talks about the sexes anymore?" (No matter that while we were writing, Celinda Lake and Kellyanne Conway's *What Women Really Want* and Maureen Dowd's *Are Men Necessary?* came out and sold big.) Others were amused. "What the heck does being female have to do with sustainable design?" asked a female architect in a respected sustainable design firm. "The topic makes me nervous. What comes to mind are images of mother earth goddesses dancing naked around a cauldron, waving T-squares in the air. Being a chick is irrelevant." Still, we asked more questions.

Some people we respect declined to discuss the book or said the topic had no interest for them. People close to people we respect said they should avoid us: "They want to marginalize you. What's more important? Your gender or your accomplishments?" An accomplished university professor put it this way: "I want to be known as a great educator in architecture, not a great *woman* educator." Nevertheless, she was generous with her time, and her input was invaluable. So we kept asking questions.

As it turned out, surprisingly few people challenged the subject, even if we didn't fully describe it. Most opened up immediately, and many told us this book should have been written years ago. Though that sentiment was encouraging, no one completely explained it. (One successful woman told us this publication would "provide inspiration for young women," while another said we should write it "so that young men read it." Who was our audience?) We listened to everyone and read between the lines.

Along the way, we learned that there are profound links between women and the environment. Consider the results of recent surveys:

- Polls consistently show that women are up to 15 percent more likely than men to rate the environment a high priority.
- In political elections, women comprise up to two thirds of voters who cast their ballots around environmental issues.
- Women are more likely than men to volunteer for and give money to environmental causes, especially those related to health and safety within their own communities.
- Women report both more support for environmental activists and more concern that government isn't doing enough to protect the environment.
- More women than men support increased government spending for the environment, while more men favor spending cuts.
- Women tend to be less lenient toward business when it comes to environmental regulation.

Sources: Yale School of Forestry, American Progress Action Fund, Institute for Women's Policy Research, and American National Election Study

What's more, according to pollsters Lake and Conway, an estimated 68 percent of American consumers have gone green, choosing health-conscious and environmentally responsible lifestyles and products. Since 90 percent of women identify themselves as the primary shoppers for their households, and women sign 80 percent of all personal checks, it's safe to say that women are leading a quiet revolution in green consumerism.

If there are links between women and the environment, what do these links suggest about the sustainable design movement? "My impression is that there is a greater percentage of women active within the green building field than in design generally," says industry insider Bill Browning, formerly of the Rocky Mountain Institute. "There is a noticeable difference between going to Greenbuild [the U.S. Green Building Council's annual conference] and the AIA [American Institute of Architects] convention." Facts support the impression that women are drawn to green design. Currently, the percentage of women involved in the AIA Committee on the Environment (COTE) is nearly double the percentage of women in the AIA overall. In COTE leadership roles at the national, regional, and local levels, the presence of women is even greater. And the percentage of women on the 2006 board of directors of the USGBC triples the percentage on the AIA's board.

A brief review of the history of environmentalism and sustainable design and development reveals that from the beginning many women—some heralded and some not—have had unique contributions to this field.

- The modern environmental movement began with a book by a woman (p. 19).
- The most popular definition of sustainability comes from a commission led by a woman who is also a strong advocate of gender equity (pp. 34,79).
- The first person to use the word "sustainability" with its current connotation was a woman (p. 34).
- Women were instrumental in the preservation and conservation movements in the U.S. as early as the mid-nineteenth century (p. 11).
- Some of the most important early proponents of systems thinking were women (pp. 139-140).
- The popular biomimicry movement was spawned by an influential book by a woman (p. 158).
- The first woman president of the American Institute of Architects was also the first to herald sustainable design as the primary mission of the organization during her tenure (p. 54).

Are these facts coincidental, or does sustainable design have some special appeal for women? Do they in turn have something unique to offer this field? These are the questions we set out to ask.

What of the worry that focusing on women as women could diminish their accomplishments? "That's ridiculous," says influential business writer Sally Helgesen. "When you shine the light on a population that has not been in the mainstream, you are met with this fear. But when similar books have been written about men, they're not seen to marginalize them. The argument implicitly assumes that nothing about focusing on women will have wider applicability. Maybe there's something here that everybody can learn from."

Something everybody can learn from—that's what we hope this book offers.

Why women? Keep reading.

Listen to the land.
Now find home.

LISTENING

On the morning of November 9, 2005, while we were in Atlanta interviewing a group of women about sustainability, Interface chairman Ray Anderson was down the street telling an audience that the future of sustainability will depend on women:

> A new day dawning will build on the ascendancy of women in business, the professions, government, and education. This is one of the most encouraging of all trends, as women bring their right-brained, nurturing nature to bear on the seemingly intractable challenges created by left-brained men and their pre-occupation with bottom lines and other "practical" considerations. After all, it's the practical and pragmatic that got us into this mess. Surely, a different kind of thinking is needed to get us out.

What exactly does Anderson mean by "the ascendancy of women"? The word choice is intriguing, for *ascendancy* doesn't just mean "rise"—it implies a social or political relationship ("when one person or group has power over another"). Is this respected industry leader talking about a cultural revolution? We asked him.

> Twelve years ago, it was women who starting asking what our company is doing for the environment, and there are increasing numbers of women in business. Men are more likely to accept business as usual, but women are more likely to push us to do more. It's not so much that they're women—it's the point of view they bring. Men, if they try hard enough, can bring that point of view themselves. It's the soft side of business we're talking about. But there are a lot of women in business who are trying to be like men, which is a pity. If they forsake their nurturing nature, we all lose.

This "nurturing nature," the "soft side of business"—do women really have a particular "point of view"? If so, is it inherent or learned, and is it proven or merely perceived?

SEX ON THE BRAIN

Anderson calls men "left-brained" and "practical" and women "right-brained" and "nurturing." Studies of brain functions do show that the left hemisphere controls logic and processes data in a linear sequence, while the right side, responsible for emotion, handles information in a more complex and varied way. Popular references to left/right brain often characterize the split as objective and analytical on one side and subjective and holistic on the other. Because ecology teaches that all things are subtly intertwined, a "right brain" disposition would seem compatible with sustainable design, which emphasizes relationships over things. As Gail Vittori of the Center for Maximum Potential Building Systems puts it, "Think of buildings not as objects but as networks or systems." John Eberhard, founder of the Academy of Neuroscience for Architecture, has written about the connections between brain theory and sustainable design. "The left brain is calculating, communicative, and able to conceive and execute complicated plans. The right brain is gentle, emotional, and more at one with the natural world—probably important to those who believe in 'green' architecture." If there is a link between "right-brain" thought and women, do they bring something special to sustainable design—a "different kind of thinking," as Anderson puts it?

The brain is "a logical place to look for gender differences," writes Deborah Blum, Pulitzer-winning author of *Sex on the Brain: The Biological Differences Between Men and Women*. "This idea is based on a somewhat controversial theory that, although the brains of men and women look alike, we use them very differently. Specifically, the theory says men are more 'lateralized'; they rely on one hemisphere or the other in doing a task. By comparison, in this argument, women use both." The idea is backed up by recent studies at Johns Hopkins, Yale Medical School, and other institutions, but what does it suggest about a possible women's "point of view"? Rita Carter explains in *Mapping the Mind*. "Because men's brains are more localized, if they are asked to do a problem, they will bring to bear on that problem very precise and localized brain skills. For example, if they are asked to do a complicated problem involving mathematics, they will just use that bit of the brain which has evolved to do mathematics. Women might use the visual part of their brain to visualize the problem or will pull on memories to help them solve the problem. They have a more creative or lateral way of thinking, whereas men tend to be more incisive and logical." Physiologically, women have more cross-wiring between the hemispheres, so their thoughts and memories are likely to touch down on the emotional areas of the brain.

NATURE AND NURTURE

Whether these distinctions are scientific fact or popular perception doesn't matter, according to Blum, because "as much as we try to separate them, biology and culture aren't mutually exclusive. They can't be. Our questions about the role of nature versus nurture form a circle in which one influence feeds the other and around it comes again.... In this loop, biology is most important as a starting place. But how do you figure out where a circle begins?" Some believe this chicken-and-egg riddle is revealed in childhood play. Is it sex (a biological designation) or gender (a cultural perception) that leads many girls to care for baby dolls and play cooperative games while boys wield toy guns and compete in aggressive contact sports? Regardless of the source, experts claim such habits instill in girls and women a focus on developing long-term relationships and, in boys and men, a tendency toward short-term fulfillment and self-gratification.

In *The Female Advantage: Women's Ways of Leadership,* her "diary study" of influential women in business, Sally Helgesen maintains that cultural impressions of how men and women think and behave are more relevant than scientific evidence because they affect how people view each other—and themselves. "Our belief in these notions is intuitive rather than articulated; we back it up with anecdotes instead of argument. Some women feel ashamed of their belief in feminine principles; some are scoffing, others proud, even defiant." *Natural Capitalism* co-author L. Hunter Lovins has her own anecdote about anecdotes. "I keep hearing from male business leaders that the presence of women in the room, their energy, makes a difference in the outcome. I don't know what that means, but I keep hearing it." This kind of personal testimony is fundamental to women's ways of interacting. As ecologist Sandra Steingraber reminds us, the most important lesson of feminism is "the authority of one's own experience." By celebrating individual experiences, a more "feminine" point of view can help sustainable design respect the differences between people. Industrial designer Amelia Amon writes, "Although there is no universal women's value system, that we are seen as less hierarchical, more contextual, and more influenced by relationships and compassion can encourage us to bring these attributes to bear in a world that needs them."

BUSINESS UNUSUAL

So what are these attributes? Anita Roddick, founder of the natural cosmetics company The Body Shop, told Helgesen that she runs her organization according to "feminine principles," which she lists as "caring, making intuitive decisions, not getting hung up on hierarchy or all those dreadfully boring business-school management ideas; having a sense of work as being part of your life, not separate from it; putting your labor where your love is; being responsible to the world in how you use your profits; recognizing the bottom line should stay at the bottom." A recent study by the independent research organization Catalyst shows that these sentiments are widely shared; surveying businesses revealed a consistent impression that male leaders "take charge" while female leaders "take care"—through networking, consulting, and team-building, among other activities.

In the past, business literature coached women to play the man's game—literally so. Margaret Hennig and Anne Jardim's *The Managerial Woman,* for example, recommended studying football to understand the male concept of strategy. But industry is changing, according to Joyce LaValle, who instigated the transformation of Interface. "At the first industrial revolution, it was only men who were at the table," she says. "This time, women are." Sally Helgesen was the first to argue that the workplace can benefit from women expressing, not suppressing, their personal values, which she describes in detail:

> ## Women have been overlooked on many levels.
>
> PAUL HAWKEN

These values include an attention to process instead of a focus on the bottom line; a willingness to look at how an action will affect other people instead of simply asking, "What's in it for me?"; a concern for the wider needs of the community; a disposition to draw on personal, private sphere experience when dealing in the public realm; an appreciation of diversity; an outsider's impatience with rituals and symbols of status that divide people who work together and so reinforce hierarchies.

This description could have come just as easily from the literature of sustainability as from a book on women in business. Contrast it with the more conventional perspective, which Anderson says economist Milton Friedman best summed up: "The business of business is business." Anderson dismisses this narrow view. "That is so left brain. It misses half the world. And he won a Nobel Prize! There is a better way, I promise you."

Does this "better way"—the "soft side of business"—pay off? Anderson says yes. "We have to care about the environment because our customers do. Our costs are down, not up. Our profits are better than they've ever been." *Biomimicry* author Janine Benyus, who helped develop Interface's popular Entropy carpet tile based on irregular patterns in nature, reports that the product line has been the company's biggest success. Says Anderson, "We're proving every day that there is a better business model." Profits aside, that better model, based on traits often identified as feminine, can ensure the on-going viability or *sustainability* of not only business but also any group or community—as well as all of humanity. "[A] concern with the long term is one of the great gifts of many women leaders," says Helgesen, though she is quick to point out that these gifts are not restricted to women. "This is not to say that men do not share these values; some share many, others a few. But these values may be defined as female because they have been nurtured in the private, domestic sphere to which women have been restricted for so long."

Women's ways of thinking and working evolved not in board rooms or on battlefields but in the home and community. This experience suits sustainability well, for, as Helgesen recounts, the goal of women-led social reform has always been "making the whole world more homelike." And home, by nature, represents "an ideal of sustenance and continuity, rather than one of progress, dynamism, or bold leaps into the void." Benyus tells us her work "is all about finding place—how you create a home, a habitat." In 1990, well before the current wave of sustainable design, Land Institute co-founder Dana Jackson declared that "the coming together of the ecological and feminist movements gives us a greater opportunity to change patterns that not only lead to the extinction of countless other species but also destroy what supports humans.... Certain attributes of women's culture must be employed to help us adapt to sustainable, ecological living patterns. What we might call a feminization of the culture will come about in response to the environmental crisis in the most decentralist social organizations of all, our families and partnerships."

THE OTHER HALF OF THE SKY

This book is less about the "ascendancy of women" than it is about the growing value of those sensibilities commonly associated with women. Without always recognizing them as such, advocates of sustainability have embraced the same qualities Roddick calls "feminine"—intuition, inclusiveness, responsibility, caring, and love. To understand these connections, we asked hundreds of women to comment on both their personal views and any qualities they relate to women in general. In addition, we looked at how women have contributed to the evolution of sustainability. Reviewing the literature of the field and talking to many of its leaders—both women and men—we have found that women are behind many of the fundamental standards, values, goals, and accomplishments of green design and development. "Looking at the genesis of sustainability," says Blue Moon Fund fellow Mary Rowe, "you can see that many of these ideas came from women." Hunter Lovins points out that the same is true today: "Some of the best work in the field is being done by gals." Who are these "gals"? Many of them are familiar names, many are not. Many are unsung, diligently working behind the scenes, building momentum. "There are a lot of women in the field who are just working hard," explains Alexis Karolides of the Rocky Mountain Institute. "They're not making a lot of money—they're just getting things done." Interior designer Kirsten Childs observes, "I see very talented people not getting recognition, especially in architecture and interior design. We've allowed the credit to be taken away from us." Yet, industrial designer Wendy Brawer insists, "Who gets credit is less important than what's getting done." While we've heard this sentiment over and over, we nevertheless hope to shed light on the depth of women's work.

Why is it important to highlight women? Kim Gandy, president of the National Organization of Women (NOW), makes the case. "Women have different experiences. We need a diversity of voices and life experiences in order to bring together the best possible whole. This is as true in architecture or design as it is in government or any other field." Do women have something unique to offer sustainable design? "Sustainability looks toward the future, and women bring a particular focus on the future. Whether it's sociological or biological, the reality is that women have been the primary caregivers of children. We want equality for ourselves, but we're really doing this for our daughters and granddaughters. It's a particularly female focus." How do you measure equality? "When I started working with NOW in 1973, women were paid 59 cents on the dollar compared to men. Today, it's 76 cents. A 17-cent increase is great, but we have a long way to go. After a century of real equality, we might not need to bring special attention to this."

In the foreword to *The International Human Rights of Women*, Hillary Rodham Clinton explains the need for special attention. "The fortunes of nations are inextricably tied to the fortunes of women," she writes. "It is this simple: where women flourish, their families flourish. And where families flourish, communities and nations flourish. Issues affecting women and their families are not 'soft' issues to be relegated to the sidelines of serious debate; rather, they are among the hardest and most important issues we face." Helgesen recalls a Chinese proverb: "Women hold up half the sky," which means that "half the work and half the thinking in the world is done by women. For the sky to be complete, both halves must work together; nothing can be truly human that excludes one half of humanity. Until recently, the half of the sky assigned to women has been the private half; the public half has been ceded to men. But as women assume positions of leadership in the public realm, they are bringing their values with them, and the ancient dichotomies— between male and female, between public and private—are dissolving."

"FEMININE PRINCIPLES"

What are the values women bring to public life and to sustainability in particular? Our primary means of addressing that question has been simply to ask it. We solicited opinions from many people of various backgrounds, all somehow involved in promoting sustainability in communities, buildings, and products. They have included architects, designers, planners, policymakers, consultants, writers, executives, educators, and students. While any attempt to summarize these dialogues with a simple list of conclusions will fail to evoke the full range of what we've heard, a consistent set of themes has emerged and may outline both the "feminine principles" of sustainability and the purpose of this book:

It's about sensibilities and sensitivities more than it is about gender or sex.

It isn't divisive; it's inclusive. It's not fragmented, it's holistic. It's about synthesis.

It's about collaboration and building community. It's not about things, it's about relationships. It's not about products, it's about process.

It's about grassroots, building from the bottom up. Not proclamations from above. It's about interaction and dialogue, not solitary vision.

It's about changing the status quo. Innovation requires new ways of thinking and doing.

It's about long-term evolution, not the quick fix.

It's about versatility and balance, adapting and improvising. It's not about single-mindedness.

It's about deep-rooted respect and wonder. It's not about opportunism, it's about opportunity for all.

It isn't conclusive; it's suggestive. In other words, all of the above must be taken with a grain of salt.

> "Looking at the genesis of sustainability, you can see that many of these ideas came from women."
>
> MARY ROWE

How might these sensibilities influence design? Quite directly, according to architect Hillary Brown. While on holiday in Turkey many years ago, she recalls, she was struck by the strong (and correct) sense that the small seaside hotel where she was staying had been conceived by a woman. "I've thought about this for years. How did I know?" A modest structure ringing a courtyard that opened to the sky above and the sea beyond, the hotel struck Brown as distinctly *feminine*—a concern for space and place over buildings and objects, community over individuals, and a strong connection to natural context. At a time when relatively few female architects existed anywhere, Brown intuitively associated that welcoming place with a women's point of view. She happened to be right.

"UNMANLY" GREEN

If a feminine understanding of sustainability exists, how does it relate to prevailing, presumably masculine views? Conventional wisdom about gender and the environment portrays men as exploiters of natural resources. For instance, Roger-Mark de Souza, director of the population, health, and environment program at the Population Reference Bureau, has said that "women tend to be more the custodians of the environment than men do, and men tend to be the extractors and consumers of the environment." The custodian/consumer split may be overly simplified, although surveys consistently reveal clear differences between general masculine and feminine attitudes toward the environment (see the preface). In the age of climate change, the sexes share a desire to address the environmental crisis—but their motivations may vary.

A "left-brain" view sees environmentalism almost exclusively in terms of energy independence—as a political or military tactic. In his 2006 State of the Union address, George W. Bush pointed to alternative fuels such as hydrogen as a way for America to wean itself off foreign oil. A few years earlier, the CIA called the environment "the national-security issue of the early twenty-first century," claiming that deforestation, water depletion, and air pollution will "incite group conflicts that will be the core foreign policy challenge from which most others will ultimately emanate." *New York Times* columnist Thomas Friedman is more emphatic: "Green isn't some 'wussy' tree-hugging thing. Green is patriotic. Green is strategic. Green is the new red, white and blue." *Wussy* being derogatory slang for "especially unmanly," consider Friedman's view to be the opposite. Call it *manly green.*

In *Manliness,* his recent lament on the loss of masculinity in American culture, Harvard professor Harvey Mansfield lists the titular qualities as aggression and risk-taking and encourages their return in society and affairs of state. Independence and control come first. "Manly men defend their turf, just as other male mammals do," writes Mansfield. By dealing with the environmental crisis as an isolationist security issue, manly green seeks environmentalism without sustainability. Manly green separates; *womanly green* unites. The unmanly view embraces interdependence, not independence. Environmentalist Vandana Shiva is a leading voice for this inclusive attitude. In *Earth Democracy,* she writes, "How can we as members of the earth community reinvent security to ensure the survival of all species and the survival and future of diverse cultures?" Novelist Virginia Woolf considered this global view to be particularly feminine. "As a woman I have no country," she wrote. "As a woman my country is the whole world."

TWO SUSTAINABILITIES

Environmental educator David Orr distinguishes between two conceptions of sustainability. *Technological* sustainability is quantitative and relies on doing the same things more efficiently, while *ecological* sustainability is qualitative and requires a fundamentally new way of doing things. To explain the difference and demonstrate how both views are necessary, Orr gives a medical analogy. If a man suffers a heart attack, doctors must first attend to his vital signs so he may continue to live. But after his recovery comes the longer process of dealing with deeper causes such as diet and life style. That manly green conforms to the first attitude is clear from President Bush's State of the Union remarks: "America is addicted to oil," he said. "The best way to break this addiction is through technology." By contrast, Janet Welsh Brown of the World Resources Institute describes a more internal task, writing that "the greatest accomplishment of the environmental movement" is the "revolution in awareness and understanding." And four decades ago Rachel Carson wrote that "we're challenged as mankind has never been challenged before to prove maturity and our mastery, not of nature, but of ourselves."

> "At the first industrial revolution, it was only men who were at the table. This time, women are."
>
> JOYCE LAVALLE

Whether or not Orr's two forms of sustainability correspond perfectly to general gender differences, the most obvious sources for these two approaches happen to be men and women, respectively. The foundation for the technical approach was laid by Buckminster Fuller. Sustainability guru John Elkington, who coined the popular phrase "the triple bottom line" (economic/ecological/social), summarizes Fuller's work: "His concept of ephemeralization [the tendency for technology to become smaller and lighter] and notion of 'doing more with less,' as with geodesic domes, were direct precursors of eco-efficiency." Today, virtually every development in sustainable materials science and green construction techniques can be traced back to Fuller in some way.

The roots of ecological sustainability, however, were planted by two women—Rachel Carson and Jane Jacobs. With the publication of *Silent Spring* in 1962, Carson single-handedly began the modern environmental movement and popularized the principles of ecology. "She had a massive impact," says environmental historian Elizabeth Blum. "The most significant thing Carson did was get people to start wondering, 'Is all technology progress?'" If Carson is the recognized representative of the ecology portion of the triple bottom line, Jacobs is the less obvious source of current thinking about sustainable communities and economies. *The Death and Life of Great American Cities* (1961) spelled out her ecology-inspired theories about livable communities relying on self-sustaining economies, and her later work, especially *The Nature of Economies,* more explicitly illustrated the relationships between socioeconomic and ecological systems.

That Carson and Jacobs were women may be less important than their positions outside the mainstream. "This isn't about men and women—it's about outsiders," says Mary Rowe, echoing many comments we've heard. Rowe has led Ideas That Matter, an organization devoted to the ideas of Jane Jacobs. "If you're not part of the establishment, you don't have to worry about propping it up. It doesn't feed you." Innovation requires questioning the establishment, and in the era of Carson, Jacobs and Fuller the establishment was 1950s culture and technology—political conservatism, the post-war domination of what Eisenhower called the "military-industrial complex," the rise of mass production, urban plight and suburban flight, heightened social stratification, and an increasing disconnection from nature. Even while championing technology, Fuller questioned the inefficiencies of modern infrastructure, architecture, and construction. Jacobs came of age during post-war activism against the local political machine in New York City. Untrained in planning, she turned urbanism and public policy upside down. And Carson, a government-employed writer, threatened the chemical industry, academic science, and public policy all at once. As a result, both Jacobs and Carson came under vicious personal and public attack, often aimed at their sex. Standing outside the edifice of authority, they could see the cracks in its structure more readily, but speaking out took enormous courage.

OVERLOOKED

Culturally, Jacobs and Carson were part of the co-evolution of women and suburbia in post-war America, as Sally Helgesen explains. "Today, you can see women's ways of thinking upon a sustainable idea about community. The typical suburb is the opposite." The suburbs' effects on women gave birth to the modern women's movement in the form of Betty Friedan's *The Feminine Mystique,* which appeared a year after *Silent Spring.* "The problem that has no name," as Friedan called women's depression, arose from the social and environmental isolation of the suburbs. In *Everyday Revolutionaries,* Helgesen writes, "It is no accident that the contemporary women's movement emerged in the same decade as the antiwar and environmental movements; each attempted to reverse in a different way the basic tenets of Western patriarchal culture." In the mid-century, as women began to emerge from the household, where she says an "ideology of separateness" had confined them since the Victorian era, they began to question and transform the public sphere in accordance with the values they had developed in the home and local communities.

Historically, women have been strong advocates of the environment and community. "From the early reforming efforts of Jane Hull to the powerful inspirational voice of Rachel Carson," writes Helgesen, "the long-term concern with the results of resource exploitation have reflected female concerns." As feminist writer bell hooks recounts, the women's movement originally included "a global ecological vision of how the planet can survive and how everyone on it can have access to peace and well-being." Environmentalist Paul Hawken concurs: "Rachel Carson was actually part of a long lineage of women who questioned the conflict between business rights and community rights," he tells us. "I don't see any difference between environmental health, community, and equity issues. The social justice and environmental movements were the same thing forty years ago—they diverged, but they're coming back together now." Yet, the efforts of women have not always gotten recognition, he says. "Women have been overlooked on many levels."

> **Sustainability looks toward the future, and women bring a particular focus on the future.**
>
> KIM GANDY

Why is this? In *A Fierce Green Fire*, his history of the American environmental movement, Philip Shabecoff writes that while male activists often focus on national campaigns, women typically act at the grassroots level, where their work may not get as much attention but has more immediate and lasting effects on their homes and communities. Helgesen attributes to Eleanor Roosevelt the remark that women seek power to address a cause, while men address a cause to seek power. Historian Elizabeth Blum reports, "Women were not allowed in national politics. But they could get involved in campaigns close to home. It wasn't seen as threatening." Their historic contributions to environmentalism include early conservation, the revival of the Audubon Society, urban social reform, early environmental lobbying, and the clean air movement. Blum notes that the rise of industrialization and urbanization in the late 1800s created profound problems in environmental, social, and public health. "People reacted in two ways. One response, often led by males, was to escape from cities. Think of Teddy Roosevelt, the national parks movement, the Boy

Scouts, et cetera. The other response, typically led by women, was to seek change within the cities." Escape-versus-reform efforts divided roughly along gender lines.

A CULTURE TORN

Shabecoff shows that while its intellectual seeds were sown in Europe in the mid-nineteenth century, the early environmental movement took root in America. "It was a response to the sudden transformation of what had been a country untouched and unspoiled by Western civilization—the retreat of the wilderness and the startling intrusion of the machine into the garden. It reflected the dismay of Americans who were discovering that, contrary to long-held belief, resources and opportunity were not limitless, even on the vast North American continent." Even early on, Shabecoff points out, environmentalists' attitudes split between scientific rationalism, which argued logically against wasting resources, and a morally based appeal to save the land. America is a culture torn between materialism and idealism.

"The most important generality about America is not to generalize about America," Paul Hawken warns us. "It's too big and too complex." Nevertheless, there are urgent reasons to dwell on American views, as we do in this book. "It's much more important for the U.S. to go green than anywhere else," says Donna McIntire, the State Department's point-of-contact for sustainability. "We're a big consumer, and we have a lot of power. With power comes responsibility—people look to us to be a model. We owe it to the world to do this right. The U.S. isn't in a vacuum. Water isn't isolated, air isn't isolated. We have one world, and it's getting a lot smaller."

Gro Harlem Brundtland, the first woman prime minister of Norway and the chair of the commission that created the most popular definition of sustainability, emphasized in a recent lecture that the U.S. has an unprecedented responsibility and opportunity to become better global citizens by providing a different model of development. "We must now fully recognize how interdependent we all have become. Only by working together, not against each other, can we have a vision of a better-managed world." Hunter Lovins echoes this sentiment. "The biggest challenge of sustainability is how to bring it to the rest of the world." Together, she and David Orr recently wrote in their article "Common Ground/Common Future" that restoring the environment is this generation's "Great Work," akin to three other significant times and events in U.S. history—the American Revolution (throwing off tyranny), the Civil War (eradicating slavery), and World War II (defeating fascism). "The challenges of our times are like no other," they write. "No generation has ever had greater work to do, and none more reason to rise to greatness."

BALANCING ACT

In *The Unsettling of America,* farmer/environmentalist Wendell Berry writes that from the early days of the European arrival on this continent American culture has been divided between *exploitation* and *nurture.* "The standard of the exploiter is efficiency; the standard of the nurturer is care. The exploiter's goal is money, profit; the nurturer's goal is health," which he describes as "rooted in the concept of wholeness. To be healthy is to be whole." He continues: "The exploiter typically serves an institution or organization; the nurturer serves land, household, community, place. The exploiter thinks in terms of numbers, quantities, 'hard facts'; the nurturer in terms of character, condition, quality, kind." Berry contends that there are gender connotations in these roles, but the division is not clear-cut. While the exploiter represents the prototypical "masculine man," the nurturer, however, "has always passed with ease across the boundaries of the so-called sexual roles." *Breeder* becomes *brooder* and back again, he writes. "Over and over again, spring after spring, the questing mind, idealist and visionary, must pass through the planting to become nurturer of the real. The farmer, sometimes known as husbandman, is by definition half mother...."

The exploiter/nurturer schism exists "not only between persons but also within persons," according to Berry, and many reiterate this view. "Each of us holds these polar opposites of masculine and feminine energy within us," claims landscape architect Lucia Athens. "Learning to balance these and see the positive attributes of each is essential." Bioneers founder Nina Simons agrees. "We are all equally wounded by the cultural mis-definition of the masculine and the feminine. We need to rediscover the healthy masculine and feminine in each of us. If we collectively redefine these as healthy archetypes, we can integrate them in a way that is balanced, joyous, and in the service of life." To bring balance, says environmental activist Dianne Dillon-Ridgley, our culture needs to embrace the feminine more than it has in the past. "The voices of women are important, especially at a time of transition."

> The sustainable design movement is about including many voices and excluding arbitrary vision.
>
> SALLY HELGESEN

VISION AND VOICE

Berry's use of the word *visionary* and Dillon-Ridgley's use of *voice* are significant. Sally Helgesen contrasts the metaphors of *vision* and *voice* as representations of, respectively, masculine and feminine ways of relating to the world. Vision detaches the observer from the observed, and Helgesen tells us this condition perfectly applies to the stereotype of the architect. "The idea of the 'master architect' is very much about one man's vision. That can be very dangerous because it's responsible for much of the dysfunction we see in our cities—it exalts the individuality of that person above what the community needs and wants. 'Visionary' speaks of a tyrant." While vision relates to a worldview in which truth is objective and abstract, *voice* represents a collective, interactive process in which truth depends on context and circumstance. Unlike the one-way act of seeing, speaking and listening suggest mutual participation. "Voices are an expression of a collaborative effort, coming to consensus through real dialogue, rather than someone imposing their view. It's more productive to have a mechanism that allows many voices to be heard. Non-hierarchical organization and collaboration are deeply subversive to the visionary."

Helgesen's metaphors relate to the process of integrated or participatory design. "Vision is not more valuable than the people you are serving," says Nina Simons. Balanced leadership, in which the feminine and the masculine come together, "means listening at least as much as you talk. You are in a relational dance with the people, ideas, and ecosystems that you are seeking to serve." Many women we've interviewed have celebrated the simple, thoughtful act of listening. "I can't tell you how many times people have told me in my career, 'You're the first architect who listens, who really cares,'" says Susan Maxman, the first woman president of the AIA. Architect Jeanne Gang expresses a similar sentiment. "It's never crossed my mind that architects wouldn't listen. Maybe it's a gender thing."

It is indeed a gender thing, according to linguistics professor and popular author Deborah Tannen. More often than not, during conversations women tend to *listen* while men *lecture*, she writes: "Women and men fall into this unequal pattern so often because of the differences in their interactional habits. Since women seek to build rapport, they are inclined to play down their expertise rather than display it. Since men value the position of center stage and the feeling of knowing more, they seek opportunities to gather and disseminate factual information." Studying storytelling habits among men and women, Tannen has found that women's narratives tend to be about *community*, while men's tend to be about *contest*. For women, "the community is the source of power. If men see life in terms of contest, a struggle against nature and other men, for women life is a struggle against the danger of being cut off from their community." Women create community through the very act of speaking to one another. At home and at work, says Helgesen, "women value listening as a way of making others feel comfortable and important, and as a means of encouraging others to find their own voices and grow."

MANY VOICES

In this book we try to find those voices. Many people maintain that partnerships and collaborations lead to better results than individual work can produce. As Helgesen puts it, "The sustainable design movement is about including many voices and excluding arbitrary vision." We see this book as a cooperation between the two of us as authors, the people we have interviewed, and the reader. In the tradition of oral histories, we hope to provide a place in these pages for all of these voices. The bulk of the book is a series of casual conversations with informed people about important topics, mostly determined by them. All we have done is gather them together in print.

Format matters. Jane Jacobs' later books are a series of dialogues in which she invents fictitious characters to represent different viewpoints. The result manages to make light reading out of weighty subjects, as she explains in the preface to *The Nature of Economies*: "I have used imaginary characters and didactic dialogue primarily because this venerable literary form is suited to expounding inquiry and developing argument, but also because the form implicitly invites a reader to join the characters and enter the argument too. A book is equipped to speak for itself, more so than any other artifact. But to be heard, a book needs a collaborator...." In *Systems of Survival,* she explains that the dialogue format also allows her to suppress her own voice in service of the subject—as Helgesen describes her, Jacobs channels "the voices of the community." Literary historians often refer to the Socratic dialogue as a feminine form (partly in reference to Greek philosopher Socrates' female teacher, Diotima). But, as Jacobs explains, she aimed for something more egalitarian, rejecting the "know-it-all" mentor for equal characters sharing a more democratic exchange. The book you're holding is a forum for this kind of dialogue.

WORDS

The concept of the literary voice has been fundamental to the evolution of sustainability. Many of the movement's most inspired voices have come not from designers or even from design itself but from the written and spoken word, often from women. Carson, Jacobs, Brundtland, Lovins, Benyus—none is a designer or maker of things. Their impact has been through ideas, not images—through voice, not vision. If Jacobs had been an urban planner instead of a writer, would her influence have been less substantive and more superficial (much as Fuller's legacy often is remembered as the geodesic dome alone)? Language sways, words create worlds. "Language infuses everything we think and do," Jacobs writes. "Where would either ancient preceptors or modern environmentalists be without the capacity to warn and persuade?"

The capacity to persuade relies on both information and inspiration, the practical and the poetic. In developing their popular book, *Cradle to Cradle: Remaking the Way We Make Things*, architect William McDonough and chemist Michael Braungart worked closely with poet Lisa Williams because, as McDonough recalls, "we wanted the book to be clean and accessible yet richly dimensioned, and that sounds a lot more like poetry than a business manual." Benyus describes poetry as "the worshipful articulation of what is around us—a quest to learn, to find out what *is* through the process of writing. If I can put something into poetic words that allow someone, especially a non-scientist, to feel the essence of an organism, isn't that just as valid as somebody who can tell me how long the falcon's claws are or what they're made of or how strong they are?"

Architect and artist Maya Lin sees the design process itself as a narrative form. "I begin by imagining an artwork verbally," she writes. "I try to describe in writing what the project is, what it is trying to do. I need to understand the artwork without giving it a specific materiality or solid form. I try not to find the form too soon. Instead, I try to think about it as an idea without a shape." Writing creates intimacy with an audience, she says. "I think of writing as the purest of art forms. When your thoughts and intentions are conveyed as directly as possible to another person, no need exists for a translation. Words can be the most direct means of sharing our thoughts."

Sharing thoughts through words is what any book is about. In this case, the words mostly belong to others—the voices of sustainable design. If we agree with Nobel economist Herbert Simon's description of design as "any course of action aimed at changing existing situations into preferred ones," the idea of *sustainable* design is potentially redundant, since at its heart sustainability is simply intended to make things better. Of course, the challenges lie in discovering which "existing situations" need change and who determines what is "preferred." You can find these questions lingering under the surface of every conversation that follows.

Just listen.

WHO WAS RACHEL CARSON?

A child's world is fresh and new and beautiful, full of wonder and excitement. It is our misfortune that for most of us that clear-eyed vision, that true instinct for what is beautiful and awe-inspiring, is dimmed and even lost before we reach adulthood. If I had influence with the good fairy who is supposed to preside over the christening of all children I should ask that her gift to each child in the world be a sense of wonder so indestructible that it would last throughout life....

RACHEL CARSON, *THE SENSE OF WONDER*

The significance of Rachel Carson (1907-1964) cannot be overstated. Her effect on environmentalism, ecology, science, literature, activism, culture, and sustainable design and development is truly immeasurable. In 1999, *Time* magazine named her one of the one hundred most influential people of the twentieth century. (Aside from anthropologist Mary Leakey, who was paired with her husband, Louis, Carson was the only woman listed among two dozen "scientists and thinkers.") When *Silent Spring* appeared in 1962, it remained on the bestseller list for two years; half a century later, it has never been out of print.

Carson has been called the "mother of the environmental movement." *Silent Spring*, the title referring to the disappearance of songbirds, exposed the dangers of DDT and other pesticides. By showing so powerfully how chemicals multiply and persist in the environment, she injected ecology into the public imagination and revived the public health debate. Environmental historian Maril Hazlett describes Carson as giving the public both more peril and more power. "She made it personal, a problem of everyday people. But she also made it popular by saying, 'You can evaluate the science. You can do something about this.'" As biographer Linda Lear has said, "It gives us hope. Rachel Carson showed how one human being can make a difference."

At an early age, Carson witnessed the environmental effects of technology firsthand. Growing up on a farm in western Pennsylvania, she saw how the growth of Pittsburgh's steel industry polluted the rural towns around her, and she began to question the nature of progress. After a master's degree in zoology from Johns Hopkins, she eventually worked for what became the U.S. Fish & Wildlife Service. In her twenties, she studied summers at the Marine Biological Laboratories in Woods Hole, Massachusetts, where she fell in love with the ocean. Her writing on the wonders of the sea, especially *The Sea Around Us,* established her voice and her fame. At first she used the pseudonym "R. L. Carson," because she felt a woman science writer would not have been taken seriously. In fact, after *Silent Spring* came out, she was viciously attacked by the chemical and agricultural industries as a "hysterical woman" unqualified for serious science. At the same time, she was supporting her extended family, as she had for years, and undergoing chemotherapy. She died two years after *Silent Spring,* and throughout her struggle, she showed amazing courage. "I have felt bound by a solemn obligation to do what I could," she wrote to a friend. "If I didn't at least try, I could never be happy again in nature."

As influential as her argument was her writing, which Lear writes "not only accurately and beautifully described science but was passionate prose that welded those two together." Other writers speak of the beauty of her work. "Hers was a very romantic voice," says poet Lisa Williams. "She brought emotion to ecology." Listen to this passage from *Under the Sea Wind*:

> To stand here at the edge of the sea, to sense the ebb and flow of the tides, to feel the breath of the mist over the great salt marsh, to watch the flight of shorebirds that have swept up and down these continents for untold thousands of years, to see the running of the old eels and the young shad to the sea, is to have knowledge of things that are as nearly eternal as any earthly life can be.

"Those who contemplate the beauty of the earth find reserves of strength that will endure as long as life lasts."

THE SENSE OF WONDER

Actress Kaiulani Lee, who portrays Carson in *A Sense of Wonder,* a one-woman play she wrote after years of research and interviews with friends, family, and colleagues, says audiences are transformed by Carson's words. "There is a hunger for her kind of passion and courage." Lee, who describes her own performance as "bringing the words back into the atmosphere," gives Carson's voice a fragile luminescence. "There's something transcendent about it. I go on stage as myself and just hope she visits. What a gift she gave me."

Was Carson a poetic scientist or a scientific poet? Ecologist and poet Sandra Steingraber says, "When you read her work out loud, you can hear the poetry. It has imagery but also tonality and rhythm—everything but the line breaks." Steingraber notes that Carson often used classic poetic structures such as iambic pentameter. The cadence of Carson's words may echo the cycles of the world, as she wrote in *The Sense of Wonder*: "There is something infinitely healing in the repeated refrains of nature—the assurance that dawn comes after night and spring after the winter." She died before the book was released.

Steingraber writes, "As a biologist and author myself, I labor in the fields that Carson planted." The similarity has not gone unnoticed—in 1999, the Sierra Club called Steingraber "the new Rachel Carson." A cancer survivor, Steingraber sees her work as expanding on Carson's legacy by tracing the lines between ecology and human health. *Living Downstream*, which explored the environmental links to cancer as a human rights issue, inspired *Ms.* magazine to name her 1997 "woman of the year." Her 2001 book, *Having Faith: An Ecologist's Journey to Motherhood*, was a personal and poignant look at fetal toxicology. In *Living Downstream*, Steingraber writes that *Silent Spring* exposed the risks of not speaking out, demonstrating "how one kind of silence breeds another, how the secrecies of government beget a weirdly quiet and lifeless world." Of Carson, Steingraber says, "I feel in awe of her."

Below, Steingraber considers Carson's legacy and relevance today. This passage is excerpted from an essay she contributed to Dennis Loy Johnson and Valerie Merians' *What We Do Now*, a collection published in response to the 2004 presidential election.

REMEMBERING RACHEL CARSON, FROM *WHAT WE DO NOW*
BY SANDRA STEINGRABER

For many years public-spirited citizens throughout the country have been working for the conservation of the natural resources, realizing their vital importance to the Nation. Apparently, their hard-won progress is to be wiped out, as a politically minded Administration returns to us the dark ages of unrestrained exploitation and destruction. It is one of the ironies of our time that while concentrating on the defense of our country against enemies from without, we should be so heedless of those would destroy it from within.

These bitter words appeared in a letter to the editor of the *Washington Post* in April, 1953. The Republicans had just won the White House, Joseph McCarthy held ruthless sway in the Senate. The long-time director of the Fish and Wildlife Service had just been dismissed.

The author of this letter was a young biologist named Rachel Carson.

Carson could not have known, when she penned it, how profound an impact her short letter would have. The Associated Press picked it up for syndication. The *Reader's Digest* reprinted it. And so her missive found its way onto front porches and breakfast tables, into living rooms and libraries and doctors' office waiting rooms across the nation. At the height of the Cold War, in the midst of an anti-Communist inquisition that had convulsed the federal government, Carson's assertion that "the real wealth of the Nation lies in the resources of the earth—soil, water, forests, minerals, and wildlife" struck a chord with the populace. In this way, she opened up a critical space in the paranoid culture of her time to have a conversation about the environment.

But Carson could not have foreseen all this when she pulled the pages of her letter from the typewriter, folded them into the envelope, and rummaged through her desk for a postage stamp. Nor could she have guessed the effect that the letter's publication would ultimately have on her own life as a writer. In 1953, Carson was the author of gentle, lyrical books about the sea. Now she spoke as a blistering critic. And when, nine years later, she combined her political voice with the poetry of her descriptive nature writing, the result was her masterpiece, *Silent Spring*, which broadly speaking, argued that the contamination of our environment with inherently poisonous chemicals is a basic violation of human rights. The publication of the book in 1962 did more to galvanize the environmental movement than any other single event. *Silent Spring*

> The more clearly we can focus our attention on the wonders and realities of the universe about us, the less taste we shall have for destruction.

SILENT SPRING

gave us the Environmental Protection Agency and inspired almost every major piece of environmental legislation on the books.

So, as I read the letter written to a newspaper editor 52 years ago ... I found the following reasons for hope ...

First, we are not the only generation of thoughtful people with an abiding appreciation for groundwater, oxygen, and birdsong to ever be ruled over by men utterly unconcerned with the ongoing destruction of ecological systems—and who indeed may be directly profiting by it. It is comforting to feel the presence of those reformers who came before us, to know ourselves as their heirs. Carson herself pays homage in *Silent Spring* to one of her own heroes, the French biologist Jean Rostand, who said, "the obligation to endure gives us the right to know."

Second, we owe it to these forebears—who sometimes labored at great personal cost to their health and reputation—to overcome our collective despair and figure out how best to carry on. Consider that Carson composed many of *Silent Spring*'s sentences after 11:30 P.M. when she finally got her household settled. She was a single mother, the sole caretaker of an aged parent, and a breast cancer patient. She took on the pesticide industry and the U.S. Department of Agriculture while on chemotherapy. Her editor was threatened with lawsuits.

Third, out of a dark period of history can sometimes emerge a redeeming idea that lights the way for years to come.

And, fourth, such an illuminating idea may not arrive full-blown on the scene. It may begin in small ways and with other intents and purposes. As when someone objects in the newspaper to the firing of a fine public servant.

Reprinted with permission from Dennis Loy Johnson, Valerie Merians, and Melville House Publishing.

WORKS
Under the Sea Wind (1941)
Food From the Sea: Fish and Shellfish of New England (1943)
Food From the Sea: Fish and Shellfish of the South Atlantic (1944)
The Sea Around Us (1951)
The Edge of the Sea (1955)
Silent Spring (1962)
The Sense of Wonder (posthumous, 1965)

WHO WAS JANE JACOBS?

Human beings are, of course, a part of nature, as much so as grizzly bears or bees or whales or sorghum cane. The cities of human beings are as natural, being a product of one form of nature, as are the colonies of prairie dogs or the beds of oysters.

JANE JACOBS, *THE DEATH AND LIFE OF GREAT AMERICAN CITIES*

Jane Jacobs (1916-2006) is not typically seen as green but, in fact, she planted the seeds of many of sustainable design's basic principles. "Though she never called it that, the idea of 'sustaining neighborhoods' began with her," recounts *Metropolis* magazine's Susan Szenasy. "Jane Jacobs was the grandmother of all of this."

Best known for *The Death and Life of Great American Cities* (1961), her groundbreaking work rejecting overblown mid-century urbanism, Jacobs has been called by the *Financial Times* of London "the leading voice of the city." She believed that city dwellers, whom she called "great informal experts," know what's best for their neighborhoods. Thinking that externally imposed plans can drain the life from communities, she preferred to draw lessons from "how cities work in real life." She renounced "the statistical city," which conceived of urbanism as a mathematical abstraction rather than a living community of people. The social justice implications were clear—the dehumanization of cities gave planners and policymakers the rationale for relocating large numbers of residents. "In the form of statistics, these citizens ... could be dealt with intellectually like grains of sand, or electrons or billiard balls."

As Szenasy suggests, Jacobs had a maternal view of communities. Humanity was her first concern. With no professional training or education in planning, she based her ideas on simple observations about everyday life. "She was a wacky housewife," says Mary Rowe, a friend and colleague. "Then she wrote this tome that changed the world." Jacobs called conventional approaches to urban problems "paternalistic" because they regard city dwellers as incapable of acting in their own self-interest. She worked tirelessly to protect older neighborhoods in both New York and Toronto, where she lived from 1968 until her death. Her protest of invasive large-scale construction projects in New York once landed her in jail but helped oust Parks Commissioner Robert Moses, the infamous "power broker" who epitomized what she called the "Olympian view" of the city.

> "Human beings exist wholly within nature as a legitimate part of natural order in every respect.
>
> THE NATURE OF ECONOMIES

Although architect William McDonough praises Jacobs as "one of the greatest design leaders ever," in fact she was not very interested in design. "It's ironic that planners love Jane's work," says Rowe, "because she's about not planning." Jacobs argued that strong places do not spring up overnight—they adapt and evolve over time, much like a natural system. Designers' instincts to build anew run against this grain. "The *antithesis* of what she was talking about was a designed community," says business writer Sally Helgesen, who knew Jacobs. "She was talking about a vernacular architecture that reflected and supported a small-scale local economy." Though she has heavily influenced New Urbanism, the new towns movement begun by Elizabeth Plater-Zyberk and Andres Duany, Jacobs did not approve of the attempt to turn her ideas into a planning template, because it contradicts the very heart of those ideas—that vibrant cities self-assemble. As she said in an interview, "I don't think the New Urbanists understand this kind of thing."

Ecology significantly inspired much of Jacobs' work, explains biologist Janine Benyus, who knew her well. "We always focus on survival of the fittest, extinction, what dies. But the real action is what survives. Life keeps what works from one generation to another. What Jane did was look at what works in great cities. She held up a mirror to this organic pattern. It's bottom up, like evolution." Sounding much like a systems theorist, Jacobs insisted that what urbanism needed most was "new strategies for thinking," because the old strategies were failing. Planning, like all modernism, she argued, had been built around the physical sciences—mathematics, statistics, and physics—but the life sciences offered a better model. In *Death and Life*, she summed up her central idea: "to think of cities as problems in organized complexity—organisms that are replete with unexamined, but obviously intricately interconnected…relationships." Says environmentalist and author Paul Hawken, "Without using the terminology, she was talking about complex adaptive systems before there was a science of it."

Though she published several staggeringly inventive books on various subjects, *Death and Life* got the most attention—her obituaries focused almost exclusively on it. "Everybody always wants to talk about her old work," notes Benyus. But her appetite for ideas was voracious. "She was about a lot more than city building and a lot more than built form," says Rowe. "She was a totally original thinker." A true polymath, Jacobs had endless curiosity and imagination. "I can't think of a wiser woman," Hawken tells us. As a result, she defies classification. Says Rowe, "In North America she's seen as an urbanist. In Europe she's seen as a moral philosopher. In Asia she's seen as an economist." Rowe, who notes that Jacobs thought a full generation must pass for an idea to take hold (hence the impact of *Death and Life* on 1980s urbanism), predicts that Jacobs' theories connecting economy to ecology will prove to be her most important legacy. In *The Nature of Economies* (2000), Jacobs wrote that "economic development is a matter of using the same universal principles that the rest of nature uses. The alternative isn't to develop some other way; some other way doesn't exist."

Shortly after Jacobs' death in 2006, we invited Mary Rowe to write a remembrance. As the former president and editor of Ideas That Matter, a convening and publishing organization based on Jacobs' work, Rowe was close to Jacobs, both professionally and personally. Currently she is the senior urban fellow with the Blue Moon Fund, a foundation that explores the relationship between human consumption and the natural world. She reflects on Jacobs, sustainability, and womanhood.

REMEMBERING JANE JACOBS
BY MARY ROWE

Jane Jacobs was unpredictable. She saw the world with such perceptive and unusual insight, she noticed what others don't. So her observations were always original and often breathtakingly provocative. Although you could not predict the content, you could sometimes anticipate the tone of her reaction, such as her response to ideology, to sweeping generalizations, to linear, easily arrived at conclusions. Of these she was fiercely critical. And her aversion to buzz words—that was predictable. She did not embrace the word "sustainability" as it is now commonly used. When such terms form part of a code, used as short-hand to indicate a complicated set of beliefs, they ultimately become meaningless. Jane would not like her ideas to be seen as part of any ideology. Sustainability included. She wasn't interested.

In the epigraph of her first classic, *The Death and Life of Great American Cities,* Jane quoted Oliver Wendell Holmes, Jr.:

> When it is said that we are too much occupied with the means of living to live, I answer that the chief worth of civilization is just that it makes the means of living more complex; that it calls for great and combined intellectual efforts, instead of simple, uncoordinated ones, in order that the crowd may be fed and clothed and housed and moved from place to place. Because more complex and intense intellectual efforts mean a fuller and richer life. They mean more life. Life is an end in itself, and the only question as to whether it is worth living is whether you have enough of it.

From the outset Jane was looking at the complexity of life—at how things interconnect. Cities and economies, and all that they encompass, were where she saw the process of life played out. She was interested in the various ways in which things work, and especially in how things work together. A keen observer of processes and interactions, she was inductive, always examining the particular, and then looking—often across her intellectual landscape to another context—to see if there were similar patterns of behavior, such as self-correcting feedback loops in termite colonies, or the perils in economic monopolies, in which feedback is artificially eliminated, blocking the natural ebb and flow of that ecology, that economy.

Where the word *sustainability* appealed to Jane is in its most basic meaning—as "long-lasting." For her that would mean things that are inherently organic, rooted to their environments in such a way—through use and contribution—that they will naturally endure and evolve through adaptation. Old buildings brought back to life through re-use. Industrial by-products becoming feedstock for needful adjacent enterprises. For her, artificial things, like publicly funded regional or rural economic schemes, or grotesquely out-of-scale condominium projects for yet-to-be-found denizens, were not part of a natural, organic occurrence and therefore were not sustainable.

If we are to understand that at the core of any of our collective notions of sustainable development is the basic premise that human life is an integrated part of ecological life, then Jane was an early identifier of this overarching understanding of connection. Where she might have parted company with some would have been her rejection of what she saw as the underlying misanthropy in "deep ecology" circles. Jane was unrelenting in her belief in humanity as co-developers with the natural world—she had an almost cosmological view. In the foreword to *The Nature of Economies*, she wrote:

> The theme running throughout this exposition—indeed, the basic premise on which the book is constructed—is that human beings exist wholly within nature as a legitimate part of natural order in every respect. To accept this unity seems to be difficult for ecologists, who assume—as many do, in understandable anger and despair—that the human species is an interloper in the natural order of things.... Readers unwilling or unable to breach a barrier that they imagine separates humankind and its works from the rest of nature will be unable to hear what this book is saying.

In that same section she dismisses others from more linear traditions—"economists, industrialists, politicians" who commit the same error in assuming that humans are separate from the natural world. But unlike their ecological counterparts who might wish to limit negative human impact, the misunderstanding of these utilitarians leads them to think it "possible for human beings to circumvent and outdo the natural order."

Both of these approaches suggest a kind of control, a curbing of human behavior to spare nature, or a harnessing of nature to suit human needs. But neither is as holistic a view as Jane's. She valued interdependency and did not judge. She challenged readers to see it as co-development and to be ever on the lookout for nuances that could help us nurture it.

A brief word on Jane Jacobs as a woman. It is true that one of the examples she chose (in *The Economy of Cities*) to illustrate how economies expand was the story of a New York dressmaker who, unsatisfied with the workings of a corset, invented the brassiere and spun off an enterprise to manufacture them. (Thank heavens.) And Jane certainly recognized in the world around her traits often ascribed as feminine, like nurturance. But she never characterized herself as a feminist—again, she was reluctant to embrace terms that smacked of intellectual rigidity.

> "I think we have to be true to the kind of species we are, and to the assets we have—ingenuity, adaptability and our diversity. We are very lucky we are not all alike, like pigeons in a flock.
>
> FROM AN INTERVIEW

Jane formed and articulated her world view from the vantage point of the household, titling one of the chapters of her final book, *Dark Age Ahead*, "Families Rigged to Fail." While feminists leapt to support her conclusions from their own analysis of gender inequality, Jane chose to cite the economics of home ownership and the erosion of spatially accessible communities as the central factors contributing to the demise of the nuclear family. So together they might have stood—Jane Jacobs and family-reform-minded feminists—but their reasons for arriving there were quite different.

Although not remotely interested in the discourse of gender identity, Jane was very much a woman interested in how people's day-to-day lives were affected by the cities and economies in which they lived and worked. In *The Economy of Cities*, she debunks seeing poverty as a pathology that should be treated, suggesting instead that we look at how to create wealth. "[P]overty has no causes. Only prosperity has causes. Analogically, heat is a result of active processes; it has causes. But cold is not the result of any processes; it is only the absence of heat."

To me this speaks to Jane's typically female approach—practical, additive, and imbued with common sense. She looked at things that worked, rather than things that did not. She was curious about the growth or flow of things rather than what she would consider vain attempts to control it. In the 1950s and 1960s, Jane eschewed any large-scale, grand plans promoted—certainly publicly, almost exclusively—by men as solutions to perceived urban problems. In an infamous conference exchange with her, Boston developer James Rouse quoted Chicago architect and planner Daniel Burnham: "Make no little plans; they have no magic to stir men's blood." Her reply: "I'm not sure big plans ever did have the magic to stir women's blood."

Finally, I return to Oliver Wendell Holmes' remarks, which Jane chose to begin her own foray as a public voice.

> I will add but a word. We are all very near despair. The sheathing that floats us over its waves is compounded of hope, faith in the unexplainable worth and sure issue of effort, and the deep, sub-conscious content which comes from the exercise of our powers.

With that invocation, Jane began what was to be a forty-five year relationship with the ideas that mattered to her and the readers who learned about them along with her. She chose to do this primarily as a writer. Her activism—she led opposition in both New York and Toronto to halt freeway expansions that would have destroyed neighborhoods—may have drawn the most media attention. But Jane saw herself as a writer. Not long after I met her, she told me that during the fanfare that followed the publication of *Death and Life*, she realized she had to choose between becoming a celebrity or doing the work. She chose the work. How fortunate for us.

Now it's our turn.

WORKS

The Death and Life of Great American Cities (1961)
The Economy of Cities (1969)
The Question of Separatism: Quebec and the Struggle over Separation (1980)
Cities and the Wealth of Nations (1984)
Systems of Survival: A Dialogue on the Moral Foundations of Commerce and Politics (1992)
The Nature of Economies (2000)
Dark Age Ahead (2004)

WHAT IS SUSTAINABILITY?

One challenge of writing a book about sustainability is that we're not certain what it is. The word itself is used in so many different ways that it virtually eludes meaning. "The term is very moldable," notes Gail Vittori, co-director of the Center for Maximum Potential Building Systems. Dianne Dillon-Ridgley explains that the use of the term reflects the breadth of the topic. "Ultimately, we're talking about the way we live. How do you name that?" Because of this uncertainty, says Mary Rowe, "Sustainability has been co-opted by everyone to refer to his or her pet thing." Ecologists use the word one way, policymakers use it another, designers another still. Many architects invoke the term as if it is synonymous with "high-performance building," which confines sustainability to one agenda within one industry. But, as Emerging Green Builders co-founder Traci Rose Rider is quick to point out, "Sustainability is not just bricks and mortar." The implications of the word, according to World Green Building Council president Kath Williams, "run the gamut from a very narrow, building-only view all the way to how you live your life and, philosophically, how you make decisions. It can take on a religious connotation."

Some see sustainability as vast in scope. "It's bigger than any of us," maintains Vittori. Artist Jackie Brookner agrees that it is treated as "too small" by the design industry. "We talk about products and technology, but really we need to change our relationship to life and death and other species, and to ourselves and each other." Natural Capitalism president L. Hunter Lovins says, "We're talking about the survival of humankind. The future doesn't work. Now what? We're going to have to reinvent every institution of business, government and society." Others, however, see the task as more personal. University of California-Berkeley professor Galen Cranz says sustainability is primarily a lifestyle choice. "This morning I walked to the post office. In the process, I saved money, strengthened my mind and body, socialized with friends and neighbors, and avoided more air pollution, fossil fuel depletion, and wear-and-tear on the roads. It's that simple."

> " Sustainability is not just bricks and mortar. "
>
> TRACI ROSE RIDER

Some say it's about responsibility and accountability. "It is not, as many people say, 'do no harm,'" insists designer Kirsten Childs. "It has to go further. It has to be restorative." If restoration is the goal, what is it we're trying to restore? Everything, says educator Jean Gardner. She measures the expanding scope of this agenda by the growing number of books she acquires. "My library, which is starting to take over my living space, is an indication of what sustainability includes. It's a way of living on the earth." But which ways of living take precedence? Consultant Bill Reed suggests that we are "evolving toward unity," seeking balance with and within the world, a state architect Anne Schopf calls "wholeness, which is the real meaning and purpose of sustainability."

Women have been instrumental in defining the "real meaning and purpose" of sustainability. Lovins claims that the first person to use the word with its current connotations was systems theorist Donella "Dana" Meadows, and research reveals no printed reference that predates the one in *Limits to Growth,* the 1972 book Meadows co-authored: "It is possible to alter these growth trends and to establish a condition of ecological and economic stability that is sustainable far into the future. The state of global equilibrium could be designed so that the basic material needs of each person on earth are satisfied and each person has an equal opportunity to realize his individual human potential." This explanation presages the most popular definition of sustainability, included in *Our Common Future,* the 1987 report from the World Commission on Environment and Development (WCED), chaired by Gro Harlem Brundtland, the first woman prime minister of Norway. "We developed the concept of sustainable development," Brundtland recalled in a recent lecture, "which means we must meet the needs of the present without compromising the ability of future generations to meet their needs."

Over the last twenty years, this simple statement has become the single most widely cited description of sustainability. Yet, despite (or perhaps because of) its popularity, the language has sparked a great deal of debate over its meaning and usefulness. Christine Ervin, former president/CEO of the U.S. Green Building Council, sums up one interpretation: "Living as if we intend to stay." Education advocate Jaimie Cloud also views it quite simply: "You can't shoot yourself and your neighbors in the foot. It's the golden rule." Yet, the simplicity of the definition is both its strength and weakness. "That's not a terribly operational statement," remarks Lovins. "What do you do on Monday morning?" And, as environmentalist Paul Hawken points out, the language isn't very inspiring. "The Brundtland Report definition is so boring. It's one of the great yawners of all time."

"Language is so important," urges Majora Carter, who works to bring green to her native South Bronx. "But it's more important to get the message right. We are trying to figure out how to make sustainability sexy but also democratize it. Right now, it's seen as something for rich people." Kath Williams agrees that many people dismiss sustainability as a luxury, "a country club topic." The elitist connotations also concern Cloud. "Low-income communities in Brooklyn think of sustainability as not gentrifying—maintaining the character of a place and its people." The association with affluence is even greater outside the U.S., she points out. "People in the two-thirds world think of sustainability as the rest of the world's desire not to let them develop. But it should mean providing a rich quality of life for all—and accomplishing this within the means of nature."

Landscape architect Kathleen Bakewell feels the differences are a matter of perspective. "Less privileged communities look at sustainability from a simple justice and fairness perspective. The privileged classes are enamored with technical solutions that address the symptoms but often ignore the underlying problems." Over-emphasizing technology is a common fear among women. "Sustainability is a social concept, not a technical or even biological one," says Cranz. "Humans made the problems. Technology alone is not a fix." So what is the fix? Jane Talkington, an environmental science student in Oklahoma, offers a simple formula: "Sustainability equals wisdom plus compassion." She calls this formula The Sustainability Equation. "Wisdom has to go beyond education and technical knowledge. It only becomes life sustaining when compassion is added. So our biggest challenge is how to teach compassion. Can you call anything 'sustainable' if it doesn't nurture?"

In this chapter, three women discuss the nurturing nature of sustainability. Lovins co-founded the Rocky Mountain Institute and co-authored *Natural Capitalism* with Paul Hawken and Amory Lovins. "This is an emergent field," she points out. "It was created in our lifetime, and we're making it up as we go." Biologist Janine Benyus is the influential author of *Biomimicry: Innovation Inspired by Nature*. "Right now we tell ourselves that the earth was put here for our use—that we are at the top of the pyramid when it comes to earthlings," she reminds us. "But of course this is a myth." And Nina Simons is co-executive director of the Collective Heritage Institute, which produces the popular Bioneers conference. "We have a tendency to factionalize, to create false separations between people and ideas," she says. "We need a shift in focus. I see this as part of the reemergence of the feminine as we work toward balance." We asked them what sustainability is and how best to pursue it. And we asked them about the word itself.

HUNTER LOVINS: All the focus groups have shown that people don't know what "sustainability" means. But, whether we like it or not, it's the word the international community has adopted.

JANINE BENYUS: It's our job now to define it. If nobody knows what it means, that's good, because we have a chance to bring the term meaning. We have to bring in the idea of flourishing—thriving instead of just surviving or hanging on by our toenails. And we have to bring the idea of thriving *equitably* into it. So, I agree with Hunter. I don't think it's time to find a new word—it's time to bring life to this one.

NINA SIMONS: It is what we have. More people relate to it in some way than any other word or phrase in our lexicon. Adding greater meaning to it is our best course of action at this point—as well as being open to new terms. We've been experimenting for some years with "restoring," partly prompted by Paul Hawken's observation that sustainability simply implies the midpoint between restoration and destruction. The state of the world is already so damaged that it's time to tip the scales toward restoration. But restoration of what and toward what? It's a challenge.

BENYUS: We can ask how nature would define sustainability. One of the problems with the standard definition is that it sounds like we're sustaining the good life for the north. When we talk about sustaining resources, it sounds like sustaining what we already have. But what we really need to sustain is biological continuity. If this movement is about anything, it's about resetting the definition of what works. And what works for life is the idea that your behavior always contributes to the continuity of life.

So, we're not trying to sustain the good life; we're sustaining that which makes life worth living—beauty, diversity, health, vitality, fertility, the capacity to heal, the capacity of life to continue. It's not so much about sustaining resources for us, it's about sustaining the capacity of the earth itself.

SIMONS: The essential disconnect we have is imagining that the environment is something outside of ourselves. But what we're really sustaining is the entire web of life. Of course, we have an amended self-interest, because it is the web of life that sustains us. A major conceptual reconnection needs to happen so we see the environment as our very ground of being.

LOVINS: Time is what's crushing us now. Things are coming at us faster and faster and faster. Dana Meadows felt that the most precious thing is the time to figure out how to live in ways that aren't destructive. So, you achieve sustainability first of all by buying time. And the best way to do that is through using resources dramatically more productively.

But that's only the first step. Then we use that time to redesign every product and process in society to achieve a vision for all living things. The third step is to manage all institutions to be restorative of all forms of capital—not just the capital that we currently count and manage, the manufactured and financial capital, but also natural capital. The integrity of intact ecosystems. And human capital, which is the integrity of cultural systems.

There are all sorts of very legitimate contributors to our economic well-being that are not counted on anybody's balance sheet at the moment. We treat them as if they have a value of zero, and that's clearly just bad economics. It's bad capitalism, it's bad business, and it's bad for life.

WOMEN in GREEN: You're all talking about sustaining the capacity of this planet. The aerospace industry is talking seriously about colonizing other planets.

LOVINS: [Physicist] Freeman Dyson once said that the meek will inherit the earth and the bold will inherit the rest of the solar system. To which Amory [Lovins] said, "You can have the rest of the solar system."

I think we should do a better job of learning to be at home in the only place in the universe where we know life exists before we have the hubris to think we know enough to create ecosystems elsewhere.

BENYUS: Our job is not to create—it's to fit in.

SIMONS: And this is the planet that created us.

BENYUS: Why do a better job here? We'll just find more of it.

LOVINS: It's the frontier mentality.

BENYUS: It really is. I understand the excitement of space, from an intellectual standpoint. But, boy, it just doesn't warm the cockles of my heart.

LOVINS: Janine, you talk about how nature uses limits as a source of innovation. And humans try to exceed limits as a source of innovation. We need to understand the value of being within limits, and one of those fundamental limits is keeping our feet planted on this place.

BENYUS: Exactly.

LOVINS: [Author and farmer] Wendell Berry says, "What I stand for is what I stand on."

SIMONS: [Author] Bill McKibben talks about cultivating a romance of limits. Part of what has allowed our culture to go awry is this ever expansionist orientation—bigger is better.

BENYUS: It's the idea of writing poetry instead of having an endless page. Someone apologized for writing a long letter by saying, "I wanted it to be shorter, but I didn't have time." It always takes more to find the essence of something. And that's what organisms do. These are the opportunities—not just on this planet but in this particular spot. In this one hundred yards or one hundred centimeters of territory, these are the opportunities, these are the limits.

What are the limits? That very simple act of asking about the opportunities in a place is an exercise we as humans, as inhabitants of our places, have not done systematically. We need a scientific method for that. We need to learn.

LOVINS: We need vision across boundaries. We need more than anything not to silo this field. We need all the disciplines. We need engineers and artists. We need everyone.

SIMONS: I'm witnessing a cultural shift from a kind of couch potato mentality, which thinks that the powers that be will take care of things, to one that actually encourages a participatory democracy—people feeling they have the resources and intelligence to pursue what comes to them through their own authority. The people who are bringing new ideas to the fore have determined that their own connection to the natural world— their inner direction and guidance—is valid and worth pursuing. That flies in the face of cultural norms.

Some say we're shifting from campaigns to governance. We need to look at a much larger picture to halt environmental degradation and restore ecological health.

LOVINS: We lack a theory of governance. The world's governments cannot agree on an implementation plan. Of the world's one hundred largest economic entities, well over half aren't countries any more—they're companies. And in an Internet-empowered world, a handful of people can de-legitimize any country or any company.

So, who's in charge here? How do you make decisions in this sort of a world? We need to invent whole new institutions, new ways of doing business, and new ways of governing.

BENYUS: One of the roles for this new governance would be to recognize and nurture what's working on a local level—the small, individual experiments that come from within, as Nina says. People are trying things on a small community level.

As individuals, we've got to get really good at recognizing what works and sharing it with others. But that's a skill that is not necessarily taught. The way science works is that somebody has a theory, and the way you get rewarded is to disprove that theory by finding the exception. The scientific method works for a lot of things, but you have a whole group of people trained to find not the common pattern you see everywhere but, rather, the odd one. What we need to find is what works, not what doesn't.

> Sustain that which makes life worth living. What makes life worth living?
>
> JANINE BENYUS

SIMONS: The progressive and sustainability movements have been attacked for being negative, for focusing on the problems. Yet, here we are in this shift towards how we cultivate awareness, support innovation, and recognize what works—the beauty of this exquisite system that has borne us. It feels like an interesting paradigm shift.

LOVINS: There really is a paradigm shift between the environmental movement, which focused on what it didn't like, and the sustainability movement, which asks what works. What is it that we want? What is our vision? Where are we going? How do we get there?

BENYUS: Once we figure out what works, we tend to sit back and relax. But actually, that's not at all what life does. Moment to moment, organisms say, "I'm feeding here, and I seem to be safe." But that doesn't mean they're not looking over their shoulder, wondering, "Is this still a safe place?" When it's not, when they see the shadow of a hawk or other predator, it's time to change the strategy.

So, there's another set of tools we need to teach. Constantly evaluate our technologies and our strategies in light of context, because the context is always changing. How do we teach people to be fully tuned in? If sustainability is the search for well-adapted solutions for a particular place, we have to understand the context fully. Otherwise "well-adapted" means nothing. Well adapted to what? Where?

So how do we teach people to check out context, correct course, and re-invent the next solution? And the next one and next one?

LOVINS: How do we teach people to be present?

SIMONS: To question their own assumptions.

BENYUS: Exactly. I don't know whether it's our culture or human nature, but we always want to find the solution that works for all time. What we need to do is find any solution rather than looking for the durable one. We need a durable solution-seeking model.

LOVINS: [Ecologist] Allan Savory says that no approach works outside the environment in which we apply it. If we assume we're right, which as humans we tend to do, we will miss early warning signs. It's much better to do the best you can, understand the system you're in, determine the goals for that particular situation, then measure that against the constraints of the environment. Assume you're wrong for being wrong. That's the approach of holistic management, and it sure works on a piece of ground.

SIMONS: I see a paradigm shift to correcting an imbalance that has been prevalent for 5,000 years. That is to over-value traits relegated to the "masculine" and to undervalue and deride those qualities associated with the "feminine."

So, in terms of abandoning the quest for the simple fast solution, I hear an embracing of not only humility but also vulnerability. And the recognition of what a young species we are, how much we have to learn.

And I don't relegate this only to people who are in male bodies or women's bodies. I really believe we all have masculine and feminine within us, but we are all recovering from a very long cultural period where things associated with the feminine have been squelched.

There are particular perspectives and perhaps even biological skills that are associated with the feminine that are called for in the societal shift toward a sustainable future.

BENYUS: Absolutely. Including our prerogative to change our minds if we screw up. I'm a flip-flopper by nature and I'm proud of it. I'll flip and I'll flop if I need to. Certainty is overrated.

SIMONS: UCLA researchers recently discovered that, biologically, men and women respond differently to stress. Men tend to react with a fight, flight or freeze response. But when women are stressed, our bodies release a hormone called oxytocin, which is also released in childbirth. Women tend to respond with a desire to connect with others—we socialize. Instead of "fight or flight," we "tend and befriend." The very act of connecting with other people calms the body's response to the stress. So, perhaps women are particularly equipped for a different model of leadership that is more collaborative, more interactive and more social. More group-oriented.

> We need to invent whole new institutions, new ways of doing business, and new ways of governing.
>
> HUNTER LOVINS

BENYUS: This idea that you're not ashamed to be dependent on other people is another one of those traits we have to tune up in our species. We're not just dependent on one another or even primarily dependent on one another—we're dependent on creatures we don't even have names for yet.

It's one thing to say, "I'll tolerate this ant's existence. I won't kill it right now." It's a different attitude to say, "Wow! Thanks for all you're doing for me, ant." It's a different way of thinking. It's tough if you are trained culturally to value extreme independence. We need to wake up.

SIMONS: [Biologist] Lynn Margulis says we're here to be a host to the microbes—which makes me nervous about antimicrobial soaps. What are you doing to all these critters? We need them.

BENYUS: We're really just making them bad asses. That's what we're doing. We're making big motorcycle gangs out of them. They'll be around a lot longer than we will.

WiG: Nina talked about the need for feminine sensibilities. How important is diversity of any kind?

LOVINS: Diversity is the basis of life and its capacity to create more life. As Janine says, "Life creates conditions conducive to life."

But I get a bit worried when we tag these skills and abilities as feminine or masculine, because if you look at most of the female leaders the world has known, they've embodied the worst traits. And we all know men who are far better at nurturing than most women.

I think we need to rename what these capacities are and take it out of the sexually charged debate. Fair enough, women have long been one of those oppressed groups, and oppression of any group is a bad idea. I've been working recently in Afghanistan, where women are very oppressed. If ever I've had a reason to turn feminist, that experience would do it. But at the same time, putting these capacities into the gender debate risks alienating a whole group of people we most desperately need to start adopting these tendencies.

BENYUS: If you think about any group of people that has been considered "other"—people of color, lesbians, handicapped, old, you name it—those are the people able to see the world from another point of view. And it helps to get other voices. People who have been "other" know what it's like—women know what it's like to live in a world that is male-centered. And gay people know what it's like to live in a world that is heterosexually-centered. You live within it and yet you are always *other*.

What if we were to turn the whole world around and see it through the homosexual viewpoint? How would the world look then? What if we were to turn the world around and have it be through the viewpoint of the South instead of the North? And what if we were to turn it around and have the viewpoint through the eyes of organisms other than humans? The human-centered viewpoint is just one of many. The biological definition of sustainability has to do with life and sustaining the plasma of the biosphere, that basketball skin. So, to see things from other points of view will become an important trait if we want to make the change from human-centered to life-centered.

> What people are yearning for is purpose. Where do we want to go? What can this world be?
>
> NINA SIMONS

SIMONS: [Physicist] Fritjof Capra says that the shift to an eco-literate society involves a shift from a focus on counting things to a focus on mapping relationships. We live in a world that has tended to devalue women, people of color, the elderly, and much of the natural world. There are all kinds of other experiences throughout our culture, and part of the task at hand is to cultivate empathy. The truth of the golden rule is biological and palpable. What we do unto others we do unto ourselves.

The sense of false separation that our culture has cultivated for so long is exactly what we need to transcend. That is true for all of us. If, in fact, women are in some ways hard wired for relationships, we may have an opportunity to model that kind of collaborative leadership.

[Environmentalist] Winona LaDuke recently told me, "If you're not at the table, you're on the menu." It went right to the core of diversity for me. What does it mean to call all the voices to the table—including those that don't have a voice? How do we exercise all of our abilities to form alliances with those other than human—whether it's with our land, our place, a tree, or a species?

BENYUS: The outsider status. You can either be seen as a real bummer or you can use it to help the voices of other outsiders be heard.

SIMONS: The experience of being an outsider—probably all of us have had it in one way or another. That experience asks us to recognize and reclaim our inner authority. There is a healing function that outsiders can serve.

WIG: Hunter mentioned her work abroad. If we're talking about different ways of viewing sustainability, is there a particularly American point of view?

LOVINS: All countries have their myths of who they are and what it is that they value. Values derive from what is adaptive, what helps you survive. We're at a time in world history in which survival of most life is in question. Two of every five creatures on earth are now endangered. So what we have been doing is politically not adaptive. Sociologically, this means we're in an extremely risky time of having to question or reaffirm core values.

If you look at American mythology, we've allowed marketers and the media to use bad myths to lead us astray. For example, where I live in Colorado there's still a strong cowboy culture. People think of the cowboy as a rugged individual male, but if you look at what cowboy culture actually was, it was people utterly dependent on each other who came together to raise barns, gather cattle together, and have communal feasts. It was in many ways very egalitarian. If you look at any rural community, you'll find this. It's much more about cooperation than it is about competition, yet we've allowed the myth to become the rugged individual with the gun, striding the planet and doing whatever the hell he wants. The macho big SUV tearing up the countryside comes out of that. To what extent are these myths being manipulated against us, and to what extent are they still adaptive? To what extent do we need to create new myths?

So, as we're struggling to find our way, it may be useful to revisit some of the core myths about what it is to be American. What do we truly value? Dana Meadows said we seek to meet non-material needs with material things. Bernard Amadei, the brilliant founder of Engineers without Borders, talks about the connection between inner poverty and outer poverty.

What is it that we all want in our lives? To have a love that we substitute cosmetics for? To have a sense of place that we substitute a football team for? To have a sense of enough-ness in ourselves that we substitute a great big automobile for? What are we trying to sustain with sustainability? What sort of a future do we want to build?

SIMONS: What we are all talking about is storytelling. What is the story of this culture and this country? What are the stories we tell ourselves, and how do we become more mindful of which stories really serve us and which don't? How do we realize that we are not our stories?

It seems that one of the most valuable capacities we could cultivate is the capacity to witness ourselves, to step outside of those things we presume to be so that we begin to understand our context with fresh eyes.

BENYUS: How do we enhance our capacity to see the world and ourselves as we really are? If we are going to innovate, how do we honestly evaluate the world as it really is? Boy, that's real truth-telling.

I think we're going to have an opportunity to do that. I've been thinking about how to tell each other the story of what's happening to the planet. As we drag ourselves through climate change, there's going to be such ecological disruption that it's going to get unrecognizable in places. So right now it's important for us to be telling the stories of the change.

My friend [activist] Howie Wolke talks about landscape amnesia. People will look at beaten down riparian areas that have no willows and say that's the way streams look around here. But then the old-timers say there used to be huge cottonwoods. We're telling each other the stories of the landscape.

Say we weren't telling the story of the obesity epidemic right now. Say, we kept quiet, and twenty years from now nobody remembered that three quarters of the people were very, very large. We'd have body amnesia. It's the same sort of thing. We have an opportunity to draw attention to what we're losing and what the new ecological conditions are—and then to tie that to our actions as a species. It's such a teachable moment.

SIMONS: The carrot is stronger than the stick. What people are yearning for is purpose. Where do we want to go? What can this world be?

LOVINS: [Author] Dave Korten says that people—Americans in particular but Western people in general—want three things: prosperity, security, and meaning. How does behaving in more environmentally and socially responsible ways enhance prosperity in a community? How does it enhance our security, and how does it give you personally greater meaning in your life?

BENYUS: Sustain that which makes life worth living. What makes life worth living?

LOVINS: [The late folk singer] Kate Wolfe's dictum was to find what you really care about and live a life that shows it. That's how you do this.

WHAT IS SUSTAINABLE DESIGN?

A perennial question about sustainable design is whether it is a design agenda at all. Is it more about sustainability or about design? Many architects and builders consider it a purely technical agenda pursued exclusively through materials and methods—the science of building, not the art of architecture. Certainly many of the buildings touted as green cannot be called inspired design, at least not by any traditional measure. What is the place of aesthetics in sustainability?

Among consumers, "green" often brings to mind rusticity, not refinement—what designer Annette Stelmack calls "granola and Birkenstock style." As a result, artist Jackie Brookner says that sustainable design has been relatively uninspiring so far. "We have to make this sexy, irresistible, and joyful! The point is to live within the climate and celebrate that." Outside the building industry, women are leading some of the most exciting efforts to bring a fresh look to environmentally conscious design. Fashion designer Linda Loudermilk's eco-couture collection gives green an edgy sex appeal. "Nature may be beautiful," she claims. "But nature is not pretty." Clothing inspired by living systems is "not about making something pretty to wear; it's about holy fearsome awe." Furniture designer Jill Salisbury feels that design should bring delight, which she considers a particularly feminine sensibility. "Women put the 'chic' in 'eco-chic.'"

Making environmentalism chic could give it greater appeal, but it also risks equating it with affluence. After all, Loudermilk named her line "Luxury Eco," and Salisbury's heirloom-quality chairs are quite expensive. Is sustainability a privilege or a necessity? "Affordable green is the key," insists Patty Rose of GreenHOME, a non-profit that promotes low-cost housing. "If it isn't economical, it is only for those with money to spare. Where is the environmental and social justice in that?" The same could be asked of good design in general, so this criticism isn't necessarily specific to green. Yet, even as women are bringing together nature and fashion, they also are being used by fashion to harm nature, according to Naomi Wolf. In her best-selling study *The Beauty Myth*, she suggests that product marketing uses sexualized images of women to spur more consumption, which directly attributes to the depletion of natural resources. Graphic designer and branding consultant Janine James says her profession has a great responsibility to consider the consequences of its actions. "How are the images we're bombarded with affecting us? Advertising is full of images of young, emaciated women. How does that affect women's self-esteem?"

But James insists the industry is fundamentally optimistic. "As designers we live in the paradigm of opportunity." Landscape architect Julie Bargmann agrees that design should be joyous. "This should be fun, shouldn't it?" Industrial designer Amelia Amon maintains that great design can encourage preservation instead of consumption. If we ignore aesthetics, she says, we do so "at our peril." Products should inspire, and lack of inspiration leads to lack of value, which leads to waste. "Our instinctual love of beauty may still be our best hope for preserving our natural environment." Environmental psychologist Judith Heerwagen attributes this "instinctual love of beauty" to biophilia, the more general human attraction to nature. The brain evolved in a particular environment, adapting to certain stimuli, and we respond to beauty because we once associated it with a survival advantage. As she puts it, "Interest and pleasure signal that an environment is likely to provide resources that promote survival and reproductive fitness." To paraphrase biologist E. O. Wilson, beauty is in the genes of the beholder.

> "Our instinctual love of beauty may still be our best hope for preserving our natural environment."
>
> AMELIA AMON

Leslie Hoffman of Earth Pledge maintains, "None of us wants to sacrifice beauty to achieve sustainability, but taste is a funny thing. What you see as beauty can change." And of course, a fixation with appearances often can lead us astray. *New York Times* columnist Maureen Dowd recounts that according to recent studies people perceived to be "beautiful" typically earn higher wages (five percent more per hour), so there is a strange relationship between beauty and equity. And the desire for natural beauty can lead to unnatural pursuits. Dowd reports that among American women there has been a 118 percent increase in cosmetic surgery over the last decade. "It's all about faking better genes," she writes. "Survival of the fittest has been replaced by survival of the fakest."

What makes design sustainable, however, isn't superficial attraction but long-term fulfillment—less eye candy than soul food. As Leslie Hoffman puts it, "The pretty picture is not enough." A number of women have told us that the best design enhances well-being for the mind, body, and spirit all at once. "It has to be a wonderful thing to occupy," says architect Anni Tilt. "If we don't connect with it, have an attachment with it, it's not 'sustainable.'" Architect Patricia Patkau says this connection has to be renewed continually. "We have to think about how buildings adapt over time. If they aren't culturally sustainable, people will tear them down for other reasons." Many consider the long view a particularly feminine tendency. "The goal is bigger than the object," explains architect Julie Eizenberg. "When you design from the other point of view, you're trying to impress people with the power of what you've done. That's about showmanship. Sustainable design is about the relationship between people and the world."

Some of the best known women designers still exhibit what Eizenberg calls "the other point of view"—an architecture of showmanship. Zaha Hadid, the only woman to win the Pritzker Prize, architecture's Nobel, hasn't done much to dispel this image—the sculptural exuberance of her work appears to be as much about self-aggrandizement as anything else. The classic persona of the heroic architect lives on, even if the hero happens to be a heroine. By contrast, another celebrated female designer, Maya Lin, famous for the Vietnam Veterans' Memorial, is known for sensitivity to natural and cultural context. According to *BusinessWeek* magazine, "If the most famous architect of our day, Frank Gehry, is all about gargantuan, computer-shaped, titanium temples to high technology, then Lin is about restraint, the environment, organic materials, and a new kind of architectural humanism. Lin is the anti-Gehry." Architect Allison Ewing wonders if such sensitivity will become more popular. "Perhaps we will see a different kind of expression coming out of a new cadre of female designers."

In the following conversation, three prominent designers weigh in on design, sustainability, and the opportunities and challenges for the industry and women. Interior designer Kirsten Childs notes that women have been at the forefront of the sustainable design movement but generally not in high-profile design positions. Architect Sandra Mendler maintains that design is the area in which women eventually could have the greatest impact by cultivating more responsive places. And Susan Maxman, the first woman president of the American Institute of Architects and a repeat winner of its Committee on the Environment awards, is known for both sensitive design and exceptional leadership. We asked them what makes good design.

SANDRA MENDLER: Design is the process of envisioning and making things—bringing into being something that doesn't already exist. People are motivated to make things for many different reasons. Design is a process, and the way people engage the process varies, depending on their values. There's good design and bad design, and good design reflects cultural values.

KIRSTEN CHILDS: For me design takes function to a higher level. There would be no design without need. Think about craft—craft came out of utility. We look at a beautiful wooden bowl and think how pretty it is, but at first the bowl was made just to hold something. For me, it was very primitive. Good design turns utility into inspiration.

MENDLER: If we focus on architecture, good design responds to the unique challenges and opportunities of a place, climate, and culture.

SUSAN MAXMAN: It addresses many issues at the same time. Is it appropriate? Is it doing everything it should do? Does it delight the senses? The most wonderful design brings it all together in a cohesive way. Bad design ignores important issues that need to be resolved.

MENDLER: Yes. Limited thinking—a limited sense of what the issues are. Good design creates something more holistic and inspired. Over time, there's been a greater realization that good design can't happen in a vacuum. Everything is part of complex, interrelated systems, and what we design affects them.

WOMEN in GREEN: Does sustainability fundamentally alter what we perceive to be good design, or does it just add to or clarify it?

MENDLER: You can't draw a line between good design and sustainable design. I haven't seen a building I can look at and say, "That's great design, but I wish it were sustainable." I would say, "There's limited thinking here. It's not good enough." How can we call it great design if it ignores the impact on people and the larger environment?

MAXMAN: I agree. I hope there comes a time when we don't have to talk about sustainable design and we can just call it good design. To me, they're one and the same.

CHILDS: Historically, there was a much greater adherence to sustainable design, partly because people didn't have air conditioning or artificial lighting. They didn't have all the things that allowed us to stray off the path—to put up buildings with enormous floors where the executives are plastered around the windows and the worker bees at the interior never see the light of day.

MENDLER: I am intrigued by the politics of what you're saying. Social justice issues are intertwined with the way buildings have evolved in our culture.

WiG: Are you saying that buildings used to be more environmentally and socially sustainable at the same time?

MENDLER: I don't think we should assume there was a golden age in the past. There were a lot of inadequate, substandard buildings.

CHILDS: Every age has had good and bad design.

MAXMAN: I'm always inspired by indigenous architecture—it has a kind of intuitive innocence. The Montezuma Castle cliff dwelling in Arizona is a good example. It really sings, because it's necessary but beautiful. It responds to its environment with a sense of style appropriate to that place. But after modern technology came along, style dominated. Climate was dealt with artificially, so no one had to think about anything but Style with a capital "S." Now we run the risk of green building becoming a style. If it does, we've missed the point.

> "You can't draw a line between good design and sustainable design.
>
> SANDRA MENDLER

CHILDS: Architects used to dismiss sustainable design because they thought it was the next fad and would fade quickly. But it's a process, not a style. It's another layer of care and attention to detail.

MAXMAN: Many architects aren't interested in sustainability because they think it interferes with pure sculptural form.

MENDLER: There's been a deterioration of architectural expression in the U.S.—the use of air conditioning and the creation of sealed buildings have made most buildings pretty boring. If design is to make positive contributions to the built environment, it should be visually expressive. Good green buildings have a relationship to their place and climate that makes them richer as objects. That's exciting. So it's not a style, but it is visually engaging.

CHILDS: It's visually engaging, and it's also subliminally engaging. We feel better in a green building. The best design relates well to its environment in every way. You can usually recognize a green building, but it can't become a style.

MAXMAN: A style in that sense is repetitive—all the buildings look the same. Sustainable design is the opposite. It evolves out of its place and time, its people and culture.

CHILDS: It's applicable to every kind of building, so it is absolutely not a style.

MENDLER: It's not a style, but the idea of the profession engaging these issues and calling them something is a good thing. It allows people to embrace a complex set of ideas. As long as we're not dumbing it down so it becomes about liking the way a double-skin curtain wall looks. Often designers do things because of the visual effect, regardless of whether it makes sense.

MAXMAN: It shouldn't be about applying surface aesthetics.

CHILDS: It's about doing the right thing. LEED has gotten the whole industry up and running, but the fact that it's not regionally weighted undermines its real value. At this time, LEED doesn't address water issues in California differently than elsewhere, for example. Doing the right or "sustainable" thing for a particular climate would also keep buildings from looking the same everywhere.

MAXMAN: The biggest problem with LEED is that it does the opposite of what sustainable design is supposed to do.

CHILDS: There is a tendency to pursue points instead of pursuing a green building.

MAXMAN: Yes. It's not a holistic approach.

CHILDS: Every firm now is trying to practice some form of sustainable design, which is great. But many of them are not being very innovative. They're using tried-and-true methods and not really pushing the envelope.

WiG: Why is innovation important? In places like Nantucket or Santa Fe, wouldn't continuing local traditions be the most responsible thing to do?

CHILDS: If you look at Nantucket houses—how and where they were built on the island, how they deal with weather and so on— they come out of a real understanding of natural systems. But today you can use that inherent knowledge and also incorporate better daylighting, better adhesives, cleaner materials. You can take lessons from the location, climate and region and put them together with new knowledge to make a better product.

WIG: You said earlier that sustainable design applies to every building type, but some projects and programs require very little, if any, connection between inside and out— small windows, little ventilation, et cetera.

CHILDS: There are a large number of issues relative to sustainable design, not all of which can be achieved within each project. But you can still make progress on every project.

MENDLER: Every project can benefit from broad, holistic thinking to make better decisions. Every architect should do that. There's no excuse not to. But over the next decade we may see buildings transform in more fundamental ways. It's entirely possible that we'll transform our urban patterns into a living infrastructure. We may end up with an aggregated grid that uses buildings as primary generators of energy in cities. As designers, we are solving individual problems for clients, but we're also advocates for a larger set of concerns. We're doing both as stewards of the built environment.

MAXMAN: Right. As professionals we have a responsibility to show our clients that they can contribute to the greater good of all.

CHILDS: To lessen the impact of the built environment on the natural environment, every designer and architect needs to become engaged in sustainable issues. Everything we do at this point is an exemplar. But designers can't have much impact unless we work together. All they can do is demonstrate and share information. We don't get anywhere by withholding it.

MENDLER: Once we've become more aware of the larger issues—the impact buildings have on health, energy use, et cetera—we can't just ignore them. Now they are part of the design exercise. Now an architect turning a blind eye is negligent.

WIG: In your own ways, you all have been innovators in this field. You also happen to be women. Is that a coincidence?

MENDLER: We tend to think women are more concerned for the environment because of their nurturing side, and we consider women more collaborative and more able to bring people together. But I know a lot of men who have those skills and abilities, too, so I don't think they are just in the female domain. That being said, those things are all important. This work does require open-mindedness, interest in collaboration, and concern about larger issues, not just self-interests.

MAXMAN: But they're probably more prevalent in women.

MENDLER: Probably, but they're present in both and, of course, we see many men in this field, too.

WiG: Susan, you were both the first woman president of the AIA and also the first president to focus on sustainable design. Was that more of a challenge or an opportunity?

> **Designers can't have much impact unless we work together.**
>
> KIRSTEN CHILDS

MAXMAN: Everyone thought I was a little crazy to go out on a limb on some strange notion. But I always felt it was easier being a woman in this field, because I was never part of the men's club. I was always the odd man out, so to speak—or the odd woman out. So for me to do something like this was easy, because I didn't care about conforming to anything. Ever. And I wasn't used to conforming, because I never had cohorts that always thought the same way I did. I was never one of the guys, so I was used to taking chances.

MENDLER: I like your point. In order to be successful, women in this profession had to be less concerned about climbing ladders and meeting expectations, because they couldn't achieve any influence that way. They needed to find other ways to be heard, and that turned out to be a benefit.

MAXMAN: It was also timing. This was the early '90s, and architects were really suffering financially. I thought environmental responsibility was a great way to elevate the whole profession with a mission people could be proud of. I thought this could get us back on our feet. This seemed like the right message at the time.

CHILDS: But it was such a hard sell in the beginning. People thought, "Here come the tree huggers again."

MAXMAN: People had such a bad image of this from the '70s.

CHILDS: In the mid-'80s, doing what was then called environmentally-informed design was such a hard sell because of the failed early efforts. The ideas were right, but the technology wasn't there yet. The whole thing had such a bad reputation. Remember solar collectors on the White House? Being a woman didn't make it easier or more difficult, either way. I mean, we were all regarded as being a bit screwball. People literally thought we were nuts.

MENDLER: I never saw it as nutty, but you're right that it was a challenge to bring in a new way of thinking. People had to address things they preferred not to have to worry about. People would refer to me as the nerd architect.

WIG: There is an image of the architect as a lone visionary genius that is clearly masculine. Does sustainable design alter that image?

MENDLER: Many architects are just solving their own design aesthetic, like sculptors or artists.

MAXMAN: Architects can't all be Frank Lloyd Wright or Frank Gehry. I'm concerned about who young architects are emulating. Who are their gods? The hope is that the profession will provide more role models who collaborate to solve these problems. And ironically, the collaborative architect could be more celebrated.

MENDLER: There's always going to be a place for both the fabric of cities as well as the occasional building as sculptural statement. Sustainable design can make every building better. We have the potential to enrich the formal aspects of design and also create a deep respect for people and place.

WHAT IS COMMUNITY?

"There is no such thing as sustainable development," Native American organizer Winona LaDuke has said. "Community is the only thing in my experience that is sustainable." In other words, rethinking how we live together is possibly the core issue of sustainability, whether the focus is the global population or a single household. Settlement patterns and the behaviors they promote are the primary human relationship with the earth. Physical and social conditions are intertwined, and development depends on community.

But what exactly is community? "Is it place-based, or is it about shared interests, values, or demographics?" asks Dana Bourland, director of the Enterprise Foundation's Green Communities Initiative. And if the idea of community is unclear, how do we begin to understand a "sustainable" community? One way is to avoid the word altogether. The Blue Moon Fund's Mary Rowe says, "We're working with the idea of creating *sustained* communities. In my mind, it's a simpler thing." Conjugation aside, most agree that community transcends physical development. According to LaDuke, "A common set of values is needed to live together sustainably on the land." Yet Mary Tucker, with the City of San Jose, assures us that respecting individual needs and desires is more important. "How can we make it easy for people to have a good environment in the way they define that for themselves?" Or as Bourland puts it, "People ultimately define their own community. Why? Because we want to feel part of something larger than ourselves."

Such inclusiveness is critical, suggests sociologist and urban historian Dolores Hayden, who maintains that what normally passes for *sustainable growth* cannot be considered *fair growth.* "Most of the literature about green building looks at how much energy goes into a building, but sustainability has a much larger economic impact than that. We don't have any sustainable communities in the U.S. if you look at economic issues. Often there's a lot of unpaid labor that goes into making buildings and communities." Her most recent book, *A Field Guide to Sprawl,* urges communities "to pursue a balanced, integrated built environment where social interaction and sensitivity to the natural landscape have not been sacrificed to mindless growth machines."

Mindless growth is a common concern. Intentionality is crucial, insists Majora Carter, executive director of Sustainable South Bronx. "No community just 'becomes' something—communities are made. You can design a community in many different ways, but what is most important is for people to become empowered and actually participate." Joanne Denworth of the Pennsylvania Governor's Policy Office agrees. "Good design is the key factor in whether a community works or not. It's still a challenge to translate this into the world of policy and political decisions." Product designer Wendy Brawer says community design is just "how we define home. It's more than my house or my block or my city." According to earth artist Patricia Johanson, every act of design is community design, whether the designer acknowledges it or not. "You have to look at everything and make it good for everyone. That is design for the whole community."

> **What is most important is for people to become empowered and actually participate.**
>
> MAJORA CARTER

"Sustainable design has as much to do with social justice as anything else," says architect Martha Jane Murray. "I have always had a feeling that if we don't sustain people and the community, the rest of it is sort of empty." Environmental consultant Joel Todd concurs: "If you are not nourishing the community and the society, it doesn't matter how good a building is." Los Angeles architect Angela Brooks, who recently started the development company Livable Places, echoes this. "I always felt that good design was more about the urban environment. The singular building is just a small part of that." Architect Jenifer Seal Cramer, who runs the New Commons Group, a progressive real estate and development company, suggests sustainable design is much greater than individual projects. "This is about how we are going to live here. The question is how to create life-enriching places with rich solutions that solve several problems at once." Geographer, planner, and professor Emily Talen sees community design and sustainable design as the same thing. "The basic idea of walkable, diverse communities is a sustainable one. You're providing the infrastructure of collective life." At the heart of this, she says, is "a female take on how community life should work, though the proponents don't discuss it that way. Women suffered most from the isolation of the suburbs—as [Betty Friedan's] *The Feminine Mystique* laid bare. They benefit most from access to services, transportation, and to having different housing types mixed together."

"The way you make things sustainable," Jane Jacobs once said, "is largely by diversification, adding things that haven't been done... [A]ny ecosystem is an extremely complicated thing. The moment we try to simplify it ... we are going to be in trouble." A community's "ecosystem," she said, relies on caregiving—everyday citizens, often mothers, keeping their "eyes on the street." In many places today, women are still the ones watching after community welfare. Los Angeles urban planner Susan Jackson Harden has worked with the Peace Corps in Senegal and AmeriCorps in Kansas City, and in each she noticed, "Women were the change agents. They were raising the kids and working at the grassroots level to make their communities what they thought they could be." This fact doesn't surprise Gail Vittori, who has worked with many communities. "Women have always played the role of protecting community health and welfare." Or, as Mary Rowe puts it, "Culturally, the kinds of skill sets that bring about sustaining communities are the skills that run effective households."

We brought together three women to discuss the nature of community. Landscape architect Lucia Athens runs the office of Sustainability and Environment for the city of Seattle. Attorney and community development expert Lauren Anderson recently served on the Bring Back New Orleans commission. And architect and consultant Hillary Brown of New Civic Works founded the Office of Sustainable Design for New York City's Department of Design & Construction. We asked them what makes a sustainable community.

LUCIA ATHENS: It's mind-boggling to think about what a truly sustainable community would require. It's much easier to focus on green building as a design problem—you can think about inputs and outputs and how to provide for as many needs as possible on an individual site. But when you extend that to an entire community, you have to look at social capital.

HILLARY BROWN: Strong civic bodies have a lot of intrinsic social capital. They work well together, and they have the political will to improve the longevity of the community. But

I struggle with definitions. What are ways we can enrich and expand without destructive growth?

LAUREN ANDERSON: I'm accustomed to working with marginal neighborhoods we're reclaiming as "places of choice." New Orleans has a much lower rate of migration into and out of the city than most cities. During Hurricane Katrina, there were people who left New Orleans who had never been on a plane before.

BROWN: Communities are brought together by common interests. Part of it is civic pride. I think of New York as an amazing aggregation of communities—some more solidified, some more diffuse.

ATHENS: There are different scales of community. I think of Seattle as part of the regional community of Puget Sound, which transcends the boundaries of the city. There is a shared sense of values and awareness of what makes our region special.

Over 60 percent of the people who live here wouldn't move if they were offered a higher paying job somewhere else. Part of it is the setting. People identify strongly with Seattle's natural environment—the water, the Sound, and the mountains that surround us. So, while we live in a very dynamic economy, people are here because they love the sense of place.

ANDERSON: In New Orleans the unifying factors are culture and family—people are here in spite of the environment, not because of it. We're totally influenced by it, but we realize how vulnerable it is. Even knowing the risks, people are coming back.

Neighborhoods are critically important to people's sense of identity and place. It's not just about being from New Orleans—it's about being from Saint Bernard Parish or Chalmette. This is a multi-generational phenomenon—in many communities, your whole extended family lives within a very small geographic radius.

ATHENS: It's interesting to look at the nexus between the natural and cultural environments. In Seattle, people spend a lot of time indoors because it rains so much. We have a great café culture, and we're very bookish—we have more bookstores per capita than any other city in the U.S.

BROWN: We sort ourselves according to a physiological or psychological affinity for place. New York is a very "high-amp" culture. There are a multitude of stressors that have less to do with nature than with the absence of it. Just as New Orleans is about family and culture, New York is about business and culture.

ATHENS: And Seattle is about nature and culture. Ann Whiston Spirn said it best in *The Granite Garden*—nature is *in* the city as well as "out there." Parks, public spaces, landscaping, and urban streams are connective biological elements in urban areas.

BROWN: Community pride is probably place-related, because it's visualized—it's experiential.

ATHENS: It's difficult to imagine a city without its physical setting—I don't think you can separate them. Seattle's setting allows us to be a big port, which is one reason it feels very different from Portland. The natural and built environments work together to create a sense of place.

ANDERSON: It's hard for me to respond to places without a clear geographic identity. Post-World War II suburban communities have very little sense of place or history. In many respects they are more vulnerable today than urban communities. The quality of building is far inferior to the housing stock in most urban areas. And the same social ills we associate with urban communities are beginning to play themselves out. So I might define sustainable communities by what they are not.

> **How do we create communities that embrace all people?**
>
> LAUREN ANDERSON

ATHENS: Bland subdivisions where everything feels the same and there's no street life.

ANDERSON: They don't unite people—they divide them. A critical factor is the overlay of race and class. Look at the evolution of cities and suburbs—their physical separation was a way to achieve social segregation. Now, as some urban areas become more popular, poor people of color are being pushed out. There are scientific solutions for many environmental issues, but not for issues of class and race. How do we create communities that embrace all people?

ATHENS: It's a tricky puzzle. In Seattle, we've been trying to create more diversity of housing types, but many people are afraid that mixed uses will impact the value of their homes.

BROWN: We think about demographics and population as being in a state of change, and what we look for in sustainability is an ecologically stable mix. The influx of new money often creates social fragility—like an invasive species in an ecosystem.

Monocultures such as gated suburban communities are not socially healthy environments. There are parallels with ecological diversity—an ecosystem is constantly being replenished by new genetic material. I would liken that to creating racially, financially, and socially integrated communities.

ANDERSON: Diversity is not necessarily embraced by everyone—not just the majority group but also the minority group. How do you encourage development that supports diversity when ultimately it has to overcome inherent personal biases?

Here in New Orleans, a troubled public housing development was demolished and replaced with what some consider a very aesthetically pleasing new community. But it created little opportunity for the former low-income residents to come back. The progressive community hears "mixed income" as a code word for moving poor people out.

> There needs to be more room for improvisation. We need to leave space for the community to evolve.
>
> LUCIA ATHENS

WOMEN in GREEN: If communities are to develop "naturally" like an ecosystem, what is the role of designers who are accustomed to creating new things?

ATHENS: There needs to be more room for improvisation. We can't create perfect communities where every last detail is figured out. We need to leave space for the community to evolve. It's not like a marching band, where everybody knows their part ahead of time. It's more like jazz improvisation.

BROWN: We can make fine-grained improvements in environmental performance that will add up to a bigger impact over time. Maybe it's a feminine understanding that change is made up of the coordination of thousands of incremental improvements. It doesn't have to be just the "big idea."

How do we create a healthy urban ecology? We think of cities as imposing themselves on nature, but urban ecology weaves together natural and built systems in ways that support the viability of each. Is there a hybrid between constructed systems and the living systems that support them?

WiG: Lauren, didn't the Bring Back New Orleans Commission consider something like this?

ANDERSON: After the storm, outside consultants made a strong recommendation to shrink the footprint of the city and allow nature to reclaim major areas. Overwhelmingly, people have rebelled against that. It's one thing to reclaim obsolete commercial or industrial spaces along a riverfront. It's another thing to buy out family homes to create public spaces in the flood plains. How can you tell people they need to give up their neighborhood so it can be turned back into wetlands?

BROWN: What are the right methods of engaging people in the conversation about what's good for the community?

ATHENS: Sharing stories. We need to define success differently, and encourage participation towards that definition. Increasing the Gross Domestic Product is not a measure of sustainability. An oil spill or war could increase GDP while depleting natural and human capital. Dialogue and awareness of the impact of our decisions is important.

BROWN: The word I use is "stock-taking"—getting people engaged in a process of looking at how well we are doing.

WiG: Did 9/11 affect New York in this way?

BROWN: It was an opportunity to re-sharpen priorities. People showed extraordinary resilience and willingness to do what needed to be done. There are intense moments, milestone moments, that bring out the best in people. These moments stretch us to think more acutely about what ties us together.

ANDERSON: Katrina created a unique opportunity for the entire region. I've made the analogy to someone who has survived a life-threatening illness—they pause and re-assess their whole lives. We had that opportunity when we were forced out of our homes last fall. The storm created a true diaspora of people who have been separated from the roots that sustain them as a people. There has been incredible grassroots organization—people coming together without government assistance to declare that their neighborhoods are coming back.

The discussions about rebuilding have everything to do with the sense of place here. People from outside of the community have not been able to appreciate how important place is to people here.

BROWN: When we're working with a community or large organization, it's important to embed ourselves in their culture and see people's own vision for ways to change. Work in tandem with community representatives and not just with externally imposed "experts." It gives them ownership.

Women's ways of thinking are important for this process. The nature of our leadership is to work in networks—it's not top-down. Women often feel more comfortable in a participatory context, and a process that is highly collaborative is intrinsic to the sustainability agenda. Allow people to define for themselves what is sustainable.

ATHENS: I have found that women are the most powerful people in the sustainability movement. What's missing is for the women to realize their power and organize. The "good old boy" network is alive and well, even in sustainability. Each of us holds masculine and feminine energy within us. Learning to balance these and see the positive attributes of each is essential.

HOW DO WE LIVE ON THE LAND?

The sustainable design community sees a growing need to forge new relationships with the earth. "We have forgotten how to live on the land," says architect Jennifer Siegal. "Our ancestors knew how to do that. Native peoples know how to do that. But we have pushed that out of our consciousness." Nature writer Aldo Leopold believed that all species belong to what he called a land community and were ethically bound to care for it. "That land is a community is the basic concept of ecology," he wrote in *A Sand County Almanac*. "When we see land as a community to which we belong, we may begin to use it with love and respect."

Ironically, architect Constance Adams, who works in the aerospace industry, says that she learned to respect the earth more when she left it behind. A space ship, she explains, is a perfect model for sustainable design, because it is a virtually closed system. "If you don't recycle your water and air, you're screwed. When we talk about the big ship—the planet—the same principles hold. If you believe in Gaia theory, that the earth is one organism, humanity is radically different from the other parts of this organism. But we are part of it all the same. The whole planet is an integrated system for supporting life. Earth is the mother(ship), and we are her offspring."

Thinking about human activity as one part of a living organism challenges the planning, real estate, urban design, landscape architecture, and architecture professions to rethink their practices. The very fact that they exist as separate disciplines is part of the problem. "If you are really looking at sustainability," explains landscape architect Margie Ruddick, "you can't draw a boundary between building and site, or between region, city, and neighborhood." Breaking down these boundaries is leading to new kinds of collaborations between the disciplines, and it has become quite common for landscape architects to work closely with ecologists, biologists, geologists, and others. Critic Ada Louise Huxtable recently said that landscape architecture has much more potential than architecture to accomplish change: "It's a frontier.... At the moment, this work leaves the ambitious navel-gazers of architecture in the dust, and it's where real progress and humane social responsibility is taking place."

> We have forgotten how to live on the land.
>
> JENNIFER SIEGAL

Perhaps that is because landscape architects are more attuned to layers of influence than some other design professionals simply because the limits of their influence are not clearly constrained. "You have to be contributing to quality of life and equity," Ruddick says, "thinking about what is economically generative and what will inspire stewardship. You don't just design a park. Creating that place involves public/private partnerships, programming, and a great deal more than the physical features that we commonly think of as 'landscape.'" Landscape architect Cornelia Oberlander built her Vancouver practice around the idea of achieving a fit between built form and the land in order to support both rural and urban activities. This fit could only be achieved, she has said, "if all our design-related professions collaborate and thereby demonstrate cooperatively their relevance in meeting the enormous developmental challenges facing our increasingly crowded urban regions."

Many landscape architects describe their first role as revealing what's already happening in a place. Julie Bargmann of DIRT Studio explains, "There are so many invisible, intangible things going on with a site. You have to bring them forth somehow. What I'm trying to do is give every site a voice." This approach benefits the conversation with clients and communities, she says, because she makes it clear that design is not about personal expression or gratification. "I'm not defending my ideas—I'm trying to defend the site, give presence to the site. Politics fall away when you talk about what's best for a place. How can it regenerate itself?" What does she mean by *regeneration?* "I struggle with these terms—*restore, remediate, regenerate*. Once I typed out *remediation*, and my computer's spell check changed it to *redemption*. That summed it up for me. I've been trying to get away from the sense of shame, guilt or denial. I don't like the purist stance—if it's not 100 percent sustainable, it's contaminated, as if there are only certain ways to go about it. It's messier than that."

For artist Patricia Johanson, nature's messiness is part of her palette. Her "earth art" consists of large-scale public projects such as Fair Park in Dallas, where paths meander through a living food chain. "The idea was that we would let nature do the work, and invite people to engage in that," she says. "Projects have lives of their own, and they mean different things to different people. In a sense, I'm trying to frame the whole world. I'm making nature accessible." Part of her mission is to keep the frame open to all. "You have to try to look at everything and make it good for everyone. My goal is design for the whole community." On a different scale, "eco-artist" Jackie Brookner creates living sculptures that use plants to clean and filter water. She reimagined the map of the world in one piece, ranking continents according to consumption. "Americans use 153 gallons of potable water per person per day, compared to 53 in Europe, 27 in Asia, and 12 in Africa," she says. "A billion people don't have clean water. Is this what we are sustaining?" In the U.S., she hopes we will get smarter about using waste water for productive purposes, such as irrigating urban parks. "This could lead to the incremental reforestation of cities and more humane places to live."

An important part of making more humane places, according to many women, is to make things in proportion to actual needs. Architect Julie Snow says that reducing resource consumption is a part of any responsible practice. "Editing materials, using less, strengthens design." Living responsibly on the land means carefully considering not just where to build or how to build but *how much* to build—so-called "right-sizing." Judith Heerwagen maintains that some of the most important innovations in workplaces are organizational, not architectural. "How can we get beyond the single building and look at how to work differently?" Telecommuting or work-at-home programs can avoid building altogether, and new information technology allows people to work from anywhere, reducing the amount of space needed in new buildings. Says Heerwagen, "That is sustainability dramatically connected with how people work."

"The thing that makes the biggest impact in a building is its size," says nuclear-engineer-turned-architect Michelle Addington. "So many of the energy guidelines are concerned about watts per square foot, but what we really need to be concerned with is how many square feet we're building in the first place." Rocio Romero, whose tiny off-the-shelf houses have helped the "prefab" movement grow, says our culture tends to confuse quantity with quality. "You don't need a mansion to be comfortable. Smaller spaces are much more livable." Sarah Susanka's *Not So Big House* books have popularized living modestly but well. "What we've forgotten over the last hundred years is the proportionality of everything in life," she says. "The super-size movement, whether it's a Coca-Cola or a house, forgets that. It fills you up without giving you nutrition."

Preserving and adapting existing buildings may be the most aggressive form of right-sizing. Architect Jean Carroon calls preservation "the ultimate act of sustainability. Preservation is about things that are in place, and making a link between past and present, giving people a heritage. This is an important part of the quality of life that we try to establish in a 'sustainable community.'" Intern architect Kim Del Rance, who has worked for the City of St. Augustine, Florida, says that preservation and sustainability are both "about preserving a way of life for the future. Recycling buildings avoids waste but also allows us to learn from what came before." Laurie Kerr, an architect with the City of New York, says, "We should turn this around and call the period since World War II the short, ugly history of *unsustainability*. Many of the old models really worked well, such as the light of the tall windows in Georgian townhouse." She sees an important intersection between urbanism, preservation, and sustainability, which is particularly visible in old, dense cities. "Over the years, I have come to have tremendous respect for how these buildings work. They really have a great deal of embodied wisdom, as well as embodied energy." Yet, as Carroon points out, many historic and modern buildings alike are not seen as valuable. "The environmental movement barely notices existing buildings. Shouldn't we consider them more precious than we do?" Architect Sharon Park suggests that there is a great deal to be learned from even the oldest architecture. Studying indigenous building traditions, she remembers, "it was apparent to me that people who lived on the land before they built on the land knew what they were doing."

In the following conversation, landscape architects Carol Franklin and Leslie Sauer talk about what people consider precious about places. As two of the four co-founders of Andropogon, the Philadelphia-based firm named for a common American field grass, they have actively promoted ecological design for decades. While they no longer work together, they share a deep commitment to an ecology-based approach to land at all scales. We asked them if "sustainability" is the correct way to view responsible land use.

LESLIE SAUER: I never use the word. It's a nice target but, you know, I'm not even sure it's possible. Sustainability has more to do with how we live. People understand on a global scale, but I find it's not very helpful when we're looking at an actual site, a landscape. We tend to focus more on ideas about stewardship, restoration, and management. People understand these things at the level of a site.

CAROL FRANKLIN: The word has caught on as a fashionable moniker and has done us a world of good in many ways. It's made this popular and accessible, and we can't underrate that. It's been a metaphor to capture people's imagination.

But it's a limited term, a negative target. I find it sort of depressing, because it suggests that what we're dealing with is already badly damaged. And sustainable design tends to be defined in terms of gadgetry—boys with toys. People pride themselves on re-circulating water or installing a bio-treatment system. But it's a piecemeal thing, and that's the great problem. The same is true of LEED. It's hard to specify *quality*.

SAUER: You start writing rules and suddenly you define yourself out of the original intent. In theory, zoning ordinances are about protecting the landscape, but they don't do it at all. They're very deceptive. You can meet the criteria of the regulations without meeting any performance standards. It's hard to stay real. Did you actually meet any real criteria on the ground?

> You can't draw a boundary between building and site, or between region, city, and neighborhood.
>
> MARGIE RUDDICK

That's always been our focus—what is happening on the ground? Look at the ground. Look *into* the ground.

FRANKLIN: That is a profound notion—it becomes about the bigger questions. Should I bulldoze this place and totally destroy it?

SAUER: Right. Is it "sustainable" to build on undeveloped land? Is it "sustainable" to build a new building?

FRANKLIN: I prefer the term "ecological design" because that has to do with systems—thinking about the multiple ramifications of what you do and how to connect them in new ways. Making these connections is the new ecological framework. And it's a community-wide issue. It's a political issue. It's an economic issue. How do we bring a new way of thinking at the very small scale, at the medium scale, at the community scale?

It's a household. Remember, *ecology* is about the household, and the household is run as a series of complex interlocking systems that are always changing, always evolving. Sustainability in buildings often focuses on materials and methods, but that's the second step. The first step is understanding the patterns and processes of a place.

SAUER: Yes. How is the site talking to you? It's not restoration unless it involves science *and* culture. How do you work with your own landscape rather than trying to make it fit some fantasy about what you think it ought to be? People are very drawn to English landscapes, which are highly simplified—mowing under trees because people are afraid of bugs. It all looks so orderly when you strip it of life. It's calendar art.

We get calls from people who want wildflower meadows, and we go out to visit their site and find they already have one. They have goldenrod and asters, but it isn't the image they have in mind. Every site has the potential to be beautiful if we work with it. If you work with the natural character, it will by definition be beautiful—because it's healthy and vibrant.

FRANKLIN: It's about working with the patterns of each individual piece of land. Being able to see those patterns is the first step. Translating them into art is the second step for the designer.

SAUER: The goal of the designer is to capture the ecological romance of a place.

FRANKLIN: Yes. It's hard to capture, and it's easily destroyed. If you really know a place, you can bring out the romance in its inherent character.

SAUER: I'm working with people on a big grasslands project, and we never talk about the environment or sustainability. We talk about how to foster specific trees and birds—bobolinks and meadowlarks. They understand immediately when we talk about where not to mow and how large an area. It's all very specific to their place. It's really about getting people to come together and know where they are.

FRANKLIN: Farmers understand that they themselves have polluted the waterholes they used to swim in as children. The giant pig farms and chicken farms are major polluters of the streams in North Carolina and Iowa and other places. But the farmers themselves are suffering most. You ask them, "Didn't you used to swim here when you were a kid? Do you feel bad about this?" It all pours out of them how horrifying these great manure ponds are. And how they see the streams being destroyed every time it floods. And how their own drinking water is now polluted because they haven't thought of alternative ideas. They're seeking other solutions now.

SAUER: Despite the fact that our behavior is appalling, Americans are deeply attached to the land. We all think we're environmentalists.

WOMEN in GREEN: What is an environmentalist?

SAUER: Anyone who feels an attachment to the environment and a desire to do good by it. That can be completely effective or completely ineffective and ill-informed.

FRANKLIN: Feeling something without understanding it and working hard at it—that's called sentimentality. Sentimentality is accepting the easy over the difficult. This is not about New Urbanism's static dream about the 19th century. Notice these new towns don't have horse manure piled two-feet high in the streets.

But the sentimental tends to evaporate when you encounter something real. Every artist, humanist, philosopher and religious person will tell you that it is the more difficult road that ultimately is more satisfactory.

WIG: Jane Jacobs thought Americans are very sentimental about nature. She said the suburbs turned nature into "a nice big Saint Bernard pet."

SAUER: I find that people often are eager to substitute the real for the unreal if it is offered to them. People are hungry for the natural world but are given few ways to experience it richly.

> The goal of the designer is to capture the ecological romance of a place.
>
> LESLIE SAUER

WIG: What's the difference between sentimental and romantic?

FRANKLIN: Sentimentality is when you say you love your children but you don't spend ten minutes with them. Romance is when you gather the family around and you have a wonderful event that transforms them internally and externally and makes them see all kinds of new things. Every great designer aspires to that kind of romance. It lifts you up. It transforms you. Romance is exciting and meaningful.

SAUER: That's where sustainability has to go. We're heading very fast in the wrong direction. We don't necessarily have to fix everything today, but we've got to shift the trajectory. We can get there slowly, as long as we're heading in the right direction.

FRANKLIN: The world is in crisis. We've got to be more responsible, and we've got to inspire. But we're not saying the whole world should be restorationists or ecological designers. I'm against ideology. This is not about sitting on everybody who doesn't share your agenda. It shouldn't be moral blackmail.

Al Gore refers to the Chinese character for "crisis," which is a merging of two characters, danger and opportunity. That's what it's all about. There's a lot of danger but there's still much opportunity. We just have to see it.

Ecological romance is seeing the opportunities for reconnecting things that are broken or fragmented. It's like growing the tendrils of the brain after you've had a bad blow on the head. It's about healing the wounded earth. It's about fusion. We have to break down the Victorian idea of everything in their separate boxes. Everybody talks about interdisciplinary work, but it's really more like a big stew where you throw in a lot of different stuff. You mix it all around, and something completely new comes out of it.

WHAT ARE HEALTH AND WELL-BEING?

Many consider health the first concern of sustainability. "This is really what people care about," says Leslie Hoffman, executive director of the Earth Pledge Foundation. "We invariably talk about how our initiatives relate to human health— pesticide impacts on fertility rates, air quality and asthma, et cetera." Rebecca Flora of Pittsburgh's Green Building Alliance explains that her core mission is to "create healthy places. I am driven by my desire to leave behind a cleaner and safer earth for my daughters." And Claire Barnett of the Healthy Schools Network defines sustainable design exclusively in these terms. "I don't use the terms 'green' or 'sustainable.' I talk about healthy buildings."

But what is health, exactly? As architect Robin Guenther points out below, it's more than freedom from illness. A more positive description is "well-being," a holistic term that involves not only physical but also mental, emotional, and spiritual health. Some people focus on well-being at the public scale, including buildings, communities, or the whole planet, while others give precedence to personal issues of body, mind, and spirit. Donna McIntire, who leads the U.S. State Department's sustainability initiatives, insists that sustainability isn't about saving the planet. "The earth will do just fine without us. It has to be about people."

Environmental psychologist Judith Heerwagen feels that women are redefining sustainable design in terms of health and well-being. "For a long time, the focus was on building science. Women helped change the focus to human factors. When we talk about health, we get into territory women have always been interested in." Architect Mara Baum, who works on healthcare design, says that "the human health aspects of sustainability may be what draw women to the field." But women may have more than just an interest in health—they may actually stimulate it in the people around them. Studies show that men's stress levels and eating habits both tend to improve when they get married or move in with women.

What's the connection between women and health? Biology, according to Sandra Steingraber. "Biologically, women are in a different position than men. Their bodies are the first environment for the next generation." Environmentalist Paul Hawken recounts that many women activists in the nineteenth century were the first to see the link between health and the environment, and many worked to establish food inspection and water quality standards. He points to Dr. Ellen Swallow Richards, the pioneering sanitary engineer who founded what became known as "municipal housekeeping." Today, American women generally have a much greater influence on the health of their families, spending three times as much time with children and being responsible for the vast majority of grocery shopping, cooking, cleaning, and laundry. In *What Women Want*, Celinda Lake and Kellyanne Conway write, "Women are health-care voters; 89 percent of them agree that the system needs a fundamental overhaul. They outnumber men as the leading consumers of healthcare services, and are the family's gatekeepers."

Studies by the Institute for Women's Policy Research suggest that women tend to be more concerned than men about environmental risks to health and safety. Why is this? "Women feel in some way responsible for creating quality of life—whether it's at home or in their community," remarks *Plenty* magazine editor Deborah Snoonian. "We're the ones who bring life into being, right? It's that instinct to ensure the survival of not just yourself but the whole." Biologist Janine Benyus puts it bluntly: "Women know that babies die. There's something about being brought up as nurturers, as sustainers of life, that carries through everything. Women's sense of what is reasonable has to do with that which keeps everything alive." In 2003, at the eighth annual meeting of her foundation's Women's Health and Environment Conference, Teresa Heinz Kerry gave four reasons why she focuses on women. First, to the extent that the scientific community has addressed links between the environment and human health, those studies tend to focus on men. Second, she cited evidence

> I am driven by my desire to leave behind a cleaner and safer earth for my daughters.
>
> REBECCA FLORA

of the growing environmental threats to women, including sharply increased rates of some cancers. "Third, women continue to play a special role as caregivers in our society. Our bodies, designed to nurture our children, can also become pathways for toxins to enter their developing bodies.... Women have a special interest in information like this—and a right to know it." Her fourth reason: "When women are informed, we act."

Many women acted when Rachel Carson chronicled the effects of pesticides on ecology and human health in *Silent Spring*. "She anchored environmental damage in the context of home, communities, health and human bodies—nature and human nature coming together," explains environmental historian Maril Hazlett. "But she also showed that we have the power to say 'no.' She appealed to a lot of women. This was a redistribution of power from scientists to citizens." In *A Fierce Green Fire*, his history of the American environmental movement, Philip Shabecoff notes that women usually lead local activist campaigns with great success, because they're unwilling to compromise: "the grassroots groups usually will settle for nothing less than complete victory because the health of their children, their own health, and habitability of their homes are on the line." Think of Erin Brockovich, who famously uncovered Pacific Gas & Electric's dumping of carcinogenic chemicals into water sources in Hinkley, California. And consider Lois Gibbs, who in 1978 organized the community of Love Canal in Niagara Falls, New York, to demand relief from chemicals in the soil and water resulting from nearby industrial dumpsites. "It's a survival issue," Shabecoff quotes her as saying. "People are going to fight like hell because they don't have a choice."

Gro Harlem Brundtland, originally trained as a physician, has long linked environmental indicators to poverty, health, and human rights worldwide. In a recent talk, she noted that "1.3 billion people have entered the twenty-first century without having benefited from the health revolution. These are the people still living in absolute poverty—that is, living on less than one dollar per day." Seventy percent of these people are women, according to Brundtland, and more than one third of all children worldwide are undernourished. Even in wealthy nations, health indicators are sobering. A 2006 Save the Children report notes that infant mortality in the U.S. is the second worst among industrialized nations, and some causes are linked to women's issues, including short maternity leave and teen pregnancy. Brundtland considers education for girls and women "the key to community health and environmental protection." According to the Agency for International Development, women are far more likely than men to reinvest their income in their children's health care and nutrition. Investment in women therefore benefits the welfare of the entire community.

Connections between the quality of the built environment and the health of the community are becoming clearer. Recent studies link the obesity epidemic to suburban sprawl, which Lauren Anderson of New Orleans' Neighborhood Housing Services calls "the least sustainable" type of development. In his book *Last Child in the Woods*, Richard Louv demonstrates that children spend more and more time indoors and therefore lack the regular contact with nature that promotes mental, physical, and spiritual health. Barnett bemoans this trend. "We spend billions without any attention to the health of our indoor environments, where Americans spend 85 to 90 percent of their time." The Occupational Safety and Health Administration reports that more than twenty million American workers are exposed to potentially serious health threats due to poor indoor air quality in the workplace. In fact, the green building movement has been motivated as much by the growing incidence of "sick building syndrome" as by any other concern. On the positive side, research repeatedly shows that access to light and views can reduce absenteeism, improve attention, and increase healing rates in surgical patients. Christine McEntee, executive vice president of the American Institute of Architects, was a nurse before moving into association management. "We were trained to think about the social environments of our patients—what kind of social unit and housing they were living in. I think that holistic view of health is what sustainable design needs to serve."

Many people suggest that the holistic approach of universal (or inclusive) design links it closely with sustainability. As interior designer Holley Henderson puts it, "Universal design is design for all. Sustainability is the logical extension of this idea." Valerie Fletcher, executive director of Adaptive Environments, says that universal design is actually a much greater challenge than wheelchair access, to which it is often reduced. "Too often, the places where we most need good design are where we get it the least. We have to be thinking in broader terms. What we are talking about is transforming human experience." Architect Marsha Maytum says specific issues highlight connections between the realms. "The universal design community has been addressing chemical sensitivity and human health factors at the same time that indoor air quality issues are becoming more understood as a key part of sustainable design." And Fletcher points out that demographic shifts are sure to bring universal design into sharp focus as the

> "Biologically, women are in a different position than men. Their bodies are the first environment for the next generation.
>
> SANDRA STEINGRABER

profession attempts to enhance the health and well-being of everyone. "Architects and designers in this country are not talking about aging, and it has huge implications."

Conversations about links between the environment and health started in the health care and design communities in the early 1990s. Architect Robin Guenther of Guenther5 in New York, and Gail Vittori, co-director of the Center for Maximum Potential Building Systems in Austin, Texas, helped bridge these communities. They worked with the Healthy Building Network, Commonweal (formerly Health Care Without Harm), the American Society for Healthcare Engineering, and other groups and were two of the authors of the *Green Guide for Health Care* (2003), a comprehensive sustainable design toolkit for the healthcare community. The Rocky Mountain Institute's Alexis Karolides, who has worked closely with Guenther and Vittori, says they "spearheaded green healthcare design. They're as important as anybody." We asked them to discuss the connections between environment, health, and well-being.

ROBIN GUENTHER: Health is more than the absence of disease. The word comes from "whole" or "wholeness." For a long time, a few medical professionals have talked about the connections between physical and spiritual health. Mainstream medicine tends to separate those issues and focus on curing disease rather than healing people. Sustainability has a role to play in bringing those worlds together. But as a culture we are in deep denial about those connections.

GAIL VITTORI: I'm interested in how to design with this broader view of connection and respecting the whole. We need to create conditions where there's more intentional recognition of the spiritual dimension. This might create different means and modes of expression.

GUENTHER: Mainstream sustainable design has focused more on physical health issues—indoor air quality, toxins in building materials, CO_2 emissions associated with fossil fuels. That's not surprising in the culture we live in. Sustainability is already challenging precepts.

But when we talk about restorative or regenerative buildings, it's hard not to see that there are physical and spiritual components.

Medicine is recognizing those connections. Physicians can't heal people, but they can help people heal themselves. That's a fairly radical shift in the relationship. I think this is the beginning of a powerful social movement.

WOMEN in GREEN: The word "caretaker" is often used in the context of environmental stewardship. Are there connections between health care and ecology?

VITTORI: Part of what we do in our work is make those connections more visible. We've been receivers of the goods and services that support our lives, and the shift ahead is for us to become more deeply engaged in the process—an active rather than passive state.

GUENTHER: Mental well-being depends on a cycle of caring and being cared for that's a two-way, interactive process. There's a lot of literature that supports the idea that when one of those directions is cut off, it has a profound effect on our mental well-being.

The healing professions are about caring for people you don't have any other connection to. In sustainability, we are often asking people to steward resources that they may feel no connection to. Reaching beyond what is familiar and close is necessary to our future together.

WIG: How do we work toward long-term health?

VITTORI: One of the challenges is to shift the dialogue and the focus to prevention rather than curing.

GUENTHER: It's hubris to believe that we could heal the planet when in fact the only thing that actually has any restorative power or healing power is nature itself. That's what we rely on to heal.

In health care, when someone is really sick it's a teachable moment. When you confront your own mortality is the moment you consider choices you've made and new ones you need to make. Health care institutions have patients in the middle of teachable moments as human beings. Are we at a teachable moment as the planet begins to go into convulsions? Can we get through denial and see a different path? That's a pretty exciting idea.

WIG: Health care divides medicine into separate categories of specialization, but isn't the point of sustainability to recognize that such things are all interwoven?

GUENTHER: Yes. Our culture spent the twentieth century parsing knowledge into silos. That's why we're all reading books about interconnectedness and webs of relationships. It sounds like a new idea. We have to learn it again because it's so far from our daily reality.

VITTORI: We need to unravel the compartmentalization of the human experience. Experiences in buildings can be part of flipping the switch. We have a rubber floor in one of our buildings. After stepping on the surface, nine out of ten people will stop and *bounce* because it's such a different sensory experience than what they're accustomed to.

As a society, we've been denied the full range of experience in a lot of ways. There's work going on now about nature-deficit disorder, especially in children—these kids are missing part of their reality. The consequences are starting to be understood.

GUENTHER: [Educator] David Orr talks about fast knowledge versus slow knowledge. I think there's a kind of reexamination of slow knowledge in medicine, as they search for ways to treat the whole person. Slow knowledge has particular relevance in sustainable design. It's a return to that sensibility.

> It's hubris to believe that we could heal the planet when in fact the only thing that actually has any restorative power is nature itself.
>
> ROBIN GUENTHER

WIG: What brought about the *Green Guide for Health Care*?

VITTORI: We recognized that health care had not been at the table in the development of green building tools and resources. The idea of creating structures conducive to human health and well-being wasn't part of the conversation outside of the health care community. This enormous sector has been isolated from the larger architecture dialogue. We saw a chance to link these two worlds. When you make the explicit connection, there are instant converts.

GUENTHER: The science linking environmental degradation and human health is developing, and the indications are getting stronger. These impacts, whether you talk about toxic chemicals and illness, air quality and asthma, or development and diabetes, are overwhelming to health care systems.

Health care could advocate sustainability very persuasively. Once the health care industry—at eighteen percent of the Gross Domestic Product—starts advocating for green building, it's likely to have a broad impact on public perception of sustainability and green building. Americans still trust their doctors.

WiG: Do we need to rethink medicine altogether?

GUENTHER: I think we do. There is a crisis of meaningful work in health care. The U.S. is the largest consumer of health care services, and yet we are not the healthiest people. Some physicians are beginning to challenge the fundamental provision of services and the scale at which we provide health care.

VITTORI: We can create places that are an expression of values and purpose. We're beginning to see hospitals designed with emphasis on the connection between place and context, views and daylight, scale that feels right, and acoustical control. Those become factors in recruitment and retention of professional staff, which itself can be a driver for change.

WiG: In coming years, how will the design community address health and well-being?

GUENTHER: On the materials front, we will see a revolution in chemicals and toxins in materials. Some large providers, such as Kaiser Permanente, are adopting comprehensive chemical policies and rigorously screening their materials. We'll also see a shift in the typology of hospital building—the deep floor plate will go away, for the most part— and growth of community-based health care. The tipping point will be when the health care industry decides they are about *protecting* health. If health care decides that PVC [polyvinyl chloride] is bad, there will be a sea change.

VITTORI: Sustainability is gaining ground, and it's becoming understood as an ethical challenge. The growing clarity of the links between the built environment and health is part of that. Design professionals will have to face this as a moral responsibility.

WHAT ARE COMFORT AND DELIGHT?

Comfort is a familiar but elusive condition — we all want it but can't perfectly describe it. What we consider to be comfortable can vary by sex, age, and even income and depends on not just physical but also psychological, cultural, and emotional nuances. Yet, this vague concept is essential to sustainable design, because there are clear links between physical comfort and environmental stewardship. Building strategies that embrace fresh air and natural light can soothe the occupant and save energy at the same time. More importantly, when people are better connected to the natural environment, they tend to feel better and have more respect for that environment. "We can rethink sustainability and ecology by focusing on the relationship between the body and the environment," says Galen Cranz, who studies design and well-being at the University of California-Berkeley. "If we think about what goes in our lungs, we have to think about what goes in the air. If we think about what we eat, we have to think about what goes in the land. If we think about what we drink, we have to think about what goes in the water."

In *A Natural History of the Senses*, Diane Ackerman points out that we interact with the environment first and foremost through our bodies. "There is no way to understand the world without first detecting it through the radar-net of our senses." As she points out, physiology research suggests that "the mind doesn't really dwell in the brain but travels the whole body on caravans of hormone and enzyme, busily making sense of the compound wonders we catalogue as touch, taste, smell, hearing, vision." In her popular *Thermal*

Delight in Architecture, Lisa Heschong celebrates the "simple pleasure" of touching a cool stone or a warm cup of coffee. "There is something very affirming of one's own life in being aware of these little pieces of information about the world outside us," she writes. "When the sun is warm on my face and the breeze is cool, I know it is good to be alive." Or, as Rachel Carson puts it in *A Sense of Wonder,* "it is not half so important to know as to feel."

Yet, our culture tends to give precedence to rational thought, not subjective experience, as if to devalue the most basic human interaction with the environment. In the construction industry, sustainable design emphasizes quality of light and air, but the professionals most directly responsible for these intangibles are engineers traditionally trained to work with mathematical calculations, not human beings. Heschong laments that too often physical comfort is dismissed as a purely technical requirement: "environmental control systems tend to be treated rather like the Cinderella of architecture; given only the plainest clothes to wear, they are relegated to a back room to do the drudgery that maintains the elegant life-style of the other sisters: light, form, structure, and so forth." But thermal qualities affect not just the functional but also the emotional experience of a space, she explains. Buildings, like food, must meet our needs but also delight our senses. "A few tubes of an astronaut's nutritious goop are no substitute for a gourmet meal. They lack sensuality—taste, aroma, texture, temperature, color."

Do the nuts and bolts of green building lack sensuality? "Within sustainable design, there is an emphasis on technology, which is traditionally a male focus," says environmental psychologist Judith Heerwagen. "The more emotional aspects are often seen as 'soft.' We invest a lot of money in the technology of buildings and not enough in the nurturing aspects of the environment." Architect Carrie Meinberg Burke wonders if sensuality in design is a feminine sensibility. "Women may be more aware of our bodies because we're more tied to the world through natural cycles. Being able to give birth to another human being is a visceral aspect of our experience." Heschong agrees: "Of course we're highly sensitive to changes in the environment because we're going through so many changes ourselves." Yet, she doubts that sexual difference is relevant. "Is that an issue for sustainable design? Probably not." For artist Jackie Brookner, all people are literally one with the world—the "permeable body," that "holey place" that constantly exchanges material and energy with its surroundings, is our most intimate relationship with nature. "I can enter other things and other things can enter me," she has written. "Even the stars can come in."

Where the stars come in is the intersection of comfort and delight, which Heerwagen feels is best pursued through nature-inspired, or biophilic, design. "It's the missing link." Life-like patterns and processes, including movement, growth, organized complexity, fractal patterning, organic shapes, and multi-sensory experience, can stimulate the mind, comfort the body, and foster an appreciation for nature. For example, biologist Janine Benyus cites research showing that people tend to respond most pleasurably to certain hues of green and yellow, colors associated with verdant fauna. Graphic designer Janine James believes that her profession can learn from chromatherapy, which studies the healing properties of color. "The neuroscientific side of design is underutilized," she says. "This is the future."

> "Variety is important to consciousness. People notice and respond to change. We get bored without it.
>
> GALEN CRANZ

But comfort and delight both depend on more than the visual. As Carson writes, "Senses other than sight can prove avenues of delight and discovery." Ackerman muses that experience is synesthetic—tasting color and smelling sound, we feel the world with literally mixed emotions. Conventional design, however, tends to focus exclusively on the visual which, according to Parsons School of Design professor Jean Gardner, diminishes the potential for architecture to engage people more fully. "The separation of the senses in design is a problem. All the things you know as a child—swimming, running, riding—the things we can't communicate visually, are lost in design." Gardner has developed multi-sensory guidelines for what she calls the "Whole Building," which stimulates the mind, body and spirit all at once. Because of the historic associations between vision and masculine domination, architectural historian Deborah Fausch has written that design based on non-visual experience "could be claimed as a strategically feminist architecture."

Architect Linda Kiisk, who is writing a book on the neurological aspects of design, says that gender can affect both physiological and emotional reactions to an environment. "I consistently find that women feel and respond to space differently than men." Yet, while physical comfort varies significantly among individuals, the design industry relies on neutral standards. Studies of "human" responses have tended to focus on the same group as representative of the entire race, Heschong recounts. "For years medical scientists excluded women from their studies because they seemed too variable. They wanted a more uniform study group so they looked at middle-aged men." Yet, to honor everyone, sustainable design can embrace the differences between us. "Variety is important to consciousness," says Cranz. "People notice and respond to change. We get bored without it."

In recent decades, the science of ergonomics has developed to study the graceful interaction of the body with its physical setting, including furniture and tools. Yet Cranz, author of *The Chair: Rethinking Culture, Body, and Design*, insists that ergonomic standards are based on statistical averages that rarely, if ever, apply to real people. "There is no one posture for human beings," she says. "People are designed for movement—we want our weight to shift constantly to avoid over-taxing one set of muscles. Comfort for us has to do with the capacity to move, but we're raised to believe that strength and maturity are about sitting still. The first thing you're taught in kindergarten is to stop fidgeting. But the body is designed to fidget. The static, mechanical fix is not the answer." The parallels between designing for comfort and designing for sustainability should be obvious, she says. "Originally, in the Latin, *comfort* meant strength," explains Cranz. "Over time, it has come to mean 'yielding ease.' I think we need to go back and reclaim the older meaning. Comfort has to do with long-term well-being, not short-term."

The conversation below brings together three people who design with the body in mind. Mechanical engineer Jennifer Sanguinetti is a principal with Stantec (formerly Keen) Engineering and manages its Concepts group, which focuses on environmental innovation. Architect Susan Ubbelohde is a founding partner with Loisos+Ubbelohde, which specializes in daylight and energy analysis. And lighting designer Nancy Clanton is known widely for her work promoting comfort through light. We asked them to talk about comfort and why it's important for sustainable design.

SUSAN UBBELOHDE: Often comfort is defined as lack of stress—it's defined in the negative. But Lisa Heschong probably put it best—buildings shouldn't be neutral backgrounds but should in fact provide delight. It's about creating an engaging environment connected to nature.

JENNIFER SANGUINETTI: We don't design a building so that people can experience its systems. When people are comfortable they don't notice the building.

NANCY CLANTON: I couldn't agree more. Sometimes people don't know why they're comfortable. They're energized, and they don't know why, but it's beyond the building. They just like where they are.

If you dig into the reasons for it, you can go through line items or the LEED checklist, but they're too linear. Comfort is more dynamic than that. It has to do with the mood and situation you're in. Are you at work trying to crank out a project, or are you at home entertaining? Or are you in a learning environment where you've been sitting in the same seat for eight hours and your butt's sore and you want to get up and move around?

UBBELOHDE: Comfort is enhanced by developing a stronger connection to the natural world, and it's not just physical. We have biological needs for solar orientation, for knowing what time it is. Good buildings are organized with a difference between north and south. But in many buildings, spaces are treated equally, as though the outside doesn't exist.

CLANTON: You would think that thermal comfort would be the first thing people would talk about in buildings. But it's the acoustics. Supposedly sustainable materials are often acoustic disasters because of all the hard surfaces.

UBBELOHDE: Many passively operated buildings are acoustic nightmares because of the exposed mass of the structure.

SANGUINETTI: Everything can work well together except for the acoustics. Opening up spaces helps daylighting, visual access to the outdoors, and thermal comfort. But it flies in the face of acoustics. As an industry we're failing horribly.

CLANTON: So how can we look at the entire building and address all of our senses, not just one or two of them?

WOMEN in GREEN: What senses are most important for comfort? Do designers overplay the visual?

> "Comfort is enhanced by developing a stronger connection to the natural world.
>
> SUSAN UBBELOHDE

CLANTON: The brain takes in a lot of visual data, but we start filtering it out or we'd be overloaded. So we probably have the best control over our visual environment. I actually think the sense of smell is most sensitive.

SANGUINETTI: The smell of wood—or the lack of smell of vinyl—is a strong cue. Smell is also important because it ties into memory.

UBBELOHDE: Smell is one of the senses that register in the brainstem, the pre-rational brain, left over from early evolution. This is why it's so closely connected to memory. It's a visceral rather than rational response to an environment.

Apparently we can smell an orange that's being peeled for about seven seconds, but then our ability to smell it begins to diminish. It's totally seductive. The same applies to thermal comfort. We go from a hot environment into a cool environment and think, "Wow! This feels really great!" The need for variability is hard for designers and engineers to get a handle on. We don't need constant stimulation—we need constant refreshment.

WiG: What about touch? There is so much literature showing that touch is an important sense for well-being. How can the built environment address this?

UBBELOHDE: One of the things I've noticed about visiting green buildings is that the materials often feel better to touch. There are more natural materials and fewer synthetics. Fewer plastics, fewer vinyls. Materials can ground you in the natural world.

SANGUINETTI: But we don't always feel we have permission to touch.

UBBELOHDE: I touch everything.

WiG: The areas of buildings we touch most often—railings, door pulls, et cetera—tend to be cold, sleek surfaces such as metal, as opposed to something that has a warmer, more natural texture.

CLANTON: It may be more indirect than what we touch with our hands. Our posteriors are always touching things—how does what we're sitting on affect thermal comfort? I was in a little shack in Montana, sitting on metal chairs—it was so cold. But I'm always cold. There is such a difference between men and women with thermal comfort. And glare sensitivity. There's a big difference in women's hormone levels and how we react to glare.

WiG: How can we design buildings to consider the wide range of people who might occupy them?

UBBELOHDE: Personal controls. Individual choice. People will tolerate a much wider range of thermal comfort as long as they can control it. If somebody has a window they can open, they will be happier in their office, whether or not they make an adjustment.

SANGUINETTI: People want to determine for themselves what is comfortable. Mechanical engineers grossly underestimate the need for people to feel they have some influence over their space. It's the only thing people have when they're in a cubical farm in a large corporate environment.

WiG: Many people have talked to us about nurturing, and there seems to be a close connection between nurturing and comfort. Is that how you would describe what we're discussing?

CLANTON: I've noticed owners and even designers are turned off by fuzzy words. Let's face it, most owners and developers are men, and to them "nurturing" is not a comfortable word. You look like a tree hugger instead of just doing the right thing for your building.

SANGUINETTI: As a female engineer, I can't use that kind of word, and it's not a word people respond particularly well to. It may be that a space is nurturing, and it may be that it does foster social capital, but it's not something I would ever use as a selling feature.

UBBELOHDE: The building industry is still a boys' club. There's no question about that, although women work in it in much greater numbers and with much greater effectiveness now.

I find "humane" to be a powerful word, because it calls on the best of everybody in the room. And it has a civic and philosophical positioning, rather than a gender positioning.

WiG: What makes a humane environment?

CLANTON: Humane is giving people a good connection to the outdoors. It's not a big window with a view of a parking lot with all the sunlight glaring off the cars. It's not forcing someone into a western exposure office where the sun beats in about 3:00, right when you're trying to get a deadline out. Humane is not giving the boss the corner office with two windows. Humane is giving everyone the best possible environment.

> How can we address all of our senses, not just one or two of them?
>
> NANCY CLANTON

UBBELOHDE: Yes. It's about recognizing that people in buildings have both bodies and psyches that are valued. It's egalitarian.

SANGUINETTI: The engineering side of the building design profession is notorious for forgetting that people are irrational. You can either try to control them or you can recognize their unpredictability and celebrate it. What can we do to allow people to experience the environment in the way they want to experience it? That's humane.

CLANTON: You're right. Don't underestimate people. They'll open their windows at appropriate times, and they'll close them afterward. And guess what, when they walk out, they usually turn off the lights.

SANGUINETTI: There's an impression that operable windows would screw up the mechanical system, as if the building and its controls are more important than the people. We forget who the building is for.

HOW DO WE INNOVATE?

Over the last ten or fifteen years, sustainable design has been propelled by new developments in research. What is research, and how does it lead to innovation? Defined simply as a form of inquiry or investigation, the word itself can be broken down to suggest a "search" that repeats itself continually. Biographer Catherine Drinker Bowen has written that research is always incomplete, because "around the corner lurks another possibility." Innovation is like this— always turning more corners to discover new possibilities. Michelle Addington, the nuclear-engineer-turned-architect and co-author of *Smart Materials and Technologies,* finds true innovation strangely absent in architecture. "Having come from the outside, the construction industry amazes me—building systems are incredibly archaic. We still try to optimize them rather than questioning their existence. Why do we have these Rube Goldberg machines for buildings? They are totally antithetical to what another industry would do to make something happen."

Yet, Addington says that the underlying idea of innovation is not to make better widgets but simply to understand how things work. "I'm interested in smart materials and technologies only insofar as they help us understand how to leverage something small and strategic." In other words, responsible research and development are guided by responsible intentions. Novelist Zora Neale Hurston once called research "formalized curiosity," or "poking and prying with a purpose." In sustainable research, what is the purpose of all this poking and prying? "What problems are we going to solve with this knowledge?" asks biologist Janine Benyus. "Are we going to make new Barbies? Are we going to build better tanks? Or is there something more? We need to think very deliberately about where we put our attention."

This renewed sense of responsibility is what separates sustainable design from conventional development as it has been defined for hundreds of years. Eco-feminist historian Carolyn Merchant writes that after the sixteenth century, the Scientific Revolution replaced the ancient image of the earth as a "nurturing mother" with an image of domination and mastery over nature. In *Biomimicry*, Benyus recounts that in the modern era the task of science became, in Francis Bacon's words, to "torture nature for her secrets." "Machines replaced muscles," she writes, "and we learned to rock the world." Sustainable design, however, must regard the environment with profound awe and respect. According to Benyus, our task now is not to learn *about* nature but to learn *from* it.

> " We invest a lot of money in the technology of buildings and not enough in the nurturing aspects of the environment. "
>
> JUDITH HEERWAGEN

Women have been championing nature-inspired innovation for years, especially in product design, where many of the most inspired advances in new methods have occurred. In the 1980s, Sally Fox's development of naturally pigmented, chemical-free cottons grew out of her experience in the Peace Corps in West Africa, where she saw firsthand how pesticides can have devastating effects both ecologically and socially. Susan Lyons was motivated by similar concerns while running the design department at Designtex in the early 1990s. "Any time you're moving chemicals through a system, you can see the impact it has on a community if it's not managed correctly," Lyons explains. "You could go up to a small mill in Maine and see a huge pool of effluence collecting out back. These people were not behaving irresponsibly; they'd conform to the regulations and do everything by the book. I'm not a scientist, but I could see that something was wrong." Lyons' concern led to her commissioning William McDonough and Michael Braungart to develop the world's first compostable fabric, the Climatex Lifecycle series, which McDonough calls "the first Cradle-to-Cradle product" and "the flag of the Next Industrial Revolution."

Lyons recalls studies showing that women, who make the majority of product selections for their families, tend to make any decision based on what's good for the community, so naturally that sensibility would influence how they conduct research and development. This blend of curiosity and empathy runs throughout the following conversation, and all three participants focus on how innovation can promote humanity. Vivian Loftness, whom Gail Vittori, co-director of the Center for Maximum Potential Building Systems, calls "a scientist with passion," is a senior researcher with Carnegie Mellon's Center for Building Performance and Diagnostics and a key contributor to the development of the Intelligent Workplace, a "living laboratory" of commercial building innovations for performance. Architect Lisa Heschong co-authored the *Daylighting and Productivity Studies*, a landmark report on the benefits of natural light in buildings. Environmental psychologist Judith Heerwagen is widely recognized as one of the world's foremost proponents of biophilic design, and her study of William McDonough + Partners' Herman Miller SQA Building was a milestone in research connecting sustainable design to mental and social well-being.

Ironically, although architecture has brought a great deal of attention to sustainability, the building industry often is considered to be one of the least progressive areas of innovation. "Construction is what you might call 'a dynamically conservative industry,'" says Hunter Lovins. "It works real hard to stay in the same place." We asked Heschong, Heerwagen, and Loftness how research and innovation are changing buildings.

LISA HESCHONG: Energy efficiency is the prime motive for almost all the work that I do, but really I'm trying to develop research that promotes comfortable, habitable environments where people can work well and be well.

JUDITH HEERWAGEN: Ultimately, the goal of any research is to change practice—to get better buildings for people and the environment. I think less about environmental technologies than the social dimensions of high-performance buildings—the impact on the human condition. Put the people back in buildings. In the "triple bottom line," this is the line least attended to—social equity, social justice, what happens inside a building as well as to communities surrounding the building. To me, that is more important than the environmental side of sustainability.

VIVIAN LOFTNESS: It's the social side of sustainability.

HESCHONG: Intuitively, buildings need to be designed so that people are comfortable and productive. The sustainability argument comes in by saying that you don't need to use brute force to make it so. We can have our cake and eat it too.

HEERWAGEN: That's a nice way of putting it. We've assumed that in order to achieve comfort and well-being, we need a high-tech solution. It isn't so.

WOMEN in GREEN: What do we mean by "well-being"?

HESCHONG: Well-being includes physical, psychological and emotional health.

HEERWAGEN: I'm interested in well-being in a broad sense. Within sustainable design, there is an emphasis on technology, which is traditionally a male focus. The more emotional aspects of this well-being that interest me are often seen as 'soft.' We invest a lot of money in the technology of buildings and not enough in the nurturing aspects of the environment.

The link between sustainable design and human well-being, rather than productivity, is the area that is likely to produce the most positive results. We emphasize productivity to support the business case, but it's hard to prove. Nobody knows how to measure it. We're proselytizing rather than finding good evidence.

LOFTNESS: People use the word *productivity* so loosely that no one really knows what it means, except in industrial manufacturing or any kind of a repetitive task that measures speed and accuracy. But the biggest issue is that buildings may only have a small impact on performance, since other factors, such as how people get along with their colleagues, have more of an influence on job satisfaction—by a factor of ten.

HESCHONG: It's true. Our studies have shown there's an order of magnitude difference between building influence and organizational influence. But the buildings are semi-permanent and continue to influence things over a very long period of time. The time dimension makes a difference.

WiG: Is there a real connection between the physical work environment and social satisfaction and other intangibles?

HEERWAGEN: There's a grand hypothesis out there that sustainability somehow is good for people—that if we design buildings with better daylight and air quality, they'll just automatically be better for people. But we don't completely understand how these things work, so we can't talk about mechanisms to make it repeatable. Some of it is just plain common sense, but the deeper relationship between environmental justice and social equity is unclear. There is accumulating evidence in different places, but it hasn't been pulled together very well.

LOFTNESS: More research would be invaluable to understand the concrete effects of more thoughtful, human-centric environments. But there's no question about the effects on physical health. If you put people in a freshly painted, re-carpeted room with lots of off-gassing or formaldehyde-intensive furniture, many will start to have throat irritations or respiratory problems.

HESCHONG: That comes under the category of avoiding negative effects, which is the flip side of designing spaces that actually improve well-being.

LOFTNESS: I agree. One of the goals would be to improve all these factors—not just manage the negatives but make real leaps into positive signs.

HEERWAGEN: In a new environment, there are so many things affected simultaneously that it's hard to study the effects of individual factors. If you're interested in a particular variable—temperature, airflow, light, or whatever—everything else has to be constant.

LOFTNESS: The U.S. has very few resources invested in this kind of study. The Danish government has found that increasing fresh air rates can affect people's perceived and actual medical health. Because they have long-term funding from the federal government, they've started to look at compound effects. Do noise and air quality relate in any way? Humans are integrators, after all.

HESCHONG: The single greatest environmental predictor of satisfaction is the presence of a view to the outdoors. When people have a better view, everything else seems fine—they have no objections to the rest of the space. When they don't have a view, they had the highest level of complaints about temperature, acoustics, ventilation, lighting, as well as health.

HEERWAGEN: Yet, if you ask people to rate things that are important, views often come down at the bottom of the list, which is surprising.

LOFTNESS: Our studies show that seated views of windows have a very strong impact on people's perceived level of sick building syndrome, or SBS, symptoms. Why is this happening?

HESCHONG: I think it's the view itself—both the content of the view and the sense of change that goes on. There's a lot going on when you look outdoors—light, sky, people walking by. There's good evidence of stress reduction if people look out the window through the course of the day. A "positive distraction" can rest your mind.

LOFTNESS: Spending all day looking at very near views—a computer screen twelve inches away or a cubicle panel two feet away—doesn't put our eyes through very much physical exercise. Distant views with content help the eye over time.

HESCHONG: A view of the outside is generally brighter than the interior and actually allows people to control their appetite for circadian [daily cycle] stimulation. As we learn more and more about human physiology, we realize that with circadian stimulation come changes in neurotransmitters and hormone levels. It makes perfect sense that greater access to views would cause a reduction in SBS symptoms. You actually can have a better-balanced physiology.

HEERWAGEN: You're on to something very interesting here. But most of the work done in this area has assumed that it is about light entering the eye. You can look at something bright in the distance, but is it bright enough to have a biological effect, or is there another mechanism that's important? It might be more psychological or emotional than directly physiological. But that doesn't mean it can't affect your physiology.

HESCHONG: It might be all of the above. Even looking at the sky through a deeply tinted window has a spectral content closer to daylight than looking across an interior illuminated space. But you're right—we don't really know what the mechanisms are. Is it the intensity of the stimulation, or the duration, or the timing? Suggestions are pretty strong that more intense blue wave lengths, especially early in the morning, have a huge impact on people's performance and physiology. The research is primarily based on light received by the eye, and it's a circadian issue rather than a visual issue, because the stimulus is going to a different part of the brain.

LOFTNESS: The U.S. is one of the few industrialized nations that do not mandate seated views of windows. But let's add another dimension. That people need a connection to the outdoors is one issue; the parallel issue is the importance of operable windows and natural ventilation. The mechanical profession is leery of having windows that open—people say it's too complicated to design a mechanical system that can cope with operable windows, so they just forget about it. The argument shuts down before we can even do the research.

HESCHONG: Typically, engineers are taught to design a system that will maintain a static condition. Having wind pressure change their system is a huge challenge because it's something that they haven't been trained to cope with. It's not outside of their capability—it's just not what gets taught. There are only a few folks out there trying to deal with hybrid ventilation systems.

HEERWAGEN: That's true. Our buildings aim for uniformity when people have evolved in a highly variable environment.

HESCHONG: It's a new paradigm—embrace your variability. People require stimulus. Without it, they start flat-lining and get bored and fatigued. They lose their creativity and motivation, because the environment is too static.

HEERWAGEN: Researchers have been talking about variability for thirty years, and there is really good evidence out there. Yet somehow that knowledge doesn't get transferred into how we design buildings. We need to figure out how to use it.

HESCHONG: There are two kinds of variability. One is the variability of the natural environment that we're adapted to and that we find stimulating. The other is the inherent variability in the population. For both thermal and visual comfort, there are huge variations in individual preferences. Vivian, you've been a champion for the importance of individual thermal control in buildings. We're finding the same thing in the lighting field—the range of preferences is vastly bigger than the opportunity we give people. If we allow people individual control, we see improvements in both performance and energy efficiency. It's a win/win.

> All the questions in sustainability are at the crossroads of disciplines. We've got to bring the disciplines together.
>
> VIVIAN LOFTNESS

LOFTNESS: This is a really important discussion that could transform architecture and practice. These areas of research could dramatically change the kinds of systems designed. But most of the innovation in lighting and natural ventilation is coming out of Europe. In the U.S. there's a paucity of both commitment and resources to study customized controls. It happens more in the automotive industry than in the building industry.

HESCHONG: You're right—the Europeans are way ahead of us there. I would like to see the same level of capability with daylighting controls that we have with electric lighting controls. Once you can provide individual controls, trying to maintain the perfect static environment with a mechanical system becomes less important. We'd save energy, and people are better off.

LOFTNESS: Imagine the transformation of practice and education if architects and students felt that part of their responsibility is to invent new technical solutions. In every other field, invention is a norm in research. We have tremendous opportunity, but buildings are not even on the map.

HESCHONG: The key is how to make the case. What kind of evidence will increase the level of attention given to well-being in the environment?

LOFTNESS: Research needs a link to health or performance.

HESCHONG: Yes. Think of the level of response that came when sick building syndrome was identified and people actually started showing up in hospitals. A recent survey showed that over the last ten years, 95 percent of all research into interior environments was on SBS. There were only three lighting studies and two thermal comfort studies. If there's a link to a medical issue, a disability rather than an improvement, funds will flow.

LOFTNESS: That's essentially trying to take the bad and make it less bad. It's not really looking at the threshold of creativity and motivation. As long as it's highly economical to slap up cheap, short-life buildings, there's very little reason to build with better quality. In the European community, there have been substantial multi-national efforts to aggregate the research and publish it. I think it will start trickling over, but we still have to build the economic case on this end. That will be the lynchpin for changing practice in the U.S.

WIG: If you're building an economic case, how do you build that around emotional or psychological well-being? Is it measurable?

HEERWAGEN: You can measure it, but can you turn it into dollars? Should we even attempt to? The Gallup Organization measures what they call employee engagement, which has to do with well-being, job satisfaction, et cetera. It's really about work life, not the environment. But they're finding that this is strongly connected to profitability, organizational productivity, and turnover. They've taken that and turned it into an overall formula that looks at organizational success. Can we do those kinds of things in the built environment?

LOFTNESS: In addition to what happens inside buildings, there's the question of viable neighborhoods—walkable communities with mixed uses and incomes in which the people working in your grocery store can actually live in the neighborhood.

HESCHONG: Issues of community layout—transportation and walkability—are huge. They link directly to physiological health through the amount of activity people get, the time they spend outdoors in the sunshine, the exercise that children get. The public health community is starting to connect these issues to the obesity epidemic in the U.S. Once the link is made between cities and public health, we will start seeing changes in policy.

HEERWAGEN: I would extend that to the design of buildings—for example, by making stairs attractive to climb.

LOFTNESS: Yes. Put windows in the stairways.

HEERWAGEN: Right. Have open stairways. Make people want to use them to talk to one another.

HESCHONG: In one of our studies we found that the more people use the elevator, the greater number of health symptoms they reported. The fewer the number of symptoms they reported, the more often they reported using the stairs.

HEERWAGEN: The links to well-being are where the leverage is. Looking at this as a public health issue is far more powerful than looking at it as an individual health problem.

HESCHONG: It goes back to the layout of the whole city. Walking up and down stairs is more feasible in Paris or Washington, DC, where the buildings are lower, than it is in Manhattan.

LOFTNESS: It's exciting to watch what happens when the health care community looks at land use—it sparks a whole new generation of thought. I'm very excited about interdisciplinary collaboration driving not just new research but also new fields and new educational directions.

> The key is how to make the case. What kind of evidence will increase the level of attention given to well-being in the environment?
>
> LISA HESCHONG

HEERWAGEN: The Department of Public Health in Los Angeles and Georgia Tech are using sensors developed for studying herd movements in animals to learn how much people move in buildings. It's a very interdisciplinary approach, but they had to go out and find people in other fields.

LOFTNESS: At this point, all the research questions in sustainability are at the crossroads of disciplines. They're never single-subject issues. We've got to bring the disciplines together.

HESCHONG: We can't get from here to there without collaboration. Absolutely the key.

HOW DO WE MEASURE PROGRESS?

In recent years, the practice of sustainable design has received an unprecedented boost by the introduction of certain standardization systems. Programs such as Energy Star, Greenguard, and especially the U.S. Green Building Council's LEED rating system have done much to raise public awareness, provide benchmark standards, and transform various aspects of the design and construction industries. Suddenly a subject that previously had been rather vaguely defined has been given clear articulation, and efforts to be "environmentally friendly" now can be weighed against a number of consensus-based, third-party methods of evaluation. As a result, the industry now faces both new opportunities and new challenges.

On the one hand, inflated claims and so-called "green-washing" are less likely with performance guidelines and governmental regulation. "I'm a big believer in regulation," says Susan Ubbelohde, a daylight and energy consultant. "You don't have to work in energy very long before you realize that codes are your best friend. Title 24 [energy efficiency standards for buildings] is one of the best things that's ever happened in California. Instead of talking about the moral need for this, we now talk about the legal need." On the other hand, the industry is far from agreeing on such standards. The various rating systems and certification programs do not all support one another, and many environmentalists complain that none goes far enough. Ubbelohde confesses that "mainstreaming the agenda can water down the ambition. There's a question of co-opting. The Ford hybrid cars get less gas mileage than good regular cars in Europe. Is that progress?"

"Standardizations are... stultifiers of development," writes Jane Jacobs in *The Nature of Economies*. Architect Julie Eizenberg complains that LEED can stifle innovation. "Programs like that become bureaucratic very fast." Landscape architect Carol Franklin agrees. "You can do something truly dreadful and still meet all of LEED's criteria." DIRT Studio's Julie Bargmann, another landscape architect, asks, "Do we really need a checklist to tell us if we're green?" USGBC Board member Vivian Loftness acknowledges that current versions of LEED have significant limitations: "The lack of any social equity variables is a glaring hole that has to be addressed in the next generation." Laura Lesniewski, a principal with BNIM Architects in Kansas City, observes, "LEED has been transformational for our industry, but it is still just 'less bad.' Many of us are interested in exploring what a truly 'sustainable' building might be." She was part of an interdisciplinary team that developed a guide to "living buildings" for the Packard Foundation. The illustrated chart that resulted, The Packard Matrix, became known as an elegant and ambitious illustration of a graduated approach to sustainable design.

Insiders say that LEED has to be seen with the right perspective. "The main purpose of the USGBC is to create a yardstick," says Donna McIntire, the USGBC's former LEED Program Manager. "They've been focused on certification, but providing a guideline is more important. So many people now use LEED as a guide without going through the certification process, and that can be good for the industry." Early USGBC staffer Kristen Ralff Douglas agrees. "The USGBC cannot be everything to everyone. Its goal has always been the same—to mainstream green building. LEED has done that by putting green building within the spectrum of normalcy. But it's a tool, and a tool shouldn't limit your thoughts. Now we have to go way beyond what LEED set as a minimum standard. We have to change the whole notion of what a building is. How do we get people to understand the real value of a building? That is a true paradigm shift!"

The notion of "real value" underlies the debate about standards—and environmentalism in general. According to playwright Kaiulani Lee, it is at the heart of Rachel Carson's legacy: "What has value? Does a cow have standing? Does a tree have standing?" Architect Bob Berkebile, who founded the AIA Committee on the Environment (COTE), says we cannot understand value through logic alone. "What we're accustomed to is trying to solve everything mentally. We need more from the heart." COTE's annual Top Ten Green Projects awards program, begun by Gail Lindsey in 1997, encourages not just environmental performance but design excellence. The program requires entrants to write essays describing their building's most sustainable features. According to the Top Ten call for entries, the narrative format recognizes that qualitative goals are often subjective and therefore cannot always be evaluated quantitatively.

In any discussion of measurement and sustainability, quantity and quality vie for attention. How do we enumerate principles that encompass everything from the number of BTUs our houses will burn this year to the spiritual well-being of our great, great granddaughters? Maurya McClintock, a façade engineer with Arup, sums it up: "Quantifying energy efficiency is easy. The other stuff is hard." Of this "other stuff," environmental psychologist Judith Heerwagen insists, "It doesn't matter that we can't quantify the human dimension. We shouldn't even attempt to put a dollar value to it." Nevertheless, new methods are emerging. "Traditional measures consider things like productivity and absenteeism," says Karen Stephenson, a corporate consultant who focuses on social networks. "More meaningful measures are social capital and cultural health." Stephenson believes that in the next five years such factors will define how organizations understand themselves and adapt over time. "Lifestyle index" tools that evaluate the sustainability of every area of life are already available on the market, and economist Hazel Henderson's Quality of Life Indicator comprehensively assesses what she calls "national well-being."

The following conversation weaves between two senses of the word *measure*—to quantify numerically or to consider or choose with care (as in measuring one's words). What are the relationships between accounting and accountability? We invited three women to consider these questions. Christine Ervin, formerly of the Environmental Protection Agency, was the original CEO of the USGBC. Kath Williams spent seven years as vice chair of the USGBC and now serves on the board of the World Green Building Council. And Sandra Mendler's experience with green standards is unique in the industry. She is co-author of *The HOK Guidebook to Sustainable Design*, former chair of the AIA /COTE, and a USGBC Board member. We asked them what it means to measure sustainable design.

> Traditional measures consider productivity and absenteeism. More meaningful measures are social capital and cultural health.
>
> KAREN STEPHENSON

SANDRA MENDLER: One of the big questions is what we're trying to measure. Is it intentions or results? The term "sustainable design" implies that we're focusing on the design process—a set of intentions and goals. Ideally, those goals translate into the built project, but not necessarily.

KATH WILLIAMS: That sounds like sustainable development, rather than sustainable design. Design is only one piece of it.

WOMEN in GREEN: What's the distinction?

MENDLER: Design focuses on intentions and the plan to implement them, and development represents the end result of that plan. LEED is a great tool, but it measures intentions and not results. We need to bridge the gap.

CHRISTINE ERVIN: That is a top priority. That's why we're seeing a lot of interest now in post-occupancy evaluations—so we can understand how these buildings are actually performing.

WILLIAMS: We have to be able to prove we are doing what we say we are—and understand when things are not working and why. There are going to be areas where we're wrong, and hindsight will tell us to work harder. In my opinion, that's the only reason to measure—so we know how to improve.

ERVIN: After all these years grappling with sustainability, there's still widespread discussion about whether it is an end goal or a process and a philosophy.

WILLIAMS: Sustainability is way beyond buildings—it's how we live our lives. LEED only addresses the basic part of this. It isn't the answer—it's just a tool. Many people want it to be even more prescriptive than it already is, but I think it should become broader.

WIG: Kath, you have said that the ultimate goal of sustainability is perfection.

WILLIAMS: Perfection is a goal you strive for—a state where everything is in balance. I see sustainability in that way, as a kind of perfection that you constantly strive for but will never reach. There are always new factors and shifting agendas. That's why we need tools that are robust and evolving.

ERVIN: Every time there's a change in technology, price, demand, or knowledge, you've got an opportunity for advancement. Sustainability isn't static.

MENDLER: That is an important point, but sometimes people use the fact that sustainability is not ultimately achievable as an excuse for not getting started.

ERVIN: The tools shouldn't paralyze action. One of the most potent things about the green building movement has been the positive, can-do message. But we can't get lulled into a false sense of success. We have to balance passion and enthusiasm with urgency. Are we really making enough of a difference quickly enough?

That's why measuring tools are important—for third-party verification. And you can see that trend emerging now in the private sector. More and more companies are reporting indicators related to sustainability.

MENDLER: The EPA's Energy Star program existed before LEED, but it was too difficult for people to see how the program could influence their decision-making process. There's a difference between a tool that provides the best measurement versus one that influences the most positive change in the industry. If we think about LEED purely as a measurement tool, we would challenge a number of things. But if we look at it as a strategy for influencing the industry, we see it differently.

WILLIAMS: We've all heard designers say that until now, there was no pragmatic method to talk to clients about sustainability.

MENDLER: Right. Part of LEED's success is its fundamental weakness—its limited scope allows people to get their arms around it. Environmental organizations used to say it was difficult to get funding for sustainable design because it's just too broad. They get funded for specific issues such as climate change, habitat, or oceans, and people don't know how to connect many dots.

ERVIN They are missing the whole point of integration, of course. I hope that stovepipe approach is changing now.

WILLIAMS: Even environmentalists don't see the connections between the built environment and the environment they're working to protect.

MENDLER: Just this morning I saw a newspaper story about rising sea levels, and it referenced emissions from automobiles and manufacturing but didn't say anything about the building sector, which now accounts for about 40 percent of total U.S. energy use. We haven't successfully communicated this to the broader public. It's a blind spot outside of our industry.

WIG: Do tools like LEED help connect the dots, as Sandy put it?

MENDLER: The goal of any measurement tool is to break something down into its parts while not losing the wholeness of it.

ERVIN: The common criticism about LEED is the checklist format, which looks at the pieces separately. But LEED is a tool, and its usefulness is largely determined by the skill with which it's used.

MENDLER: When we change the way we design, we can create benefits in many areas at once—saving energy, creating healthier spaces, improving communities, and so on. But that holistic nature also makes it difficult to understand, so ideally we're addressing both of those things simultaneously. LEED lets an owner say it's not a zero-energy building but it is a LEED platinum building.

ERVIN: There's always been the tension in LEED between aiming high enough to capture the leaders and being within reach of the mainstream market. That's a good, healthy tension. That keeps us looking for more.

WILLIAMS: As we expand the understanding of what sustainability means, we can include more. Green buildings today don't do much spiritually, for example. I like accepting that the more we know, the more we know we don't know.

MENDLER: You're saying that you know where you want to go, and you don't want people to be frustrated by the partial successes. Even with all the incredibly hard work, we're only getting part way there with each project.

WILLIAMS: And that's okay. I like working with companies who are saying they are going to go as far as they can, because it's a long-term journey.

WIG: Some refer to this as a "stair step" approach.

MENDLER: The stair-step analogy is appropriate, but it's a long staircase, and we're at the bottom. There are opportunities in the process to leap-frog, so it's not as linear a process as climbing a staircase.

WILLIAMS: I totally disagree with the stair-step model. The process can be three-, four-, and five-dimensional. It's far more complex than taking it step by step.

MENDLER: A single built project that demonstrates the potential of sustainable design can have a profound impact. There are projects that over time have begun to change people's minds about what's possible in the building industry.

ERVIN: Incremental stair steps alone aren't going to generate the market changes we need. Those projects that raise the bar and show what's possible play a huge role in lifting aspirations—and expectations, for that matter.

WIG: What might we be trying to measure in five years that we aren't measuring now?

WILLIAMS: Incorporating life-cycle assessment data into our tools will become more critical. That's a long journey itself.

ERVIN: Hopefully, carbon emissions will be routine reporting in five years. But our economic system has a long way to go to reflect the values of sustainability. Even incremental steps in that direction would pay huge dividends.

> Sustainability is a kind of perfection you constantly strive for but will never reach.
>
> KATH WILLIAMS

MENDLER: Quality of life has a huge impact on the value of real estate. The cost of living index varies across the country, and some communities are considered more desirable than others. It would be interesting if there were a way to measure the impact of the built environment on people's perception of those places.

WIG: Sandy, you have written about "humanistic sustainability." Is the mainstream practice of sustainable design effectively promoting well-being and other issues that aren't as tangible as materials and energy?

MENDLER: People addressing sustainability are largely motivated by human issues. They want the numbers and the math to come out well in the end, but the reason they're doing it is because they want to create a fundamentally better place.

WILLIAMS: LEED only addresses the quantitative aspects of this, and that's important for many people, particularly Americans. It's pushed us along the way.

MENDLER: When you listen to what people say about their buildings, in the end what delights them are these qualitative issues. People love coming to work here—it *feels* different.

WILLIAMS: No one but the facilities manager jumps up and down and says, "I'm saving so much energy!"

MENDLER: One of the reasons why the focus on energy efficiency in the 1970s wasn't very successful is because it produced some very ugly buildings. And now there are LEED-certified buildings that aren't wonderful places. Qualitative and quantitative goals need to be addressed at the same time.

WILLIAMS: People are motivated and satisfied by different things, but quality is what really matters. And that's what satisfaction is, anyway. It's not a bunch of numbers, and it's not something you can quantify. It's saying, "I love this building, and I'm proud of this building." We don't talk much about pride. People are proud of green buildings. That's pretty cool.

WIG: Kath, you mentioned spirituality. What will it take to include more of that aspect of sustainability?

WILLIAMS: New blood! More diversity in the industry. We keep saying we have all of the building industry represented, but it's not really true yet. There are more angles than we're seeing right now. As more people get involved, we get new ways of looking at this.

HOW DO WE WORK TOGETHER?

Sustainability's emphasis on interdisciplinary work presents a challenge for architecture, which traditionally is compartmentalized by discipline and responsibilities, both in education and practice. Architect Moira McClintock explains that the profession currently isn't built for sustainability. "The star system in architecture—a pyramid with the architect at the top—does not lend itself well to the deep collaboration needed for sustainable design." Kate Schwennsen, 2006 president of the AIA, sums up the state of the profession. "In the twenty-first century, you can't be the lone hero architect and succeed."

Architect Nancy Malone says the old, lone visionary model is divisive and counterproductive. "When something goes wrong, there's blame and finger pointing. We need a change in the structure of how we do things so that we can collectively solve problems and take responsibility together." Landscape architect Carol Franklin remarks that designers often neglect to recognize the value of other disciplines. "Architects have a hard time with something women have always understood—that ideas come from everyone and everywhere." Architect Jeanne Gang agrees. "It's more important to recognize a good idea than to author it." AIA CEO Christine McEntee suggests that diversity is the key. "The more diverse the team, the greater the productivity and creativity," she says. "Given the challenges architects are facing, including the challenge of sustainability, we need those perspectives more than ever to get to better solutions." Activist Dianne Dillon-Ridgley offers this advice: "Whenever you encounter a vertical hierarchy, turn it on its side—make it a horizontal. Then it is a continuum and allows us to have the capacity to engage each other and work together."

Many people feel that women are particularly adept at creating new ways of working. "Business as usual is broken," declares Gail Vittori. "And women are often the ones rallying about broken systems." Studies support these impressions; surveys conducted by pollsters Celinda Lake and Kellyanne Conway for *What Women Really Want* show that men and women agreed that female-led organizations typically focus more on collaboration and personal relationships. "Women generally tend to be more willing to work collaboratively, work behind the scenes, and spread the credit around," says sustainability consultant Christine Ervin. "In the sustainable design movement, these methods and ways of working are gaining more respect." Gensler's Nellie Reid says she's noticed that "women clients buy into green before designers even bring it up. They don't always need the justification. Men seem to want more of an argument for the business case." Architect Katherine Austin sees design evolving into an inherently "feminine profession": "It is a group process and not a single 'star' process, no matter what the awards say. Who best to lead a team? Who can leave their own ego behind and do what's best for the whole? Nine times out of ten, women will fit the bill."

Architect Sylvia Smith finds that the goals of sustainability encourage deeper connections. "Clients understand that buildings are systems informed by issues they care about, not by the arbitrary vision of the architect. Sustainability gave us a way to have a rich, complete discussion." An example of this richer discussion led to the C.K. Choi Building at the University of British Columbia. Architect Freda Pagani was a campus architect in the early 1990s, and the way she organized the project is considered a model of integrated design. "We didn't use that term," Pagani says. "We thought it was just a good management idea to get all the players together very early on to ensure that everyone had an understanding about shared values." Pagani later studied the process as part of her Ph.D. work. "Most of the participants said it had been the most fun they had had in their professional lives. People love to be asked to engage their minds and hearts in a positive way." Architect Mary Ann Lazarus, who recently put together large charrettes in New Orleans, says that it is often the women in such groups who are the organizers. "Sustainability and green design demand a great deal of listening and facilitation. Women may be more willing to hear and include differing voices."

Schwennsen says this process often stems directly from the sensibilities women bring to the process. "I think we are getting more comfortable bringing our values to work." However, she also feels that the conflict between those values and conventional ways of working discourage many women, who "are finding they can't be in traditional practice and live their values." Architect Joyce Lee says this conflict presents both challenges and opportunities for the profession. "Women who have children will always be more time-challenged than many of their male counterparts to go the extra mile in this field. Yet the wisdom that comes from nurturing children can be the fuel that empowers a more sustainable future." McClintock says that many of the women who attended architecture school with her several years ago are no longer practicing architecture at all—because many of them are forging new paths. "They found ways to use their skills that offer more creative control, more flexibility, more quality of life, or more money than they were finding in traditional paths."

Alternatives to those traditional paths have begun to appear, along with new possibilities for women. For example, architect Hillary Brown believes there may be more opportunities for women in government than in the private sector. "There is a quality of female leadership that seems to be a good fit in government," she says. "This has direct application in sustainability, because it is a large, public idea. Women are often good at conceiving an organization's mission in terms of sustainability, and generating support, so the idea will persist." Landscape architect Lucia Athens agrees. "Public sector work affords the opportunity to work on many fascinating projects, but also to take a larger systems view. Working for the public as the client means taking a commitment to serving 'public health, welfare, and safety' to a broad, strategic level."

> Sustainability and green design demand a great deal of listening and facilitation. Women may be more willing to hear and include differing voices.
>
> MARY ANN LAZARUS

More generally, many people have suggested that women are less likely to conform to the limitations of any traditionally defined profession, regardless of the field. "Some women are comfortable being unclaimed in a career," says Dillon-Ridgley, explaining that because they often are the primary caretakers of their children, they tend to seek more of a balance between work life with home life. As a result, they are creating new careers but also allowing themselves the flexibility of changing their careers along the way. Mary Catherine Bateson has written that this variation actually may be stronger than traditional linear models. "These are not lives without commitment, but rather lives in which commitments are continually refocused and redefined... The circumstances of women's lives now and in the past provide examples for new ways of thinking about the lives of both men and women." Architect Sandra Mendler suggests that women may adapt to multiple career phases more easily than some men. "Those whose identities are strongly linked to achievement may be less likely to move across disciplines." Attorney and environmental advocate Joanne Denworth, who now works in the governor's office in Pennsylvania, realizes that it was her husband's linear path, in fact, that freed her to pursue a varied one. "He worked all his life at the same firm. I was lucky, therefore, to be as creative as I wanted to be."

In recent years, one of the new roles to emerge is green consulting, which has had special appeal for women. "There are a large number of women in consulting," says Sandra Leibowitz Earley, who runs Sustainable Design Consulting in Virginia and Maryland. Five of her six staff members are female. Mechanical engineer Jennifer Sanguinetti runs a sustainable design consultancy of twenty professionals, of which she says half are women. By comparison, fewer than 10 percent of all engineers are women, according to the National Science Foundation. Architect Sigi Koko estimates that most of the consultants she knows are women. Why is this? "It's a newer field, even though it is based on old concepts, so perhaps there are fewer expectations about who the face of it will be."

> Women are getting more comfortable bringing their values to work.
>
> KATE SCHWENNSEN

The role typically offers more flexibility, which can be especially attractive to women with families. "Women professionals often end up going out on their own as a way to avoid the glass ceiling in firms," offers Earley, who welcomes the freedom. Koko worked at the corporate architecture firm HOK before starting her own consulting business that centers on "healthy and ecologically sensible" building principles. "I have created a business that *is* my value system." Women also offer skills that are well suited to the role, says Earley. "Consulting relies on communication, coordination, and collaboration. Culturally, these are skills that women tend to have." Elizabeth Floyd, who works with Earley, has a similar view. "Women may be wired to address a variety of issues at once, while men seem to focus more on single issues or projects. The feminine approach works well with the integrated design process and with involvement in several stop-and-start projects at the same time. Men are often less comfortable with being limited to a supporting role."

"When you decide to become a consultant, you are letting go of the ego thrill of putting your name on the building," says Sanguinetti. "There are many architects, both men and women, who would not be comfortable with that. But it wouldn't surprise me if more women than men were willing to let go and find satisfaction in making the team effort stronger and the result better." Yet, architect Sandra Mendler wonders whether this trend limits women's opportunities. "I worry that many women get drawn into a consulting role when it may not be the most effective way to work." She notes that while at least half of all architecture students now are women, there is still a great imbalance in professional practice. "Generally, women have less firm ownership, less partnership, and less design leadership than men." She's convinced that design is the area in which women will eventually have the greatest impact.

We asked three successful sustainable design consultants to talk about the nature of their roles and what led them to it. Since 1993, architect Lynn Simon has run Lynn Simon Associates in San Francisco; Holley Henderson is an interior designer who runs H2 Ecodesign in Atlanta; and Barbra Batshalom is founder and executive director of the Green Roundtable in Boston, a non-profit that promotes sustainable design and development through advocacy, education, and consulting. We asked them how they discuss "sustainable design" with their clients.

LYNN SIMON: I don't worry much about the terminology. I use "green building" and "sustainable design" interchangeably, depending on the audience. I am more concerned with the activity than what we're calling it. But we're always talking about much more than a building.

BARBRA BATSHALOM: I often relate it to baseline conventional practice. That hooks people into thinking about green design as a way to add more value.

HOLLEY HENDERSON: I tailor the dialogue for the client. Getting the conversation going is what's important—then getting to awareness and commitment.

WOMEN in GREEN: How do you see your role?

BATSHALOM: I think I function as an educator and a change agent. Direct consultation is a small part of what I do.

SIMON: The word "consulting" has a business context that's not a perfect fit here. I think about how to have the greatest impact and making green part of standard practice. We usually work for owners, but sometimes for architects. However, we turn down work for firms who don't want to internalize sustainable design. Our goal is to mainstream green building. I work with clients who want to incrementally move that way and others who want to be really aggressive.

HENDERSON: As an interior designer who is now in a consulting role, part of my role is to empower designers. I show them the tools, the resources, and how they can collaborate on projects and education. I also work with owners, looking at their global standards. It's exciting to help push the field towards sustainability. I try to keep it real with people and say, "You don't have to be perfect." What can you do to move the needle?

WiG: What was the appeal of the consulting role? Why go outside of a traditional design firm?

HENDERSON: The architecture industry is an old model. I worked in a firm that had the commitment, but even their progress on this agenda was slow. I felt I couldn't reach enough people quickly enough. Now I feel like I have more agility and the ability to make the movement stronger and faster.

SIMON: I enjoy the diversity of working with all disciplines, and that's not something that happens in most firms. I also love the flexibility of having my own firm, especially now that I have a child.

BATSHALOM: I was initially attracted to architecture because it included so much. Historically, architects had so many roles outside of traditional building. But I worked in firms for twelve years and felt disconnected. For me, green consulting is exciting because it brings back an infinite menu of possible roles for the architect. Our education and policy work is just as important as green building consulting—they all enrich us.

Lifestyle flexibility is also important. In those twelve years, I worked in five firms. In none of those did I think there was room for balance.

WiG: If sustainable design, and the deep collaboration that enables it, becomes part of mainstream practice, are you putting yourselves out of business?

SIMON: I'll always try to be strategic about my role. There is great demand. I'm busier than I've ever been.

BATSHALOM: It's part of our mission as an organization to become obsolete. We want to empower other organizations so they are not dependent on us. I started in a firm and realized it was hard to have impact from within. But now a large part of my business is a "boot camp" for firms who want to restructure and align with green project delivery.

What jazzes me is intervening in systems and changing them. There are many messed up systems!

HENDERSON: I don't see our jobs becoming obsolete, though I wish they would. And then I'd just do something else.

SIMON: We are all very adaptable. We have diverse skills and could do lots of things.

WiG: Of the women you trained with, how many are in design firms today?

HENDERSON: About 85 percent of my classmates were women, and about half of them have gone into firms. The others are still involved in the field, typically, on other paths.

BATSHALOM: Many women I know are still practicing in firms. They have not risen to the position of principal as quickly as the guys that we were at school with us.

SIMON: Lots of the women I know have moved beyond the firm track. One reason is that traditional practice does not typically support working women who have families. Many friends I know are leaving traditional practice because they can't get flexibility and real support. A woman has to give up a lot to get to the top of a traditional architecture firm.

WiG: Have you experienced barriers to women in your practice?

BATSHALOM: Some clients have expectations that a green building consultant will be an older, white male—the gray-haired engineer—because this is a technical topic. They don't appreciate that it's not just technical, or that a younger woman might have technical capacity.

> "Almost all of my competitors are women, and I have talked to almost all of them about collaborating. We don't see it as competition—we see opportunities."
>
> HOLLEY HENDERSON

SIMON: I'm often the only woman in the room. But I typically get respect.

HENDERSON: Barriers are there if you choose to see them. Even in a very traditional architecture and interiors firm, where it was mostly male at the top, I feel I could have gone as high as I wanted.

WiG: Do women bring something unique to green consulting, especially facilitation?

BATSHALOM: It's tricky to generalize. Some women are more comfortable with process-related issues. Women may be more comfortable mapping the emotional topography of a team setting and dealing with conflict management.

SIMON: I find that many women have an interest in and a strong ability to multi-task.

BATSHALOM: Some women are skilled at communication with others in a way that makes them comfortable. For me, that means interpreting what that person values and talking around that.

HENDERSON: Almost all of my competitors are women, and I have talked to almost all of them about collaborating. We don't see it as competition—we see opportunities. I'm not sure that all men would be the same way.

SIMON: Most of my competitors are men, but it's very friendly competition. People involved in green building consulting tend to be sensitive individuals, supportive of women and men in the profession, and open to flexible hours. There's a certain type of person that goes into this. My peers are open to partnering, and we recommend each other all the time, even though we compete for jobs.

WiG: What's next?

HENDERSON: I'm seeing movement away from the old model of the team just washing their hands of the job when the building is "done." Interface's Atlanta showroom got the first LEED-CI Platinum rating, but it has very poor acoustics. The Center for the Built Environment at Berkeley did a post-occupancy evaluation, and it reveals the gap in LEED, which doesn't touch acoustics. The whole team saw the value of the feedback and learned from it. It's an important part of the process.

BATSHALOM: I think that we'll see a growing emphasis on training people to be active listeners, mediators, and other roles that are not traditionally part of our training as architects or business people. We have to get people competent to work collaboratively in teams. Right now, this is not in our grade schools or our university education, where architects are isolated from all others, learning only how to talk to each other.

SIMON: I hope people begin to understand the truly integrated process. Most projects are traditional practice trying to shoehorn the green features in. There's value to that because we're educating people. But there's not yet a realization that this is not business as usual. This is about mindset.

HOW DO WE LEARN?

"People no longer know how things work," says Karen Butler, an architect with the Environmental Protection Agency. "My grandparents were not biologists, but they knew how soil and light made plants grow." Education is the key to change, according to many people in various fields. "Most Americans spend at least thirteen years in school," says Jaimie Cloud, of The Cloud Institute for Sustainability Education. "That's where they learn the mental models that will frame their lives. Education is central to sustainability, because it's about learning how to live together."

Traditional educational methods, however, isolate subjects and therefore are not ideally suited for ecology, which teaches that everything is interrelated. Educators such as Oberlin College's David Orr advocate a different approach, which they call ecological literacy, in order to break down barriers between fields and between the classroom and the outside world. An early proponent of this approach was Maria Montessori (1870-1952), whom Orr calls "a real luminary." Emphasizing learning through direct experience, Montessori education connects ecology to individual potential and awareness. "All things are part of the universe and are connected with each other to form one whole unity," Montessori wrote. Her voice presaged Rachel Carson's by celebrating the joys of nature: "There is no description, no image in any book that is capable of replacing the sight of real trees, and all of the life to be found around them in a real forest."

Studies suggest that children and adults learn better when ideas are taught across subjects and disciplines. Anthropologist Mary Catherine Bateson has written that "the most creative thinking occurs at the meeting places of disciplines. At the center of any tradition, it is easy to become blind to alternatives. At the edges, where the lines are blurred, it is easier to imagine that the world might be different." Hunter Lovins, co-chair of sustainability at the Presidio School of Management, asks, "Am I a business professor? Am I an economist? Am I an engineer? I'm all of these." Business schools are catching on to sustainability. Beth Robinowitz, a Columbia University MBA candidate, thinks that business offers the greatest potential for sustainability. "My goal is to create products that benefit people and the planet, jobs people don't feel guilty about, and markets in which companies will compete to be the greenest and most socially responsible." Ann Goodman, who founded the Women's Network for a Sustainable Future, teaches a graduate business seminar called Corporate Power and Responsibility at New York University. The course explores the evolution of business responsibility and its convergence with sustainability over the past twenty years. Last semester, ten of the eleven students from various programs were women, which surprised her. "One reason may be because women, like other groups historically peripheral to the center of power—in this case business power—are likely to be sensitive to shortcomings of the status quo and therefore interested in its roots and the possibilities for change."

At the architecture schools, which are notoriously insular, there are signs of the walls breaking down. Under the leadership of dean Karen van Lengen, the University of Virginia recently merged its architecture and landscape programs and actively promotes dual degrees in both fields. More diverse multidisciplinary majors can still be a challenge to arrange, partly because funding centers on individual departments. But outside the schools, the Department of Energy's Solar Decathlon, a biannual design-build competition for green housing, has pushed many programs toward interdepartmental coursework. In both 2002 and 2005, University of Colorado professor Julee Herdt led the winning teams, which included students in architecture, engineering, business, journalism, and environmental studies. "We couldn't have won without very strong collaboration," she says. University of California-Berkeley professor Gail Brager brings guests into her classes to help dislodge stereotypes. "Some students—and some faculty—have no idea what a mechanical engineer can bring to the table."

Design programs in all disciplines are struggling to incorporate sustainability. The National Architectural Accrediting Board (NAAB) recently added it as a competency requirement, but there are no stipulations about how it should be met or woven through an already packed curriculum, and many schools fulfill the requirement solely through environmental systems courses. The authors of this book recently conducted a study for the AIA and found that not one school of architecture in the U.S. has transformed its curriculum to ensure that every student is steeped in the principles of sustainability. Sandra Leibowitz

Earley recently published *Ecological Design and Building Schools,* the only directory of its kind in North America, and drew similar conclusions. "There's a lot more to be done."

Demand is growing. "The students want more," according to Herdt. "They're hungry for this." An example is Tammi Wright, a recent graduate of the architecture program at California Polytechnic State University-San Luis Obispo. "I can't justify being an architect without being more responsible," she explains. "Sustainability is the primary issue my generation will face—the more we are aware, the more impact we can have." Even at schools known for this subject, it has yet to permeate. "There is an understanding that it should be fully integrated," notes Suzanne Charest, a master of architecture student at the University of British Columbia, "but it's still taught as something separate." Mary Helen Neal, an undergraduate architecture student at Alabama's Auburn University, which is known for its progressive Rural Studio program, says she has noticed a general failure to "put architecture basics and sustainability together."

Many aspects of architecture education have remained essentially the same for years and may not prepare designers for the sustainability challenge. University of Minnesota architecture professor Mary Guzowski, who helped develop their sustainable design master's program, maintains that bringing ecology and ecologists into the studio is not enough. "The next leap is understanding that we cannot teach the same way anymore. We need ecological and systems thinking to inform the teaching methods." Margot McDonald helped create the interdisciplinary "sustainable environments" minor at Cal Poly and was a key author of the Sustainable Environmental Design Education (SEDE) project, which produced a groundbreaking model curriculum for sustainable design education. "The old way was abstract, all about form, and not about site, client, or anything real," she says. "The new way is place-based, problem-oriented, and participatory. It is grounded in real life."

> **Education is central to sustainability, because it's about learning how to live together.**
>
> JAIMIE CLOUD

As these examples show, women are making a difference as both faculty and students. The majority of college students now are women, and studies show that girls and women outperform boys and men at every age. In addition, growing research shows that girls actually learn differently—more through social interaction than through the simple transmission of information. Studies suggest that on predominantly female campuses both men and women get higher grades. What's more, on those same campuses the men lean toward uncommonly progressive views on sociopolitical issues and the environment. As UCLA professor of education professor Linda Sax has put it, "What we're talking about here is the impact of women's attitudes and values." In *What Women Want*, Celinda Lake and Kellyanne Conway report, "Research consistently shows that women are more focused on education issues than men. They are more likely to vote in school-bond elections, and to take education issues into account when voting in national, state, and local elections. They are also more likely to tell the men in their lives how to vote—even if they do not have children in school. By a wide margin, women reelect candidates who support early childhood education and who vote to reduce school size."

If women are more focused on education issues generally, more students are women, and women learn differently than men, how will education adapt? Is the growth of sustainability in education related to the rising number of women students and teachers? Enrollment in many architecture schools is now split evenly between the sexes, though NAAB estimates that, nationwide, 38 percent of students and only 16 percent of full-time teachers are female. Nevertheless, many programs have higher percentages, and a third of the members of the Society of Building Science Educators are women. Will these trends alter the nature of design education? Beyond formal education is the question of learning through life. Hunter Lovins asks, "How does a person learn in a world where everything is changing so rapidly?"

> The best way for students to experience themselves as part of 'nature' is with physical experience—body knowledge.
>
> JEAN GARDNER

This chapter brings together three educators who face that question every day. Vivian Loftness is a professor and former dean of architecture at Carnegie Mellon University in Pittsburgh. Jean Gardner is a professor of architecture at Parsons School of Design. Michelle Addington has taught at Harvard Graduate School of Design and recently joined Yale's School of Architecture. We asked them about education and sustainable design.

MICHELLE ADDINGTON: Teaching sustainable design is not about teaching students to apply a set of pre-determined strategies—it's about developing a deep understanding of how things work. This requires that we learn from the science-based disciplines, including physics, biology, chemistry, and human physiology. These are the disciplines in which the knowledge most needed for sustainability resides. We are comfortable working with professions with whom we have some overlap, such as structural engineering or landscape architecture. But we have to learn to communicate with physicists and atmospheric chemists who are not subordinates in our process and will not be focused on our end product. It is a completely different way of working, but it has the potential to open up many new exciting opportunities for designers.

VIVIAN LOFTNESS: Sustainability requires a shift in our overall thinking. Right now, it's difficult to get a physics faculty member to think about the built environment and to get architecture faculty to think about how physics and chemistry affect their decision-making. ·

JEAN GARDNER: It does require a shift. In curriculum for all ages, it's powerful to call attention to the fact that we are living systems. We are not outsiders—we are a living part of what we're engaged in reworking. We have to get away from making the environment and our activities into objects rather than engaging them as part of our own subjectivity.

The best way for students to experience themselves as part of "nature" is with physical experience—body knowledge. After a visit to a farm, I asked a kindergarten class to draw by hand an animal they'd seen. The hand is a powerful part of knowing oneself and connecting oneself to things that seem outside us. The response was extraordinary. The children started to smell the pigs in the classroom as they were drawing; they were bringing back the physical experience.

LOFTNESS: Hands-on, kinetic, field-related learning is the richest way to build a common vocabulary between disparate disciplines. Students building a green roof on campus must engage issues of water, energy, and ecosystems.

ADDINGTON: Immersion in the tangible is very important. A group of Harvard students went into the Ecuadorian Amazon to meet with Indians about an eco-tourism project. It was one thing to be able to think about it in the abstract, neatly truncated as a design exercise. But once the contexts were exposed, it became a messy problem. At first, this paralyzed the students. They began to realize that eco-tourism was not necessarily the right answer, ecologically speaking, yet they had to think about the Indians' survival. Looking for balance was profound.

GARDNER: Our educational system creates informed, analytical thinkers who have looked at things as separate from themselves. We need our students and ourselves to be immersed in real, living, everything-hinges-on-what-I-do-next moments. Neurology studies on students working with high-powered computers suggest that they don't know how to make decisions—how to choose—because they have no body knowledge prior to their thought knowledge. You're right—it's a paralysis.

ADDINGTON: Faculty members, on the whole, feel somewhat comfortable opening up a dialogue in regard to explicit choices—one material or another, whether or not to use a shading system. But very few of the design faculty have the comfort level to bring sustainability more substantively into design beyond the implementation of preset strategies and solutions. We have to figure out a methodological approach that allows for a deeper inquiry and exploration or we'll lose a generation of students who are committed to addressing these issues.

GARDNER: The way my generation was taught does not address the problems we want our students to engage. I don't want to lead students to believe that if they design a solution in the studio, they will have an answer. The most I can do is to help build their ability to see themselves as capable of an open-ended exploration.

WOMEN in GREEN: For example, if you are talking about wood as a building material in a design studio, shouldn't you also discuss forestry and land management?

GARDNER: I helped develop a curriculum between Black Rock Forest, which is a 3,500 acre forest on the Hudson River, and schools in New York City. The Forest Consortium works with elementary and high schools and universities. We put monitors in the forest so students can access data from the classroom. This would be a rare thing to have in an architecture school, but it would be a wonderful way of teaching about design for context.

ADDINGTON: We have a capability, or at least a desire, that other professions do not. We *can* move from context to context. We may not yet be able to seamlessly slip into these other realms, but we recognize the need to do so. Other professions are so atomized that contexts are extraordinarily rigid.

LOFTNESS: Architecture students should develop their abilities to be integrators—the conveners of the integrated process.

GARDNER: One challenge is that the students see everything as highly mediated—to them, everything is an artifact. My graduate students think there is no such thing as authentic experience. Waking them up requires putting the nexus of responsibility in their hands. When it happens, it's magic. They begin to realize what they are capable of.

LOFTNESS: If we're going to get universities moving over hurdles toward collaborative process, we need to move away from the polarity of either/or. Schools of architecture talk about design and technology, or design and science, as opposites. This is crippling the thought process. That art, science, and religion are separable is a basic Enlightenment proposition, and the university as we know it is modeled on that disciplinary segregation.

If you draw an ecological cycle and realize how interdependent things are, you see that education should itself be a cycle of activities. Universities are set up to depend on people providing their sole value, not the collective value.

GARDNER: At The New School, we've started something called Transdisciplinary Bridges between schools and departments. It's a parallel universe at the university. We have a new commitment that every student who graduates from The New School will be eco-literate.

ADDINGTON: There is questioning along these lines at universities around the country. What's interesting is that the question of cross-disciplinary thinking, in many places, began with the subject of the environment.

I worry about how the polarity Vivian mentioned focuses the sustainability conversation on choices, as if it is all about choosing one thing or avoiding another. That's something we need to get away from. The difficult decisions don't fit neatly into those categories.

> Teaching sustainable design is not about teaching students to apply a set of pre-determined strategies—it's about developing a deep understanding of how things work.
>
> MICHELLE ADDINGTON

One of the interpretations of the new NAAB sustainability guideline is that studio projects should show certain didactic elements that "represent" sustainability. This suggests that if thermal mass or passive ventilation are part of the project, that's sustainable. This is a gross oversimplification.

LOFTNESS: This is reminiscent of prescriptive versus performance standards. For code officials, it's easier to have prescriptive standards—check the box for the right glazing or insulation. A performance standard requires that you have comprehensive knowledge. It's ironic that the accreditation body for a school of architecture would use a prescriptive standard for the very field in which performance goals are key drivers. Teaching performance is a huge challenge. It requires more knowledge, more exploration.

WiG: Less than 20 percent of full-time architecture faculty members are women. Yet women make up between a third and half the architecture student body at most schools. How will gender affect teaching?

LOFTNESS: Sustainability is being pursued as aggressively by male and female teachers and students.

ADDINGTON: But studies show that women faculty tend to have more contact hours with their students. I wonder if that relates to how we approach teaching more generally. I don't want to casually assign this to gender, but this subject does demand a great deal of discourse, give-and-take, and time.

GARDNER: Are there practices that women bring to this agenda that shift our sensibility? For a teacher to pay attention depends on whether he or she is conditioned just to look at things or to engage life—students, trees, or streets.

LOFTNESS: The generational divide may be more important. Each generation seems to have less contact with the environment, less understanding of their region. Things are increasingly homogenous. Kids spend birthdays at Chuck E. Cheese rather than the local park. How do you get emotional responses back into a generation that never had them?

GARDNER: I ask my students to buy something at the farmer's market and compare that to what they're eating at McDonald's. Suddenly they are thinking about the difference between an onion just pulled from the earth and the one that's on their hamburger. The next step follows naturally for students—they realize that the architecture they put their bodies into affects them as much as the food they put into their bodies. Sustainability is not an add-on—it's part of everything we do.

WHAT STORIES DO WE TELL?

Communication—personal and public—is at the heart of social change, and the written and spoken word has done much to spread the word about sustainability. Architect Jeanne Gang sums it up: "We have to get into the public imagination if we are going to transform how people think." Yet, educator Jean Gardner warns that public discourse often relies too much on rhetoric that limits thinking and reinforces existing attitudes. "Our need to tell stories may be one of the problems. Stories are culturally based. The global community is so diversified now. If we are talking about a unified effort for the whole planet, what stories do we tell?" Avoiding mythmaking merely requires a bit of self-examination, according to designer/contractor Catriona Campbell Winter. "A certain amount of dialogue needs to be happening at the personal level. This agenda draws from the very foundations of what it means to be human, what one needs to survive, what one can do to have a positive impact. I look daily for that nook where the personal and professional meet."

Many types of print, television, electronic discourse, and events and conferences have been instrumental in stimulating conversations about environmental issues at both the public and personal levels. In 1962, Rachel Carson's *Silent Spring* was a poignant and important wake-up call to the American public. Ten years later, systems thinker Donella "Dana" Meadows and three colleagues wrote *Limits to Growth*. The 1992 sequel, *Beyond the Limits,* was an even more influential articulation of the impact of human activity on natural systems. The clarity of Meadows' voice reached many people through the *Global Citizen*, a newspaper column she wrote for fifteen years. "Hers was the quiet voice of reason," recalls Hunter Lovins. "Hers was the first definitive word that there are limits, and that the job for us all is to find the fulfillment of our lives within them." And Janine Benyus says of Meadows, "She taught us to think like a system." Today, Meadows' article "Leverage Points" is a staple of sustainability reading lists. Anthony Cortese, an advocate for sustainability in education, says he uses that article in every workshop he gives. "Dana is one of the unsung heroes of this movement," he says. "Without her systemic way of thinking about health, economics, and the environmental challenges together, I don't think we'd be where we are today. She had a quiet way of putting things and connecting people that made a huge difference."

In the design community, *Environmental Building News*, published advertisement-free since 1992 by Building Green, earned a sterling reputation for its authoritative voice about the products and processes behind sustainable design. Around the same time, interior design magazines began paying attention. Katie Sosnowchik was editor of *Interiors & Sources* in 1992, when the magazine began covering the work of designers Randy Croxton, Kirsten Childs, and William McDonough. "I thought, 'This is what the future is all about,'" Sosnowchik says. In 1996, she and two of her publishers produced the first EnvironDesign conference, which brought together sustainability thinkers and designers; this was a must-attend event until the USGBC's annual Greenbuild conference started in 2002. Four years later, she started *Green@Work* magazine to tell stories of companies embracing sustainability.

> **We have to get into the public imagination if we are going to transform how people think.**
>
> JEANNE GANG

Coverage of the topic was not yet mainstream, but it was growing. In 1994, following the grassroots tradition of Meadows and others, consultant Chris Hammer started *GreenClips*, a free, bimonthly summary of news about sustainable design and construction. Today more than 10,000 people subscribe. During this period, the American architectural press only occasionally mentioned the topic. *Architecture* had a short-lived column, "Green Sheet," limiting coverage to one page. *Architectural Record*, the magazine affiliated with the AIA, addressed the subject in building technology sections and sometimes featured projects (mostly European) with advanced energy or curtain-wall systems. The design press was beginning to take notice but still addressed the subject only sporadically.

That limited coverage spurred alternative publications to tackle the subject more thoroughly. Kristin Ralff Douglas became editor/publisher of *Environmental Design + Construction* in 2000, after helping David Gottfried get the USGBC off the ground. "I felt there needed to be more dialogue in the industry amongst leaders who knew what they were talking about. I wasn't seeing the topic addressed in the design press, and I felt that we really needed to be sharing information." Many designers feel that to whatever degree the media does cover sustainable design, it tends to overplay the technical aspects. According to architect Lisa Mathiessen, "There is a joy that informs much of the green movement that is not yet being communicated to the industry as a whole."

Architect and freelance writer Nancy Solomon says the media has a special role in the pursuit of sustainability because it depends on public awareness. "The media has the best chance of inspiring and educating at a personal level so that people begin to learn how to ask critical questions and tap their creative powers." If design magazines have not been covering the topic thoroughly, it may be because much of the industry has been torn about how sustainability affects design. That lack of coverage may be changing now. Since devoting a special issue to sustainability in 1996, *Metropolis* has embedded the subject in all its content, treating sustainability as an integral part of design and culture. In the last several years, *Dwell* magazine, founded around the idea that "good design is an integral part of real life," has almost single-handedly started the modern prefab movement, which is setting new standards for combining efficiency, affordability, and good design. The current popularity of prefab is due, in large part, to the attention that Allison Arieff, *Dwell's* former editor, brought to designers such as Jennifer Siegal, Michelle Kaufmann, and Rocio Romero. "People thought I was off my rocker," Arieff recalls.

Beyond periodicals, books have brought more and more attention to sustainability within the design community and the public at large. Some of the most influential and eloquent include Paul Hawken's *Ecology of Commerce* (1993); Janine Benyus' *Biomimicry* (1997); *Natural Capitalism* (1999), by Hawken, Amory Lovins, and Hunter Lovins; and William McDonough and Michael Braungart's *Cradle to Cradle* (2002). All of these books built on the legacy begun thirty years earlier by Carson, Meadows, and Jane Jacobs. In the meantime, many popular books about green design and construction have appeared. Sarah Susanka published the first of her successful *Not So Big House* series in 1998, making the eloquent and beautifully illustrated case for quality over quantity. "It is important to make this accessible to average home owners," she says. "Architects often skip the little guy. True change happens when people incorporate these things in their everyday lives. When you help people in their houses, sustainability filters into the rest of their lives." Writer Jennifer Roberts' first book, *Good Green Homes*, was called by *Dwell* magazine "a superb introduction to the concept of green building." She says her passion is to use her voice "to make sense of abstract issues and make them more real to a larger audience."

Poet and ecologist Sandra Steingraber, who has been called this era's Rachel Carson, had a larger audience in mind when she wrote *Living Downstream* in 1997. It was designed as a blueprint for tracing toxins in communities. "I thought that if I could lay bare what went on in my home town, it could be a method people could use anywhere." She notes that Rachel Carson was intensely private and rarely wrote in first person, as she herself does. "There's a part of me that is convinced of the authority of one's own experience. I think feminism has taught us that. And the world has changed since *Silent Spring*. People need a narrator, someone they can relate to, to take them through this territory."

We invited three magazine writers to discuss the role of the media as an advocate for sustainable design. Susan Szenasy has edited *Metropolis* for most of its twenty-five years and recently has championed younger designers through the "next generation" design prize program. Penny Bonda writes and edits *Interior Design* magazine's "Green Zone," a section of the magazine's Web site, and has been a vocal proponent of sustainable design in the interiors industry. Deborah Snoonian spent five years at *Architectural Record* where she often covered sustainable design. As a writer and engineer, Snoonian's voice mediates between worlds. She is now senior editor at the green consumer magazine *Plenty*. We asked them how the design media is covering sustainability.

> When people turn a phrase well, it grabs the emotions of people, it catches them. It's much more compelling than spouting statistics.
>
> PENNY BONDA

SUSAN SZENASY: Generally it's being discussed in a superficial way. When design magazines cover green, it's very rudimentary, and much of it is lip service. We must refer to more than architecture and buildings. We're talking about the idea of sustaining community and all its people. It's about ethics. But it's not in everybody's consciousness yet.

PENNY BONDA: What's happening with the media is the same thing that's happening in the design industry right now—green is an add-on, and it shouldn't be. It should be integrated in everything that we do. Sustainability shouldn't be something that some projects do and some projects don't.

People ask me how to convince their clients. My answer is, don't convince them, just do it. Integrate green principles into everything you do. And then when the media writes about design, they will write about it as an integrated part of every project—interiors, buildings, communities, or automobiles.

SZENASY: *Metropolis* grabbed on to this idea early on. Because we seek out these kinds of jobs and ask these questions, it may seem that there's more out there than there really is. It's a very strange position to be in. We're telling a particular story that we choose to tell.

DEBORAH SNOONIAN: *Plenty* was founded as an eco-friendly lifestyle magazine. We cover a wide range of subjects and promote green as good for people and good for the economy. At consumer publications where there is no eco focus, we are starting to see single issues focused on the topic. *Vanity Fair*, *Elle*, and *Wired* just did these.

WOMEN in GREEN: Obviously, *Plenty* and *Architectural Record* have completely different missions, but have you noticed that there are differences in the *way* this topic is discussed?

SNOONIAN: *Record* is written for a trade audience. They're using technical terms. *Plenty* is written for a mainstream audience in their twenties and thirties who don't necessarily know about sustainability, so the language is simpler.

At *Record*, I saw a kind of dual evolution—the staff was getting better at asking questions about sustainability, and architects were getting better at doing these things and telling their stories.

WiG: Do you think the broader human issues about lifestyle and community are being covered more in the general media than in so-called trade magazines?

SZENASY: The media that reaches most Americans, television, doesn't do anything on this. There might be an occasional piece on the price of oil, or a one-off show on PBS, but it's really not part of the mainstream conversation. Those of us who subscribe to the electronic newsletters have this idea that there's a lot of coverage on sustainability because we get that daily cache. But that's partly because it's worldwide, and the rest of the world is covering it far better than the American mass media.

Something has shifted in the past two or three years. Global warming is no longer referred to as a theory. Now you see occasional pieces in the *New York Times* on LEED-certified buildings. But I don't think the larger issues are resonating. When oil prices went up, there was no discussion at all about the way things are made, designed, distributed.

SNOONIAN: Television, in many ways, is a better medium for conveying green information than a magazine or Web site, because it's active and visual. And it helps to have a very strong three-dimensional component to what you're seeing and hearing. There's a new network, Lime, that's covering green topics. HBO is doing a documentary on global warming, and there are a series of films on that topic out right now. And now Brad Pitt is hosting a green design show. I guess in our celebrity-obsessed culture, that's what it takes to draw the viewers.

SZENASY: I helped to put that show together. Asking Brad Pitt to narrate is interesting. In this star culture, everybody is paying attention to celebrities instead of the real issue—choking ourselves to death on all that we make and throw away. That's the world we live in right now.

BONDA: We are not going to start paying attention to the global issues that are a problem—global warming, water shortages, land use, air quality—until there are disasters. I believe that Katrina and the hurricane season in 2005 were responsible for renewed interest in global warming. It's unfortunate that it takes loss of human life and massive loss of property to get us to talk about these issues. The sustainability issue started with the industrial revolution, and it's not going away. Our attention to it is what ebbs and flows.

SZENASY: For a brief time, there was reporting about people and their tragedies, but soon we moved on. And there has been no talk of the real issues that forced that to happen. We have terrible denial in the mass media about anything that is difficult.

WIG: There seem to be three ways that design magazines cover this topic. There are whole magazines devoted to it, and a lot of those that have popped up in recent years. Other magazines devote certain sections or columns to this matter. A few try to have it inform every aspect of the magazine without always calling attention to it. Are some strategies more effective than others?

BONDA: Magazines that are totally centered on green issues—*Environmental Design + Construction, eco-structure,* or *Green@Work,* which I used to work for—are not wildly successful, but they should be.

Every year at *Interior Design* we survey the top one hundred interiors firms. This year, 97 percent said their firms are specifying green products, and 74 percent said that firms are initiating the concept of making projects sustainable. There is interest here, and yet publications on these topics are struggling. The design world, it seems, is paying lip service to sustainability. People think that it's politically correct to say they care about sustainability.

The media has to feed what its audience wants in order to sell magazines and attract advertisers. The green magazines' lack of success speaks volumes.

SZENASY: People used to want to do a women's page or a children's page, and now it's a sustainable page, a technology page. All those things are a part of everything that we do and we are. I have a hard time calling those out. There is a personal and philosophical decision that everybody makes on that score. Right now, whatever is being done is great, because the more of it that's out there—no matter the form—the better. But I hope that in the next five years, it will turn into something much more organic.

SNOONIAN: To some extent, if we're doing our jobs right, then all the green magazines should just go away. Publications focused on this topic might be informing mainstream publications about what's out there. Once the issues are prevalent and mainstream, there will be no need for niche publications.

BONDA: There is an education component that the magazines help fill. For example, there's a lot of technology that has come about with the growth of green building that we never learned in design school. I was a practicing interior designer for thirty years, and I never learned about displacement ventilation, because that was the purview of the mechanical engineer. As a green designer, I need to know it. Through specialty articles, the design trade is learning about the chemistry of fire retardants and other things we never considered to be part of our trade.

> **If we're doing our jobs right, all the green magazines should just go away.**
>
> SUSAN SZENASY

SZENASY: You're absolutely right. The trade magazines have to relate these things to their professions in a very specific way. There is very little talk about industrial design and sustainability, but the architecture and interior design publications are trying.

BONDA: There has to be a commitment to what kind of language you're going to use, but also to how you're going to illustrate certain stories. An informative story about ventilation is going to require illustration. There needs to be a commitment for resources to make that an effective educational tool, if that's really the goal.

SNOONIAN: This is one reason why television and the internet can be so effective—animations can often convey technical information in a visually engaging way.

SZENASY: We use illustrations a lot, because there are things that need to be shown somehow. We've finally gotten into a habit of saying, "It's not visual, but we have to *make* it visual."

WiG: What's the best way to illustrate sustainable design? How do you demonstrate fresh air and human comfort in a photograph?

BONDA: You can't take a picture of green. For that matter, there are beautiful green projects and there are damn ugly green projects. You can take a picture of a light shelf or a raised floor, but you can't take a picture of good quality air.

SZENASY: The traditional way of presenting design, using beauty shots, is working against sustainability, especially in interior design and architecture. You have to show beautiful pictures, but the supportive material has to be there. For me, if design magazines don't use schematics to show how light comes in or how air circulates, they're not doing their job.

WiG: What we're talking about is effective communication. In writing about sustainability, how important is a persuasive voice?

BONDA: When people turn a phrase well, it grabs the emotions of people, it catches them. It's much more compelling than spouting statistics. When Ray Anderson starts listing disappearing species, one at a time, it grabs people's imaginations and fears and hopes, and that's what does it.

SZENASY: Once you're caught, you're really caught, and you want to know more. You are intellectually and emotionally involved and your work and life take on a more meaningful stance. That's where the passion comes from for a lot of people, and I think that's very appealing.

WiG: Would the message be more persuasive if it were less doom and gloom?

SZENASY: We need to be hopeful. Every time I write about what could happen with the power that designers have, I get a lot of positive mail. Looking at the world, people can get depressed, and they want to be inspired.

I have always been astounded by the fact that *Business Week* and *Fortune* don't have a column by someone like Paul Hawken, who has written about this beautifully for years. American business could have leapt ahead on these issues.

BONDA: I hope the mainstream media will feature more about sustainability. I was disappointed when *Organic Style* stopped publishing. They had a nice voice that spoke to the ordinary person. I just hope this continues to spread. I also hope it isn't disasters but genuine interest and passion that make it happen.

SNOONIAN: I see a lot of promising enthusiasm on the part of younger people coming out of school—not just in design, but in many disciplines. They are asking the right questions, maybe because they've been raised to recycle.

SZENASY: We need to tap that enthusiasm to inform practicing designers right now. Something has to open up in the profession to welcome this new generation, because they have an innate understanding of social and environmental issues. They need to be brought into the conversation. We can't wait for today's twenty-year-olds to be thirty-five. It might be too late.

HOW DO WE LOVE MORE?

"What really makes sustainability work?" ask architect Gail Lindsey and environmental consultant Joel Ann Todd. "What are its deeper core values, core purpose, and core process?" Having worked with many organizations and co-authored a guidebook to integrated design charrettes, they are experts on facilitation, so we asked them about working with people. Instead, what they talked about was love.

What's love got to do with it? Everything, as it turns out. In *The Sacred Balance,* geneticist David Suzuki writes that love binds together everything on earth. "Built into the fundamental properties of matter is the mutual attraction that could be thought of as the basis of love. For human beings, love, beginning with the bond between mother and infant, is the humanizing force that confers health in body and mind. Receiving love releases the capacity for love and compassion that is a critical part of living together as social beings." Such love should also be the basis for design, according to Jane Talkington, who is pursuing her doctorate in sustainability. Everything is energy, she says, and hand-hewn keepsakes affect us differently than mass-produced artifacts. "When items are handcrafted with great intention and care, those objects are embedded with 'embodied love.'" Call it the emotional version of the technical term "embodied energy."

Elizabeth Sawin, a biologist and systems analyst affiliated with the Sustainability Institute, lists three simple steps toward sustainability: "let reality in," "speak the truth," and "stay in love with what you love, even when it hurts." Of the last, she continues, "As long as we stay in love with our world, there's really nothing to do but keep on trying to figure out how to live within its limits." Sociology professor Denise Lach of Oregon State University writes, "Sustainability is like love and democracy—multiple meanings, not always perfectly realized, but always struggled for, at least by most of us." Others suggest that it's not merely *like* love. "Sustainability is love," write Patsy Benveniste of the Chicago Botanic Garden and Jan Kaderly of the Wildlife Conservation Society.

How can we realistically begin to translate "sustainability is love" into a workable set of strategies? If trying to understand sustainability seems challenging, dissecting love seems virtually impossible. Described as "an ineffable feeling of affection," it is by definition indefinable. That may be the point—care that knows no bounds. But care for what? For the earth, each other, and ourselves, says Donna McIntire, the U.S. State Department's liaison for sustainability. "We're disconnected from nature now more than ever, and we're also disconnected from our inner selves. But we are all connected to one another. How do we tap into that?" In his famous 1992 talk to the United Nations, Haudenosaunee Faithkeeper Chief Oren Lyons spoke of giving thanks to "All That Sustains Us" and described his people's "compassion and love for those generations yet unborn... We were instructed to love our children, indeed, to love *ALL* children." Humanity, he said, can be judged by how we treat our children. Echoing this sentiment, architect William McDonough condenses all of sustainability to one essential question: "How do we love all of the children of all species for all time?"

Put another way, these descriptions of sustainability sound like maternal love. Architect Bob Berkebile tells us that's exactly what it is. "We are learning how to love one another and our environment and the next generation. That requires more femininity and nurturing—more leadership from women and from the feminine side of all of us. There are damn few men who will be able to get us there." He points to biologist Janine Benyus as someone who understands the integration of science and spirit. "She sees that we are informed by energy we have yet to understand. That openness and ability to love takes courage and integrity." Benyus tells us, "I think what I'm carrying is love for the natural world. It's sacred fire."

> **People** wish for an easy technical fix, but this issue is really about a change of heart.
>
> JOEL ANN TODD

As Lindsey and Todd describe below, this sacred fire is the answer to sustainability's questions.

GAIL LINDSEY: I spoke on a panel at a conference recently, and a student asked, "What can we do to make a huge change very quickly?" The panelists mentioned several important things—fuel efficiencies, technology, daylighting and passive strategies, and so forth. And I said, "All we have to do is *love more*. Love ourselves more. Love the ecosystems more. Just love more." I had been a little afraid to say it, but I think that is the crux of it. The students really responded. I got a standing ovation!

WOMEN in GREEN: Why were you afraid to say it?

LINDSEY: Our society is left-brain dominated. The logical and scientific have primacy. In the context of that, it sometimes sounds strange to ask, "How do we measure love?"

JOEL ANN TODD: People wish for an easy technical fix that our left brains can understand. But this issue is really about a change of heart—changing the way we live, not just the way we design buildings.

LINDSEY: A mentor once told me that to change the world, I should change myself. But that's hard! Sustainability is most profound when you find it personally. Once you respect and love yourself, you start respecting and loving and valuing everything else—other people, the planet—because you know that you are connected.

TODD: The real magic is that you need people pushing forward in their own ways. When you bring that together, it's more powerful than having everyone in lockstep. It's messier and more difficult but much richer. We need emotion and reason. We need it all.

LINDSEY: It's a balancing act. Let us all be whole and let us all be integrated. It's a cultural challenge. Kids are incredibly intuitive, and it seems that our education system is training them away from intuition and connections with nature. Are we cutting down that real knowledge and connection to nature?

TODD: Things in nature just automatically do their best. The ant is carrying leaves, and the plant is reaching for the sun. We're the only ones making a conscious decision *not* to do whatever we can do, the best way we can do it.

LINDSEY: What we really mean by sustainability is making our highest and best choices, every day with every thing.

WiG: How do we decide what's highest and best?

LINDSEY: People ask me about how to deal with people who think their best choices are McMansions. I believe we respect everybody where they are. We might find out that what we're doing now is not, after all, highest and best. You have to be open—respect everything and continually question.

TODD: That's how we learn more about what's highest and best. There's the highest and best for me personally, and then there's the highest and best thinking more broadly.

LINDSEY: Thinking broadly involves understanding implications. When consequences are revealed, people get it.

WiG: Are you saying that sustainability itself needs to be questioned?

TODD: There is the possibility that we may not be doing the right things at all. We talk about this all the time, as we travel by airplane to conferences all over the world. We're still not behaving holistically and thinking beyond the building. An energy-efficient building may be having negative effects on its community for some reason, and that's certainly not sustainable.

WiG: You're both talking of left- and right-brain thinking. Is this related to men and women, respectively?

LINDSEY: Yes, but also to cultural and other differences. The Japanese encourage women and men both to engage in right- and left-brain thinking, but American culture emphasizes the left brain. If someone is a great deal more intuitive, whether female or male, that is likely to be discouraged in our school system.

TODD: One thing I love about working in this field is that there tends to be less stereotypical division along gender lines. You find men who are very open to the spiritual side of the work and are very articulate about it, too.

LINDSEY: This field does seem to be very trusting and open—it's a very good community.

TODD: People tend to be very collaborative instead of competitive.

LINDSEY: It may be that we all have masculine and feminine sensibilities and this topic empowers us to cultivate both parts.

TODD: I definitely have both—I want to know how to measure how well we're doing.

LINDSEY: Diversity of any kind is critical—then the effort functions like an ecosystem.

WiG: There appears to be greater gender balance in sustainable design than in the design industry at large, but racial and ethnic diversity are still very low.

TODD: Diversity is growing, but it's still low. What will change that is when we stop thinking about green design as the technical side of things and we start thinking more about its relationships to community. That's when we'll include professions that are more diverse.

LINDSEY: It may also be that we are not yet working closely enough with other groups, some of which are very diverse. Some of the groups just coming into this field are more diverse. And student populations are more diverse, too.

WiG: How can people with diverse backgrounds, views, and agendas work well together?

TODD: You start by having the conversation with people you trust. And then you provide opportunities for the conversation for other people. Community visioning workshops are one of those opportunities for people to talk about their values, what they really want for their community. It's up to people organizing these events to provide a trusting and comfortable environment.

> All we have to do is *love* more. Love ourselves more. Love the ecosystems more. Just love more.
>
> GAIL LINDSEY

Look at where you agree and disagree and look at the ways to work on that. How do we get something positive out of resolving the differences?

LINDSEY: Look at what we want to accomplish together. What we all need now for positive evolution is the highest energy we can have. Tapping that energy is critical.

TODD: I think most people that are doing this kind of work have these impulses within them. We're a bunch of do-gooders even if most of us won't admit it. Most people welcome a comfortable opportunity to have these discussions.

WiG: How do you begin to talk about sustainability with someone who has never considered any of these issues?

LINDSEY: I think if you open up, others will too. Remove the judgment and have the conversation openly.

TODD: People will surprise you. Gail and I have worked with people you might think would be hard to convince and they get it quickly, with a depth we didn't expect.

LINDSEY: [Environmentalist] David Brower once told me, "Whatever you do, make it fun. If you are passionate and you want others to join in, make it fun." I heard that before age six we laugh 400 times a day, but as adults we barely make it to four.

WiG: The two of you have worked hard to demonstrate what an integrated process looks like and how it relates to what you call the core values and purpose of sustainability. What is the distinction between values and purpose?

TODD: Values are the basis on which you construct a purpose to go forward or a purpose to do something. They are the basic underpinnings of everything you do.

LINDSEY: Joel and I are working with different universities. Yale is viewing sustainability from the biophilia perspective—their purpose is to engage the human connection to nature. But at MIT, they are focused on infrastructure and technologies that enable sustainability. These groups can have very different core purposes but shared values.

TODD: Our goal is to get people talking about values, not just the technological fix. Most of our conversations happen to be about making a building more efficient, but if we start talking about values, we can probably get to a much better place.

LINDSEY: I gave my "love" talk to a policy group—lots of three-piece suits. The first guy that zoomed up to me, a retired military guy, said "I loved your talk. We need more love in everything."

TODD: It would be great if we were having more conversations about what it really means to love more. If people were thinking about that personally and professionally, things would really shift.

FINDING HOME

"We have lost our senses."

Dayna Baumeister's voice is assuring but makes us curious. "In our two-dimensional world of books, television, and computers, we have forgotten how to experience the world with anything but our eyes. So let's close them for a few minutes."

We do as she says, and on her cue we rotate three times, eyes shut, as if we're about to take a swing at a piñata. "*Stop.*" We do. "Now point toward the ocean." On this spring morning, two dozen of us are gathered in an open-air pavilion on a bluff overlooking the Playa del Arco on the Pacific shore of southern Costa Rica. Below, the surf rushes against the rocks.

"Now close your eyes again and turn three times in the other direction." Before we complete the third rotation—"*Stop.*" More disoriented now, we still can hear the sea behind us. "Can you tell where the wind is coming from?" The moist spring air is heavy and almost doesn't move at all, but a warm breeze faintly brushes our backs. We point. Again, we shut eyes and turn. "*Stop.*" Now we are really turned around. "Listen. Wait for the loudest sound you can hear." A cell phone rings. Nervous laughter. Then, in the distance, deep in the rainforest, a hoarse cry wells up in the throat of something primal. Just a howler monkey. They're harmless. (Aren't they?)

One more set of blind turns. "*Stop.*" Baumeister pauses, bugs and birds sing, the rainforest rings with life.

"Now point toward home."

After a long silence we open our eyes again. We're all gesturing in roughly the same direction, which turns out to be far west of North America, somewhere over the Pacific. Home may be where the heart is, but our fingers can't find it.

As the first event in a week-long workshop, this activity introduces us to what biologist Janine Benyus calls "quieting"—calming the mind and body to open ourselves to the world around us. Twice a year, Benyus and Baumeister, also a biologist, organize excursions for designers and other professionals to immerse themselves in nature and witness its wisdom and wonders firsthand. While Baumeister may intend her instructions on this morning as a simple preparatory exercise, later we realize that its message could be a mission statement for the human race:

> Listen to the land.
> Now find home.

Benyus and Baumeister met in 1997, after Benyus published *Biomimicry: Innovation Inspired by Nature*, in which she profiled the growing practice of emulating living systems in human enterprise. (Literally, *biomimicry* means "imitation of life.") The book shows how farms can emulate prairies, how businesses can operate like woodlands, how bridges can span like spider webs. Its irresistible mixture of humor, marvel, and scientific detail led the *San Francisco Chronicle* to call it an "answer to the wake-up call that Rachel Carson sounded." A Montana graduate student when it came out, Baumeister read it in one sitting. "I shook for three days," she recalls. Immediately she located Benyus, who coincidentally lived an easy drive away, and arranged a meeting that ended up lasting hours. Their kindred spirit and common sensibility eventually gave birth to the Biomimicry Guild, a consulting and research organization that promotes nature as "model, measure, and mentor." Calling themselves "biologists at the design table," Benyus and Baumeister spread a simple idea: For every problem we encounter, nature can provide elegant inspirations for a solution.

> If the age of the Earth were a calendar year and today were a breath before midnight on New Year's Eve, we showed up a scant fifteen minutes ago, and all of recorded history has blinked by in the last sixty seconds. Lucky for us, our planet-mates—the fantastic meshwork of plants, animals, and microbes—have been patiently perfecting their wares since March, an incredible 3.8 billion years since the first bacteria.

In that time, life has learned to fly, circumnavigate the globe, live in the depths of the ocean and atop the highest peaks, craft miracle materials, light up the night, lasso the sun's energy, and build a self-reflective brain. Collectively, organisms have managed to turn rock and sea into a life-friendly home, with steady temperatures and smoothly percolating cycles. In short, living things have done everything we want to do, without guzzling fossil fuel, polluting the planet, or mortgaging their future. What better models could there be?

Janine Benyus, *Biomimicry*

There is ancient wisdom in the world, Baumeister assures us. "Life has been around for nearly four billion years. She's figured a few things out." (Nature's a she? "You bet," Baumeister quips.) We need only open our eyes, ears, and other senses to decode the messages all around us. How do we do this? The biomimics have a ready answer—"go outside." The irony of this simple imperative escapes us at first, but then an unavoidable truth dawns. Many of us hoping to help the environment don't actually know much about it. Designers and other professionals spend more time in conference rooms and corridors than in fields and forests. But to build a better relationship with something, we need to get to know it up close. This realization stirred something in Suzanne Charest, a Canadian architecture student who attended the Costa Rica session. "It's liberating. We're used to sitting at a desk, trying to figure things out. But this way seems so obvious now."

> Life has been around for nearly four billion years. She's figured a few things out.
>
> DAYNA BAUMEISTER

We have traveled to Costa Rica from different places and lives. Eight biologists, nine students of architecture, industrial design, and business, and fourteen professionals, including architects, interior designers, industrial designers, business owners, an engineer, and a writer—all discovering this place together. Biologist Corina Logan came to biomimicry as an undergraduate—she sees it as "my bridge between science and society," a way to connect biology to the broader goals of sustainability. Industrial design student Kim England heard Baumeister speak on campus. "Biomimicry is so positive," she says. "Much of what is written on sustainability is depressing. This is empowering. It's inspiring to think about creating something nourishing, rather than low- or no-impact." MBA student Beth Robinowitz (whose favorite "critter" is the sponge—because "it's structurally patient") is here because she sees "tremendous potential in the business community for products designed with the whole life cycle in mind." Mary Helen Neal, a thoughtful architecture student from Alabama, came here because of Benyus' book. "It's the only thing I've ever read that makes sense." Eileen Stephens, a consultant with degrees in mechanical engineering and business, came to learn the methodology. She was "mesmerized" when she heard Benyus speak at a green chemistry conference. "It instantly resonated with me. I am trying to use all my senses to embrace the idea that everything in nature has adapted to further survival."

The biomimicry workshop is designed to create this kind of resonance in all of us. A week of intense immersion and exploration, it's a crash course in the living world. Costa Rica, the biodiversity capital of the world (with an area about a fifth of Colorado), offers a lush laboratory—in a handful of days, we experience eight different tropical habitats with literally thousands of species. In a temperate zone, like most of the U.S., there might be half a dozen types of trees on every acre, but the same space in the tropics can host more than a hundred. "We do this in Costa Rica because it is existence proof that a sustainable world is not only possible—it's already happening," Benyus explains. "What we have to do is learn from what's out there." The biomimics hope "to create a way for biology to flow naturally into the design world," she says. "We're building the flow structure." This week, the site of that flow structure is La Cusinga Lodge, built from reforested woods, operating on solar and hydropower, and family-run with help from locals eager to share their knowledge of the abundant wildlife.

In fact, that's exactly what biomimicry is—"learning from the locals," as Benyus puts it. A self-proclaimed "nature nerd," she never tires of her subject. She laughs often, waving her arms excitedly, especially when talking about creatures—or "critters"—which is most of the time. Chatting with us, Benyus keeps one eye on the sea, hoping for humpback whales, down from North America for the calving season. When one surfaces, she squeals like a giddy child. It's hard not to share her euphoria here. Monkeys, lizards, wolf spiders, toucans—this place literally teems with life. A coati—a longer, thinner cousin of the raccoon—sneaks up on Tony Tranquilli, an aptly named, quiet architect from Illinois. Below, lightening-fast sand crabs blanket the beach. Their bodies look mechanical, but they move with grace, and the way they leap from rock to rock is unbelievable. Californian Tom Boyd, another workshop participant, lulls one with his gentle voice. "He's a crab whisperer," declares Benyus. If nature is our mentor, this environment is the perfect teacher, classroom, and lesson all in one.

It is new terrain, this bridge between biology and design, but it sounds deceptively simple—design is about making things, so how does nature make things? The biomimics suggest a four-part method—consider a goal in design, identify its underlying purpose, break it down to its functions, and then *ask nature* what it would do. Since *Biomimicry* appeared a decade ago, the simplicity of its method has appealed to many but made others skeptical. Some designers react negatively to the second part of the word, saying that *mimicry* sounds like superficial copying. Others object to the first part of the word. Architect Bill Reed says that "as long as you are still using 'bio' you are acknowledging some kind of boundary between humans and nature. I hope we can shift that to a co-creative state, a real wholeness." Benyus suggests that both objections miss the point. "This is really about building *chimeras,* pulling many solutions from many organisms, not slavishly mimicking one thing." It's not about separating people from nature—it's about working within it. Still, mechanical engineer Fiona Cousins says she's unsure about biomimicry, "because nature is not the only place to look for decent design ideas. Design synthesis can occur in the absence of a natural reference." And even if you agree that nature is the best teacher, biomimicry singles out only one part of nature—life. "By 'nature,' we mean the other thirty million species," says Baumeister. The rest of the environment is not their focus—there's no *geologist* at the design table, after all. Is this nature elitism? "Guilty as charged," Benyus rejoins. In fact, explains Baumeister, "Biomimicry is one tool—but not the only tool. It's a method you can apply, not a prescriptive list of design strategies. It is one path to restorative, regenerative, sustainable designs."

Benyus and Baumeister are very clear about their role as stewards. "Biomimicry is an idea that acquires people," Benyus says. "It just happens to be on our watch. Do we want to play with it a while? Sure. But as in nature, there has to be succession." She says that biomimicry has been around for centuries. "Leonardo da Vinci. Bucky Fuller. Even Frank Lloyd Wright, in a way, was a biomimic. But the idea stalls when it's treated as part of a Great Man movement. Or Great Woman. Sustainability in general should be leaderless. It has to be democratic. I happened to write a book pointing to some interesting things people are doing, and that brought some attention. But Dayna and I will have to get out of the way and let the idea pass through." Such modesty is a far cry from the egotism that is all too common among designers. "Once we learn to see nature as our mentor, hubris becomes humility," Benyus says. "We've got to get over the idea that all of this is here for us."

Biomimicry is but one method—an increasingly popular one—in a broader investigation that environmental psychologist Judith Heerwagen calls "bio-inspired" design, the core of which is the concept of *biophilia*—love of nature or, as she puts it, "fascination with life." It relates as much to emotional desires as it does to scientific inquiry. "Understanding what it is about nature that attracts or repels is at the core of bio-inspired design," she writes. "It is this link to emotions that we need to understand better, because design strives to evoke particular kinds of emotional experiences." Native American poet and novelist Linda Hogan has written of the need to find a new language that brings together science and spirit. "We are looking for a tongue that speaks with reverence for life, searching for an ecology of mind. Without it, we have no home, have no place of our own within creation. It is not only the vocabulary of science we desire, we want a language of that different yield. A yield rich as the harvests of earth, a yield that returns us to our own sacredness, to a self-love and respect that will carry out to others." Could biomimicry provide this new vocabulary? Benyus calls it nature's pattern language, and she makes it sound like an invitation to something wondrous. "Organisms are the answers to the questions the land is asking. These are a set of opportunities and limits, and the organisms have the answers. For any design challenge, you can look for natural teachers." It is easiest for people to see these functions in animals or plants, though they exist in organisms at all scales. The red sweat of a hippopotamus offers UV protection. The fuzzy side of a leaf can retain water. Purple leaves may be sunscreen for new growth or an adaptation to harvest low light near the forest floor. A seabird known as the Brown Booby has something called a "gular patch" at its throat that it can move without using any muscles—inspiration for an energy-efficient ventilation device? Nature's pattern book is endless.

The biomimics insist that their goal is not finding definitive answers—it's "learning to ask the right questions." So what are those questions? The methodology that Benyus and Baumeister propose, which they stress is always evolving, suggests that the right questions begin with "biologizing" the design problem—finding a bridge between biology and design. That means talking about function. You can't ask a biologist to design a better cell phone. But you can ask how nature communicates. Once you know what you are looking for, you can begin the search for the best natural models. The key first step to this, Benyus and Baumeister insist, is to *go for a walk outside*. That sounds easy. We try this on the first day of the workshop, and we're not sure what we're looking for. Sure enough, another walk after some work tuning our senses seems to reveal more. The rainforest is brimming with inspiration—there are thousands of adaptations to study at every step. After one watchful walk, we embark on what Baumeister calls "a safari through the literature" (perusing secondary sources) and then settle in to talk with biologists. We are developing a taxonomy of life's strategies, Benyus explains: "This is the amoeba-to-zebra analysis, where you look across all classes of organism for a specific function." The best sources are often the organisms most challenged by that function—"champion adapters," Benyus calls them.

Now we're ready to "play," letting the functional inspirations suggest design ideas. Then we deepen the conversation, looking for other aspects of form, process, or system for inspiration, and considering scale effects and context. Next, evaluation begins. "In the simplest terms, life creates conditions conducive to life," Baumeister says. "Incorporating that into the evaluation phase is how you get to sustainable design." What does that mean? Life builds from the bottom up, fits form to function, is cyclic and recycles, is locally attuned and resourceful, adapts and evolves, coexists with a cooperative framework. "Look at your design and ask if it's using benign manufacturing and life-friendly materials," she urges. "If a designer can say, 'what we are doing is enhancing the biosphere,' then we're there."

> "What we have to do is learn from what's out there."
>
> JANINE BENYUS

We are busy with biomimicry from first light to last. Lessons are interrupted for sightings of all kinds; binoculars rise in unison as someone shrieks "Whale!" or someone gasps and points to a hummingbird feeding on flowers just a few feet away. Benyus loves to talk about functions in nature, and they all seem to amaze and inspire her. (She also delights in watching our eyes open to this world.) On the second day of the workshop, she tells us that one of her favorite "critters" is the wolf—because "it moves like smoke, it plays a lot, and it is an excellent communicator—it has fifty-seven facial and body messages!" Of humans' current "heat, beat, and treat" manufacturing methods, she is incredulous. She talks about Kevlar, the super-strong material used to make armored vests: "We pour petroleum-derived molecules into a pressurized vat of concentrated sulfuric acid and boil it at several hundred degrees Fahrenheit. We then subject it to high pressures to force the fibers into alignment as we draw them out. The energy input is extreme and the toxic byproducts are odious." By comparison, she points to organisms that make materials right in their own bodies. "A spider produces a waterproof silk that beats the pants off Kevlar for toughness and elasticity. Ounce for ounce, it's five times stronger than steel! But the spider manufactures it in water, at room temperature, using no high heats, chemicals, or pressures. Best of all, it doesn't need to drill offshore for petroleum; it takes flies and crickets at one end and produces this miracle material at the other. In a pinch, the spider can even eat part of its old web to make a new one."

When Benyus tells the stories of biomimetic successes, her voice fills with emotion and a kind of pride that sounds almost parental. These are products, chemicals, and systems that would seem mundane to most of us. She describes how Pax Scientific has been inspired by mollusks to redesign car and computer fans to use a third less energy and operate with a quarter of the noise. And how a redesign of the Japanese bullet train based on the Kingfisher beak made it faster, more efficient, and much quieter. Columbia Forest Products looked at the mussel's byssus—a string-like protein that binds it firmly to wave-buffeted rocks—to create a soy-based adhesive that enables plywood without formaldehyde. The water-shedding properties of the lotus leaf inspired scientists at Sto, a German company, to create Lotusan, a self-cleaning paint. These are not fantasies—they are real solutions on the market.

But Benyus and Baumeister stress that this agenda is not about designers simply seeking out innovative products and materials, as helpful as they may be. For Benyus, learning how nature functions also involves learning about ourselves. She tells us that no elephants died at the Yali Wildlife Refuge in Sri Lanka after the 2004 tsunami—because they listened to the land. "They headed for the hills. Indigenous peoples followed suit and also survived. These animals have sensors in their bodies, and right now there are scientists in China working to mimic them. I think we have sensors, too. Like when we feel spooked, or feel a strong spiritual connection. But these days, we are ignoring them."

She urges us to use our time in Costa Rica to revive those connections. To do so, we must be willing to exercise our senses. In *A Natural History of the Senses*, Diane Ackerman writes about how engaging the senses is key to understanding the world we live in. "[W]e still perceive the world, in all its gushing beauty and terror, right on our pulses. There is no other way. To begin to understand the gorgeous fever that is consciousness, we must try to understand the senses ... and what they can teach us about the ravishing world we have the privilege to inhabit."

At first, our senses are simply overwhelmed by the diversity and beauty of this place. We mingle with morpho butterflies, tree frogs, ospreys, parrots, parakeets, hawksbill turtles, and those ferocious-sounding howler monkeys (they wake us before dawn). The flora is equally diverse and almost impossibly lush and full of life. Temperatures hover in the eighties during the day and the humidity is very high; the first afternoon, our faces are flushed and moist. But we settle in, finding comfort in our own bodies, hoping to free our minds and senses.

To do this, Benyus and Baumeister instruct us in four activities they call quieting, listening, echoing, and stewarding. Sight, the sense we're most dependent upon, is not nearly enough to "listen" deeply. Ackerman writes, "Seventy percent of the body's sense receptors cluster in the eyes and it is mainly through seeing the world that we appraise and understand it." To tune up our senses, we start by rebalancing them. To learn to "see" more clearly, we have to lose our sight for a while—bring out the blindfolds—and displacing it revives our hearing, smell, touch, and taste. Once we open our eyes again, we struggle to quiet our minds. One morning, we plant ourselves in one spot and watch one thing for thirty minutes. (It's amazing what you see in the last minute that you never could have detected in the first.)

Our work this week is to be curious students in nature's neighborhoods, these bustling ecosystems. We learn about their challenges and how the organisms that live there survive and thrive. We paddle through the mangrove forest, noticing complex root systems and massive stands of bamboo. Our Costa Rican guide, Jimmy Rodriguez, is a biology student who knows and cares for this place as if it's part of his own body. "We study where we live and live where we study," he tells us. "This is our job *and* our habitat." As we glide through the forest on kayaks, we look all around—into the water, on the muddy banks, and high up in the treetops. Rodriguez points to the opposite shore and we all fall silent, searching for what he sees. Finally, we see it—a sloth, making unusual progress from branch to branch. Eyes widen, paddles still, while we watch it ease out of sight.

An exploration of the tidal pool begins with a lesson on the solar system from Rose Tocke, a Guild biologist who, back in the "real" world, signs her e-mails, "Life!" On the beach, she draws the planets in the sand so we remember (or discover) what's driving the tides. Soon we are fixated on the watery world of water slugs, limpets, and chitons. A wayward ant roams the rocks, a tourist among the barnacles. A long night walk in the forest reveals another new world, alive with armies of leaf-cutter ants, luminescent mosses and molds, industrious wolf spiders, and slender snakes. Someone spots another sloth a hundred feet over our heads, dangling from the branch of a 1,000-year-old Aho tree. A last-day hike in the cloud forest is yet another world, one where plant life has adapted to altitude, dryness, and exposure—the opposite of the lush rainforest.

The Way Nature Works, a favorite of the Guild, is a beautifully illustrated book about function in nature. We pore through its pages, damp from the humidity, along with piles of other reference books. But our surroundings are our best reference. Together with the biologists, we take long walks through the rainforest, cataloging forms, functions, mutualisms, patterns. Our soggy notebooks are filled with sketches and misspelled Latin names. Later we tackle design problems and present solutions on the last night at La Cusinga. The all-girl group of students designs a biodegradable, honeycomb-shaped organic yogurt container that is extremely efficient with both material and space. Their beautiful drawings, irresistible prototype and spirited presentation steal the show.

One of Benyus' most compelling examples, and her presentations are filled with them, is the story of the ancient Live Oaks in New Orleans. Hundreds were hurt by Hurricane Katrina, but only four died. "We could build on this model," she says. "I'm not talking about a building that looks like a tree. We can study how their plumbing spirals, allowing them to bend and twist, and how their roots are linked to other root systems. These are fault-tolerant devices." She says she wasn't thinking about designers as her audience when she set out to write *Biomimicry*, her fifth nature book. "I was curious to know who was learning from adaptations in nature. The sustainable design movement was the farthest thing from my mind." But perhaps it's no surprise that designers responded to someone who sees art and science as "conjoined twins," as Benyus likes to say. Product designer David Oakey says, "I couldn't see the future until I read *Biomimicry*. Then it started to make sense to me that everything we make and do has to fit into the natural cycle." Interior designer Kirsten Childs, with us in Costa Rica, agrees. "It's all out there if we are just smart enough to engage it."

It was Jane Jacobs who drew Benyus out of Montana and onto a public stage when she invited her to give "a little talk," Benyus remembers, at the Ideas that Matter conference in 1997. "It was like being on stage at Carnegie Hall," Benyus says. She recalls finding Jane's round, smiling facing in the audience and pretending she was speaking with her alone rather than the hundreds of people who listened that day. Today, Benyus is a popular keynoter at design conferences. She is a mesmerizing speaker, as comfortable with poetic, emotional language as she is with hard science, and many have found her talks transformative. Paul Hawken says that Benyus has a deep, warm, and loving presence. "You want to follow her home." Benyus has been surprised at the reactions. She tells us: "Men often come up to me at the end of presentations and say, 'Thank you for permission to bring passion, emotion, and heart to this.'"

> **Biomimicry is an idea that acquires people.**
>
> JANINE BENYUS

Green consultant Bill Browning says he was there the first time Benyus spoke to the building community, at a 1999 AIA/USGBC event in Chattanooga, Tennessee. "When she finished, the room was dead silent," he recalls. "There were 450 people sitting there, mouths hanging open. It just blew them away. It's the only time I've seen anything like that." Today Benyus sees designers as an important audience. "The design profession is essential to the task of what [writer] William Kittredge has called 're-imagining desire.'

Today, a gorgeous building or chair may be leaching toxins into your body. That is a bait and switch. It is deceit of the worst kind. I'd love to see this realigned so that the beautiful is truly good."

Within the design professions, awareness of the potential of this conversation is growing. Architecture and engineering firms are beginning to hire biologists, ecologists, and environmental psychologists, and universities are establishing new, cross-disciplinary programs. Georgia Tech oceanographer Jeannette Yen and her colleagues had been thinking about "how to transform what we learn about nature into better designed solutions." They took a Guild workshop in 2005, and soon the Center for Biologically Inspired Design was born. The enrollment in their first course was half biologists and half designers and engineers, but they got off to a slow start. "They can't talk to each other right away. They don't know what words to use," Yen says. But the conversation deepened; now the Center is part of the collaborative Georgia Tech team competing in the Department of Energy's Solar Decathlon design/build competition.

In the early 1990s, architect Elva Rubio was designing a building for David Oakey's Pond Studios, searching for ways to make it "one with nature," she says. She learned about biology-inspired design and now applies those principles in her work and her teaching. "Janine and Dayna offer a scientific way of understanding the natural world and systems. What is so amazing about biomimicry is that it works." She notes that very specific engineering is needed—she worked closely with an optical engineer to design a bioluminescent ceiling based on a Biomimicry Guild analysis. "This is the beginning of the conversation," she says. "Architects need to work closely with many more consultants in many different disciplines." Ecologist Sandra Steingraber agrees, calling biomimicry "the supreme example of the cross-talk we need between designers and scientists."

For a week, we spend most of our time exploring the first three parts of the process—quieting, listening, and echoing. But Benyus and Baumeister keep reminding us about stewarding. Without a hint of irony, they ask us to thank the organisms for what they teach us. For the Biomimicry Guild, this gratitude extends to their business contracts. A percentage of the profits for every product they help develop must go to the restoration of habitats that inspired the design. For workshop participants, gratitude means living mindfully while we're here and appreciating the habitats. (And maybe spreading the word once we leave. Though Costa Rica is known as an eco-tourism paradise, many habitats are degrading due to development and agriculture.) This thanking is a part of deep respect for earth, something familiar to many indigenous peoples. Benyus describes it as respectful attribution, whether in writing, science, or design. "This is an important, civilized ritual of thanks. Good writing and good science depend on this. Part of the design process needs to address this, too. How do we give attribution to the organisms that taught us?"

If humanity's task is to form a new relationship with nature, where do we begin? Many leading thinkers, many of whom are quoted in these pages, suggest that it must start with deep ecological literacy. The word *ecology*, after all, stems from the Greek word for house. We need to find, know, and nurture our house—the place we live. Ecology itself is about finding home. As landscape architect Carol Franklin puts it, "The earth is one large household we have responsibility for." When Winona LaDuke, an activist with the Anishinaabeg, a Native American people, talks about sustainability, she starts with *keewaydahn*, her culture's word for "going home." And Diane Ackerman has written that "the twentieth century will be remembered as the time when we first began to understand what our address was. Learning our full address may not end all wars, but it will enrich our sense of wonder and pride."

What all of these voices are describing is finding our proper place in the world. It's about *belonging*, says Benyus. "We're homesick. For a long time, we thought we were better than nature. The earth is abundant and resilient, but she is not *endlessly* abundant and resilient. We need to learn to dance within it, like other species do. We have a chance to fit in—we have a chance to come home."

If we look to nature as a guide, we may realize we are already there. It's not about creating a new home—it's about rediscovering the one we have. To find home, it seems, we need just go outside.

A good place to begin.

PROJECTS

The following case studies illustrate the range of projects representing women's contributions and sensibilities in both design and development. The projects were selected to demonstrate a variety of scales and types, as well as a variety of ways that women are making a difference as designers, consultants, clients, and advocates.

THE CHILDREN'S MUSEUM OF PITTSBURGH
PITTSBURGH, PENNSYLVANIA

At the Children's Museum of Pittsburgh, the walls literally dance. The skin, composed of thousands of hinged acrylic scales—more kinetic sculpture than building façade—shivers in the wind and shimmers in the sun. The effect manages to be both playful and transcendent, perfectly in keeping with the museum's mission—"to nurture joy, creativity, and curiosity." Executive director Jane Werner says the aim was to honor the child's experience, not play down to it. "We don't do 'cute.' Kids can appreciate good design. They get it. They feel very comfortable here, and there's not a pink balloon or a clown anywhere."

A Chinese proverb inspired both the educational program and architectural form: "Give your children two things—roots and wings." The animated skin appears literally like wings, and the new structure delicately knits together a restored neoclassical post office and 1930s-era planetarium—*rooting* the museum in its historic context. Werner understood that the museum could do more than educate children. "Good design can completely change neighborhoods. The whole community can get involved." They nearly did. Rebecca Flora of the Pittsburgh-based Green Building Alliance coordinated the competition and helped frame the project goals, and Teresa Heinz Kerry, long an advocate of green initiatives in her community, was instrumental in drawing support and funding. "She's a mover and shaker in green building," Werner says of Heinz Kerry. "Her influence has been huge."

One of the most innovative American buildings in recent memory, the museum works on virtually every level—as figurative architecture, as an expression of the natural environment, as an educational tool, as a community builder, as a thing of pure delight. The design jury that gave the building an AIA Honor Award said it "inspires wonder" and "expresses the energy of children—youthful and optimistic." According to *Metropolis* magazine, the museum "feels more like a birthday party than a field trip." Architect Julie Eizenberg of Koning Eizenberg says this is exactly what the team had in mind—design from a child's point of view. "A cardboard box can be more evocative than many toys because it can be so many things. It's not limited. We wanted the museum to feel like that. Adults have forgotten that sense of wonder."

Albert Vecerka / Esto; design architect; Koning Eizenberg; executive architect, Perkins Eastman

Albert Vecerka / Esto

Albert Vecerka / Esto

BENJAMIN FRANKLIN ELEMENTARY SCHOOL
KIRKLAND, WASHINGTON

When the Lake Washington School District asked Mahlum Architects to design a new elementary school as a model for future facilities, architect Anne Schopf understood the opportunity to create a powerful teaching tool and a top performer. "Learning is about creating connections," says Schopf, who led the design team. "The design allows students to make a direct connection with the environment." They are not just seeing it, though large windows seem to bring the forest right into the room. These students feel the air, touch the rainwater gardens, and hear birds that populate the adjacent forest—but they don't hear any mechanical equipment.

Responding to the site and the forest grove context, Schopf's team designed a permeable building wedded to its site. The energy, light, and air strategies are woven tightly together and optimized to bioclimatic conditions. Thanks to rigorous modeling and the stack effect created by thermal chimneys and well-placed louvers, the building is naturally ventilated (only the gym and commons have mechanical systems). All learning spaces benefit from daylight and have operable windows—if the power goes out, learning goes on. The aggressive strategy had multiple motives. Low energy bills are a plus, but the team was also driven by the impact of daylight and indoor air quality on student well-being and performance.

The local climate made it easy to open to the outdoors. Winter daylight is predominantly overcast, and summertime direct sun is high in the sky. Glazing and roof slopes are oriented to north and south, and the south façade has deep overhangs and sunshades. Courtyards are landscaped with native plants and function as outdoor classrooms. Carefully detailed "butterfly" roofs sheet water into collection points and feed a stream. Stormwater is used on site in the rainwater gardens, which are also hands-on teaching laboratories. Schopf and her team are eager for data on how the students and teachers respond to the building over time. "We have much to learn from every project," she says. "If you are not making mistakes, you are not innovating."

Benjamin Benschneider

Benjamin Benschneider

176 WOMEN in GREEN

TIMEPIECE HOUSE
CHARLOTTESVILLE, VA

The Timepiece House turns the typical residence inside out and upside down. The living areas sit above the cooler sleeping spaces below, and the entire interior is shaped by daylight—through an oculus at the central skylight, a beam of light seems to carve the upper space. Aligned precisely with solar north/south, the house demonstrates the daily, seasonal, and annual cycles. The living room ceiling is a conical section traced by the arc of the sun on the winter solstice, and the central stairwell bathes in noon light on the summer solstice. A disc of light moves surprisingly quickly across the concrete floor, and this cinematic animation transforms the living room into a *living* room.

"At first, I was struck by how dizzying the effect was," confesses architect Carrie Meinberg Burke. "But after a while, it began to be comforting—it made me feel connected." Designed with her husband, Kevin, the house is home for the two of them and their daughter, Ava. Burke talks about the womb as a human being's first interior space, but in this case she literally conceived the house as a nurturing environment for her family. "Women may be more aware of our bodies because we're more tied to the world through natural cycles," she says. "There's something about the female body as a vessel—the ability to give birth to another human being is a visceral aspect of our experience."

The house also inspires a rethinking of the relationship between a private residence and the community. The subtly unique exterior blends in well with the historic neighborhood—the inverted cone roof could be mistaken for a modified gambrel, and from a distance the copper cladding resembles cedar siding. The property was purchased jointly through a unique agreement with their friend and neighbor, historian Marla Ziegler, to whom the Burkes gave final design approval. The arrangement, says Burke, "redefines what a property line can mean." On the four cardinal dates of the year, the Burkes invite people to watch what happens. On the solar equinox, children can chase the sun across the floor and try to trace its outline into the concrete with chalk. The game gives new meaning to "catching rays."

Prakash Patel for CM Burke

Equinox – 10 a.m.

Equinox – Noon

Equinox – 3 p.m.

FORD CALUMET ENVIRONMENTAL CENTER
CHICAGO, ILLINOIS

What can buildings learn from birds? This is the question architect Jeanne Gang set out to answer in the competition-winning design for the Ford Calumet Environmental Center. The site sits in both a heavy industrial zone and a 4,000-acre wetlands preserve located on the Mississippi Flyway, a 3,000-mile aviary migration route running from South America to the Arctic. The design, which the team called "Best Nest," tells a story about industry and ecology coming together.

"We wanted to make a building like a bird makes a nest—with materials that were abundant and nearby," Gang says. For the structure, the team salvaged discarded steel from nearby factories. A combination of bundled interior columns and a basket-like exoskeleton make the design actually appear nest-like. She explains, "We realized that the form would come from the process of making this." The exterior lattice doubles as a screen to prevent birds from colliding with glass, a common occurrence that kills 97 million birds every year, according to ornithologists.

Landscape architect Julie Bargmann was on the competition jury. "Studio Gang's proposal was clearly the most intelligent and inventive in terms of giving compelling form to ecological principles. The forms were not the usual 'wanna-be nature.' They're an abstract and productive interpretation of ecological processes. Their research-based approach demonstrates how design can respond to an evolving understanding of the site's dynamics."

Chicago Tribune architecture critic Blair Kamin says this process ties all of Gang's projects both to their immediate settings and to the broader history and culture of Chicago. "Her work is driven by program and research, not form. She's reaching for larger gestures in the environment, but at the same time the work is grounded by materiality in the pragmatic tradition of Chicago's architecture." Reclaiming local materials, some of which are marked with labels and text from previous uses, Ford Calumet illustrates the evolution of culture in the context of natural cycles. Native switch grass, blue-joint reed grass and winterberry provide an attractive habitat for birds and other fauna. As new plantings grow in, they are selectively harvested as biomass to power the building, which is conceived as an integral part of the ecology of the place. Gang relates the building to the principle of succession. "Time brings changes to the site. Our approach is to identify and magnify these 'clues' in the landscape."

STUDIO/GANG/ARCHITECTS

STUDIO/GANG/ARCHITECTS

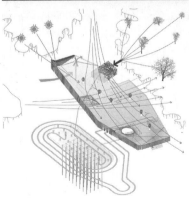

THE MOTHERHOUSE
MONROE, MICHIGAN

Sustainability is a moral mandate, say the women of the Sisters, Servants of the Immaculate Heart of Mary. In 2003, the Catholic congregation completed a $58 million renovation of the historic Motherhouse on their 280-acre campus along the banks of River Raisin in Monroe, Michigan. The 376,000 square foot building houses 220 sisters, many of whom require supportive care. "We see this renovation project as a continuation of our mission," says Sister Janet Ryan, of the congregation leadership council. "We always felt that if we educated women, we were educating a family. There is a natural progression of our mission to be concerned about the earth, which is the common home of the entire web of life."

Committed to preserving the original buildings while accommodating new needs, the congregation hired Susan Maxman Partners, a firm known for sensitive design. The project's goals included a long list of preservation, universal design, economic, environmental, and social aims. To suit the current and future occupants' needs, the renovation provided efficiency residences with private baths; the smaller units are more popular among the sisters, who prefer to live modestly. A greywater system enables three times the fixtures but half the potable water used prior to renovation. A geothermal system (with a long payback) was selected because it was the most fossil-fuel effective choice and because the sisters wanted to educate their neighbors about its availability. As Maxman recalls, "they embraced community education right from the start."

Kath Williams of the World Green Building Council was on the jury that named the Motherhouse one of the 2006 AIA Committee on the Environment Top Ten Green Projects. "The sisters' approach to sustainability as a moral mandate is compelling," she says. "Too often, preservation and renovation projects are not the ones we celebrate as green. Reusing old buildings is always a better place to start than building new. This project also shows a real sensitivity to aging occupants and how they will use the building." According to the ministry's project manager, Danielle Conroyd, the team always understood universal design as an integral part of sustainability. "We hope we are helping to link those two issues," she says. "Making the Motherhouse useful for the present and the future is central to the sustainability mission."

Barry Halkin

DOLLARD DISCOVERY HEALTH CENTER

HARRIS, NEW YORK

Sustainable design is essential in medical facilities, says Robin Guenther. "Healthcare deals with vulnerable people. The imperative is greater, so the strategies are heightened, specifically concerning indoor environmental quality." Guenther sees the Patrick H. Dollard Discovery Health Center, a 28,000-square-foot outpatient facility and residence she designed with her firm, Guenther 5, as an expression of the principles she and Gail Vittori laid out in the Green Guide to Healthcare. Sustainability, they say, is about protecting health—of the building occupants, of the surrounding community, and of the global community, human and otherwise.

Surrounding the Dollard is an organic farm that supplies residents with both fresh produce and an opportunity to learn about the land. The landscape extends literally to the edge of the building, so farmers work the ground right next to the building's walls. "This transforms the building into something completely unlike a typical hospital," Guenther says. "In the old model, the ill would be shut away behind gates. Here, we bring the community in. We bring the environment in." The architecture weds naturally with the surrounding farm while maintaining its own unique identity. Guenther calls it "a barn with attitude."

Guenther stresses the importance of the building not looking or feeling like a hospital. "People are uncomfortable in most healthcare environments—they're nervous about their conditions and what's going to be done to them. It's inevitable that people will associate their physical condition with their surroundings—our memory connects pain with the setting in which we feel it. This is especially the case with developmentally disabled children." Warm materials, plentiful daylight, fresh air, and especially a strong connection to the outdoors create "a healing environment," according to Guenther. "For people who are looking at institutionalizing their children for life, this place represents hope. It offers a vision of wholeness."

Inside, the receiving area, designed as a café-like setting, feels more like a community or social space than a hospital waiting room. Many design details empower the physically challenged. Raised planting beds allow wheelchair-bound people to cultivate their own gardens. A specially designed "FlexTable" divides into multiple leaves that adjust to various heights to allow people with differing needs to work together. One staff member says he's never worked in such a comforting environment. "I'll never leave here. They'll have to pry me out of this building."

David Allee

David Allee

NOAA PACIFIC REGION CENTER

FORD ISLAND, HAWAII

More than 600 people work for the National Oceanic and Atmospheric Administration (NOAA) in Hawaii, handling fisheries management, marine mammal protection, oceanographic research, and weather services at various sites. They will soon work together at a new campus, the Pacific Region Center. The 370,000-square-foot Center is an adaptive reuse of historic World War II aircraft hangars combined with new construction on Ford Island in Pearl Harbor on the Hawaiian island of Oahu. It is designed to use at least 50 percent less energy and water than conventional projects when it opens and to become progressively more efficient each year.

HOK's Sandra Mendler is the lead designer on the project. "Our design addresses the World War II history that permeates this site," she says, "as well as the cultural context of Hawaii." The new building, between two large hangars, was developed with nautical references in mind and references to traditional Hawaiian architecture. A ship-hull shape (which will be zinc-clad) links to a canoe-like form (finished in terra cotta). "I think people will be able to read and understand this building well," Mendler says. Deep overhangs yield shaded gathering areas. A path curves through the site and new building, linking to a waterfront park. "This path defines a metaphorical meandering stream," she explains, "making visual reference to the tributary streams that feed *Pu'ulua,* which is the traditional name for the deep stream channel that became Pearl Harbor."

The building will have a passive ventilation system, unusual for a hot, humid climate. "We will pull in the air through wind scoops on the roof," Mendler says. It will move across a hydronic system to cool and dehumidify. Large lagoons and interior garden water features will be part of the water recycling system. Skylights will bring daylight into the large-floorplate workspaces. Mender says that the sustainability of the project will be a part of daily life. "A great deal of what's happening in terms of site ecology and water and energy will be very visible to the people who work here every day."

courtesy Studio 2a / HOK

courtesy Studio 2a / HOK

THE EPICENTER
BOSTON, MASSACHUSETTS

In the summer of 1991, artist Susan Rodgerson gathered some Boston teenagers, gave them a crash course on art history, handed them paint brushes, and set them to work on a public mural. When it was done, several of them stayed on, painting in her studio in Boston's South End, and she watched a transformation. "I saw their subjects change from violence to freedom in a few weeks," she says. From this beginning, she developed Artists for Humanity to train young artists to participate in the world of business. "They create art for sale to sustain the organization, and the organization in turn pays and sustains them. We see sustainability as a human concept."

When they lost their rented loft, Rodgerson knew it was time to realize her dream of a permanent home for the group—a self-sufficient building that exemplified and supported the organization's mission. To reassure her skeptical board, she raised $1 million and lined up significant grants, including half a million dollars for photovoltaics from the Massachusetts Technology Collaborative's Renewable Energy Technology Fund. "I was thinking long term. Creating this building as a model has invigorated everything we do. We watched every penny and made careful decisions all along the way," she says. The building's angled roof positions the PV array optimally. A 5,000-square-foot space with 18-foot ceilings and a mezzanine art gallery is the centerpiece of the building and the business plan; event rental is an important revenue stream. The upper floors are roomy studios and offices. The building has an industrial loft feel with high ceilings, concrete floors, and salvaged materials. It's the city's first commercial naturally-cooled building, an important milestone, thanks to a night ventilation system and paddle fans that provide evaporative cooling in summer.

The project, called the EpiCenter, cost less than $200 per square feet and was certified by the U.S. Green Building Council's LEED rating system at the highest level (Platinum). "We built certification costs into the budget," Rodgerson says. "We wanted our learning laboratory to be an example for others. To really walk the talk of sustainability requires thinking on so many levels at once. That's inherent in female DNA. And that's how we made the building work."

Richard Mandelkorn

Shawn McLaughlin

AUDUBON HOUSE

NEW YORK, NEW YORK

When the National Audubon Society needed a new headquarters in New York in the late 1980s, then-president Peter A.A. Berle saw an opportunity to demonstrate the organization's mission in a real-world way by building a model workplace that would also be a model of environmental responsibility. He spoke with several nationally known architects but, he recalls, "They didn't know what I was talking about." Then he talked to architect Randy Croxton and interior designer Kirsten Childs, of Croxton Collaborative Architects, who had been applying what they called "full-spectrum design," by comprehensively addressing energy, materials, and human factors. "Kirsten was so good at enabling me to understand the possibilities," recalls Berle. "She understood the environmental issues but also the human side."

Kirsten describes Berle's commitment as absolute. "He wanted a workplace that really pushed boundaries. He wanted the building to *be* the mission." Completed in 1993, the renovation saved the sandstone and terra cotta façade (preserving its embodied energy) and created a comfortable workplace designed to use less than a third of the energy of conventional buildings, thereby cutting two-thirds of the association's annual energy costs. Recycled and natural materials were used to ensure that indoor air would be healthy—an innovative strategy at the time. The project was completed within market rate, and paybacks on energy saving systems took less than three years. These were important metrics to prove that a model of sustainable design could be affordable.

In *The New Yorker*, Brendan Gill wrote that Audubon House demonstrated "the means by which at least the beginnings of sustainability can be achieved." The *New York Times* praised the design team's comprehensive approach: "Ms. Childs boasts that her wood comes from 'nonendangered' sources. Yet she turns humble wood into a precious material by reminding us of its rich history: the people, land, energy, ideas, and time it takes to grow a tree and fashion it into tables or pencils. History ... isn't just a matter of landmark buildings and period details. It is also a record of the ordinary objects that circulate through daily life."

Otto Baitz, courtesy Croxton Collaborative Architects PC

Jeff Goldberg/ Esto

TOFTE CABIN
TOFTE, MINNESOTA

Attorney and Jungian analyst Medora Woods bought a 4.7-acre parcel on the north shore of Lake Superior and embarked on an adventure that goes far beyond the walls of the now-renovated 50-year-old summer cabin. Woods had been exploring the writings and teachings of indigenous peoples. "I was thinking about people who knew where everything they needed came from—the food, clothing, and shelter," she says. "We have lost that knowledge. We no longer operate out of gratitude." She thought her cabin project might be an opportunity to work with the respect that comes from deep knowledge of a place. Woods' passion led her to write a project goal statement detailing her aim that "the process of construction, operation, and maintenance of this cabin would be respectful of all the communities that will be touched by those processes." Woods gave a copy to everyone who worked on the project to make them aware, she says, "that this was the ethic of the project."

Woods hired architect Sarah Nettleton, who took her cues from the site and the sun. The seasonal difference in the angle of the sun's rays prompted her to lift and turn the roof to maximize warmth and light in winter and minimize it in summer. Trees shelter the cabin from winter winds on the west and north side. Interior spaces are designed to relate to the horizon line outside. "Developing that connection to the outdoors and the horizon in particular, both directly and in subtle ways, was important," Nettleton says. One visitor told her that it felt as if the cabin was "telling the story of sustainable design to even its most casual occupants." That was part of the plan. "We hope that people experience with their bodies and spirits the power of site-sensitive ecologically-based design in an extraordinary natural environment," she says. Woods calls it a "soul-satisfying retreat."

The cabin draws less than two percent of its annual energy load from the grid, due in part to photovoltaics on the garage, geothermal wells, and a heat pump. Several other passive and active sustainable design strategies were employed, including an aggressive approach to recycling at the site. "The only thing that went to the landfill was the insulation," says Woods, praising her contractor. She doesn't use the term "sustainability," which she finds limiting. "This is about being mindful of every person and every thing that is affected by what you do."

Peter Kerze

SUSTAINABLE SOUTH BRONX SMART ROOF

BRONX, NEW YORK

When Majora Carter, executive director of Sustainable South Bronx (SSB), first heard about green roofs, she knew she wanted one. "In an urban setting, putting a landscape on the roof made so much sense." Carter founded the organization in 2001 after defeating a new waste transfer station planned for the South Bronx as Fresh Kills landfill closed. After hearing a talk by landscape architect Kathleen Bakewell, Carter approached her about working together. That was the beginning of a close collaboration and friendship that soon included Joyce Rosenthal, who was studying urban environmental and health issues at Columbia University. The result of this relationship was the Smart Roof Demonstration Project, which opened in 2005 on the top of SSB's headquarters in the Banknote building.

"The roof has been a wonderful education tool for students," says Rosenthal. She has been working with graduate students to collect and analyze data on the costs and benefits of green and cool-roof projects in order to promote neighborhood-based energy conservation and heat island mitigation measures. Carter hopes the project, which demonstrates how rooftop vegetation can divert storm water and contribute to cooling, will inspire similar projects as a model of both product and process. "Collective creativity is vital to sustainable design," according to Bakewell. "This is what we strived for with the roof—it's a modest project, but the foundation of the working relationship is fertile."

Carter is committed to sustainable development and entrepreneurship in low-income communities of color, she says, "in a way that is supportive of human and other life." She organized visioning charrettes to get neighborhood residents thinking about a greener future for their waterfront community and raised funds for a major feasibility study. In 2005 she was awarded a MacArthur Foundation "genius grant" of $500,000 over five years, which may help turn up the volume on her message. "We want to democratize sustainability and make it sexy. Right now, it's for rich people—organic food and nontoxic cleaning products. Environmental justice is about *people*." Bakewell says that working with SSB helped her to reframe sustainability. "Design professionals often focus on environmental sustainability, which is a privileged viewpoint that misses key things about basic rights," she says. "You don't hear much about environmental justice in a white collar office."

James Burling Chase

James Burling Chase

FULLER LOFTS

LOS ANGELES

Architect Angie Brooks founded Livable Places, a nonprofit developer in Los Angeles, "to promote healthy communities through local policy reform and development of compact, affordable housing that incorporates a mixture of uses and income levels, as well as sustainable building practices in Southern California." In 2004, scouting sites for its second project, her team found an underutilized building in Lincoln Heights, a neighborhood north of downtown, just a few blocks from a new light rail line.

The W.P. Fuller Building is a five-story, 131,000-square-foot 1920s-era, cast-in-place concrete industrial building, which will become 102 live/work loft housing units and commercial workspaces. Two new levels on top will be market-rate housing for sale, and the units below will be affordable for sale. Pugh + Scarpa Architects, where Brooks works with her husband, Lawrence Scarpa, designed the project. They created a new core to bring light and air into the building. The units will have loft-style floor plans ranging from 650 to 2,700 square feet with high ceilings. Some units will be reserved for households earning below $83,000 per year. LEED certification at the Gold level is expected. "We had support from the city council," Brooks says, "because they understood the value of bringing in new for-sale units at various levels, and what that could do to help strengthen the neighborhood."

Brooks expects that the Fuller Lofts project will have greater impact as well. "Wherever we go, we talk to the planners and city officials about changing their regulations to encourage the development of mixed-use urban projects and housing in particular." After Livable Places helped change the zoning in Long Beach, land prices rose precipitously. "That priced us out, of course," Brooks says. "But it's part of our mission to bring these changes about in a broad way, as well as one parcel at a time with the projects." She says that they are also trying to do projects without subsidies to show how building a mix of market-rate and affordable housing can be economically viable as well as beautiful and sustainable.

Pugh + Scarpa

Pugh + Scarpa

PEOPLE

Our research included hours of conversations with many women and men who were generous with their time and thoughts. This list includes those participants we interviewed and quoted, briefly or at length.

ADAMS, Constance

As a designer of human habitats in the aerospace industry, Constance Adams calls herself a "space architect." Having worked with Lockheed Martin and NASA on such programs as the TransHab inflatable habitation module, she is convinced we will colonize other planets. "This will happen. It's not a matter of if, just when—and how. We already have the ability to go to other planets and terraform them—remake them literally in the earth's image—but will we do it responsibly? We are the means by which this planet will reproduce. We are the instruments of the next biological phase of the earth. Mother Earth is an empty nester."

ADDINGTON, Michelle

Michelle Addington says she thought she was the only nuclear-engineer-turned-architect—"until I met another one at a party." Having recently joined the faculty of Yale University's School of Architecture after several years at the Harvard Graduate School of Design, she teaches courses in energy, environment, advanced technologies, and new materials. Her research focuses on the human thermal environment and the potential for architecture afforded by new scientific theories in heat transfer and fluid mechanics. With Daniel Schodek, she co-authored *Smart Materials and Technologies*. Addington is interested in transforming building technology, but she is quick to point out that technology is a tool, not an answer. "Sustainable design is not a series of strategies or techniques; it's about understanding how things work."

AMON, Amelia

Industrial designer Amelia Amon develops solar, water, and energy-efficient systems, from solar streetlights to alternative energy products for rural communities. "We have to be making systems that operate on renewables *and* are beautiful," she says. She says that the sustainable design community is more open and friendly than design communities generally and predicts that the pace of change will increase. "We're at the beginning of this. Oil is ending."

ANDERSON, Lauren

Lauren Anderson is executive director of Neighborhood Housing Services of New Orleans, a nonprofit housing corporation established in 1977. She is an attorney and has worked in community development since the 1980s. She was co-chair of the Housing subcommittee of the Bring Back New Orleans commission. "I have a commitment to urban areas and to making them a place of choice," she says. Anderson played an active role in Women of the Storm, a group of 140 women from Louisiana who "stormed" Capitol Hill after Hurricane Katrina to urge Congress members to visit their city and witness its ruins firsthand. They carried blue umbrellas to symbolize the ubiquitous blue tarps protecting damaged roofs in the Gulf region. Anderson recalls, "Katrina was the largest natural disaster in the history of the U.S., and less than 30 percent of Congress had visited. So we visited them instead."

ANDERSON, Ray

Ray Anderson is founder and CEO of Interface, the world's largest carpet tile manufacturer and a company widely acknowledged as a sustainability innovator. He has been very vocal about the influence of women—in general and in particular—on Interface's mission "to be the first company that, by its deeds, shows the entire industrial world what sustainability is in all its dimensions." The company began focusing on sustainability at the urging of Joyce Lavalle, now a senior vice president. What exactly is sustainability? "With or without a name attached to it," says Anderson, "it's simply doing well by doing good."

ARIEFF, Allison

Allison Arieff is the co-author of *Prefab* and the former editor-in-chief of *Dwell* magazine. "In 2001, when I mentioned prefab," she says, "people thought I was off my rocker." Now modern prefab has become extremely popular, partly due to the attention Arieff has brought to designers such as Jennifer Siegal, Michelle Kaufmann, and Rocio Romero. She says prefab construction avoids extensive transportation to and from a building site, but the idea has a long way to go. "The hype precedes the implementation of these goals. That's true of prefab and sustainable design both."

ATHENS, Lucia

Landscape architect Lucia Athens is the Green Building Team Chair for the City of Seattle, where she has also worked with Paladino Consulting. Previously she helped implement pioneering green community efforts in Austin, Texas. There she also worked with Pliny Fisk and Gail Vittori at the Center for Maximum Potential Building Systems. "The public sector needs to set an example and provide the leadership to enable the private sector to embrace sustainability," she says. "The role of the public leader transcends that of a regulator, and it can be one that provides vision, hope, and empowerment to any global citizen." She says that the public sector's constituents or "clients" need not be human. "Think of the endangered salmon of the Pacific Northwest. They can't write checks, but they provide an enormous amount of the ecological wealth of our region."

AUSTIN, Katherine

Architect Katherine Austin worked for three firms for nine years before founding her own firm in Sebastopol, California. She now focuses on affordable housing, or "providing attractive, dignified homes for families of modest means." She says having her own firm also allows her to control her schedule and be a more active part of her sons' lives.

BAKEWELL, Kathleen

Studying film in Chicago, surrounded by great architecture, Kathleen Bakewell wound up in landscape architecture "because architecture seemed male-dominated and professionally problematic." Bakewell worked for HOK in the late 1990s in New York and worked on the green roof on the Staten Island Ferry Terminal. Today she is with Hart/Howerton. "I'd like to move the conversation to the next step and talk about how we attack the greater, more entrenched problems of sprawl, inequity, and consumption."

BARGMANN, Julie

Time magazine called Julie Bargmann an innovator for the twenty-first century. This landscape architect works with teams of many other disciplines to designs regenerative landscapes, coaxing beauty from disturbed, forgotten, or contaminated sites. The DIRT studio stands for Design Investigations Reclaiming Terrain … or for Dump It Right There. In multidisciplinary studios at the University of Virginia, she challenges students to deal with real places in real time. "They have to address these places, often degraded landscapes in marginalized communities, as they exist now. Then they can introduce systems that will regenerate the sites. But to grasp the whole context, students have to take on the role of design citizen."

BARNETT, Claire

When her son suffered a pesticide injury, Claire Barnett put her journalism skills to work seeking answers from the school where the injury had occurred (she had been a reporter with *Time* magazine). "One day, a bureaucrat told me 'We're not allowed to talk to parents,' and hung up. And my life changed." After advocating a study about the health of schools, she put together a coalition that became the Healthy Schools Network, a clearinghouse of information for parents, teachers, and schools.

BATSHALOM, Barbra

Architect Barbra Batshalom is founder and executive director of The Green Roundtable (GRT), an independent non-profit whose mission is to mainstream green development and, according to her, "ultimately become obsolete." As the New England affiliate for the USGBC, GRT works with healthcare institutions, universities, community development corporations, cities, and nonprofit property owners. According to architect and fellow consultant Bill Reed, "Barbra is working at the mental model level. She is one of few people capable and willing to tackle this issue at the deeper level."

BAUM, Mara

Mara Baum was the U.S. Green Building Council's 2006 Mark Ginsberg Sustainability Fellow and now works in healthcare design with Anshen + Allen in San Francisco. She has noticed that there are many more women in sustainable design than in design and construction generally. "I think of women as being better able to balance different ideas and disciplines. That is what sustainability is all about."

BAUMEISTER, Dayna

Janine Benyus says that Dayna Baumeister, with whom she co-founded the Biomimicry Guild, "is perfecting the art of biomimicry in motion." While in graduate school, Baumeister was exploring the idea of a wall that could breathe when a professor recommended Benyus' book, *Biomimicry: Innovation Inspired by Nature*. "I see it as a triangle: ethics (conservation biology, sustainability), science (pure biology), and application (forestry, wildlife management). Biomimicry is in the center." Baumeister speaks widely and has consulted with Interface and other companies to bring biology and design together. She coordinated the biomimicry workshop in Costa Rica in March 2006.

BENYUS, Janine

Science and nature writer Janine Benyus is the author of the influential *Biomimicry: Innovation Inspired by Nature,* which over the last decade has single-handedly spawned a movement of biologically inspired design. According to the *New York Times,* "The colors of Benyus...contain far more shades of green than of chrome." While doing field research in Montana, she "fell in love" with its mountains and stayed. She believes Montana may have triggered a genetic memory of the High Tatras in Slovakia, from which her grandfather immigrated to the U.S. at age fifteen. Architect Bob Berkebile says that Benyus sees the "part of the large pattern that is informed by spirit and intelligent energy that we have yet to understand. It's that openness and ability to love that holds real potential for the movement. It takes courage and integrity to be in that place." With Dayna Baumeister, she runs the Biomimicry Guild and dedicates herself to educating people about the wonder of the natural world. "The better people understand the genius of the natural world, the more they will want to protect it," she says.

BERKEBILE, Bob

Bob Berkebile, a founding principal of BNIM Architects in Kansas City, Missouri, was the founding chairman of the AIA Committee on the Environment, and has served on the board of the U.S. Green Building Council (USGBC), from which he received the 2005 Leadership Award. "This is the time for women," he says. "We need a more holistic, integrated approach that's more about nurturing. That will take more leadership from women or from the feminine side of all of us."

BERLE, Peter A.A.

Lawyer Peter A.A. Berle served three terms in the New York State Assembly. He was president/CEO of the National Audubon Society and publisher of *Audubon* magazine from 1985 to 1995. Today, he is president of Sky Farm Productions.

BLUM, Elizabeth

A history professor at Troy University, Elizabeth "Scout" Blum studies women's history and environmental issues. Her Ph.D. dissertation was "Pink and Green: A Comparative Study of Black and White Women's Environmental Activism in the Twentieth Century." She says that in the 1960s and 70s many women used environmental activism "as a way to react against the feminist movement, which they saw as anti-children and anti-family." She also says that the role of black women has not gotten enough attention. "Minorities have played a significant role in environmental movement—it just hasn't been visible as the civil rights movement."

BONDA, Penny

A prominent writer and lecturer, Penny Bonda currently serves as "eco-editor" of *Interior Design* magazine and contributes monthly to their online resource, The Green Zone. She authored *Creating Sustainable Interiors*, a monograph for NCIDQ and co-authored, with Katie Sosnowchik, *Sustainable Commercial Interiors*. She is past president of the American Society of Interior Designers and chair of its Sustainable Design Council. She serves on advisory boards for Antron, Greenguard, and the USGBC's LEED training faculty. Bonda is the recipient of ASID's 2007 Designer of Distinction award and the 2003 USGBC Leadership Award. She started the USGBC's LEED for Commercial Interiors program and acted as its founding chair. "While the LEED system was being developed," she recalls, "I mentioned that maybe we should have a version for interiors. One of the board members said, 'Why? Interiors don't matter.' I said 'Well, actually, that's where the people are.' "

BOURLAND, Dana

As senior program director of The Enterprise Foundation's Green Communities Initiative, Dana Bourland managed the development of the Green Communities Criteria, a collaborative effort between The Enterprise Foundation and the Natural Resource Defense Council, and other organizations. She previously worked in the Maryland Department of Planning and is a frequent speaker on green communities.

BRAGER, Gail

Mechanical engineer and professor of architecture Gail Brager is the associate director of the Center for the Built Environment at the University of California-Berkeley. She researches thermal comfort, interior environments, and climate responsive building design and currently serves as the chair of the USGBC's Research Committee. Colleague Cris Benton calls Brager a "serious advocate for design" who has bravely challenged standards and conventional wisdom about thermal comfort, including pushing the American Society of Heating, Refrigeration and Air-Conditioning Engineers (ASHRAE) towards an "Adaptive Comfort Model" she has developed with Richard de Dear. She calls sustainable design "the golden rule applied to buildings—do unto others as you would have them do unto you."

BRAWER, Wendy

Designer Wendy Brawer founded Modern World Design in 1990 to create products and systems that promote ecological stewardship, including the Green Map System for cities all over the world. Of barriers and glass ceilings, Brawer says, "Why dwell on those? It's better to ask forgiveness than permission. We all can only do so much in a day, but if we say 'I can't do that' then we're not doing much of anything."

BROOKNER, Jackie

Eco-artist Jackie Brookner's "biosculptures" clean water naturally, whether indoors, such as at the offices of the Cloud Institute for Sustainability, or outside at monumental scale. For *Of Earth & Cotton*, an installation involving portraits of the feet of people who had picked cotton in the 1930s, Brookner interviewed people all over the South, trying to understand "what we had lost by not having people working the land directly."

BROOKS, Angela

Architect Angela Brooks is a principal with Pugh + Scarpa Architects in Santa Monica, California. Brooks founded Livable Places, a non-profit development company dedicated to developing sustainable mixed-use developments on under-utilized land in Los Angeles County. Her graduate thesis, focused on increasing density in existing development, earned *Progressive Architecture* honors for unbuilt work. "One jury member said it was not politically viable to do what I was suggesting," she recalls. "Twenty years later, I'm actually doing it through Livable Places."

BROWN, Hillary

Architect Hillary Brown is the founding principal of New Civic Works in New York, a consulting group dedicated to sustainability in public works and the institutional and nonprofit sectors. Previously she worked with the City of New York to establish its first green building program, and she was a key author of the New York City Department of Design and Construction's high-performance guidelines for buildings and infrastructure. Women have been effective on the government path for a variety of reasons, Brown suggests. "There's something enabling there. The public sector seems better positioned to benefit from women's styles of leadership." What are those styles? "There's an affinity that women have with sustainability—they're as interested in the process as the product. But it isn't about gender—it's about a sensibility. It's about empathy with the earth as a living process."

BROWNING, Bill

Bill Browning founded the Rocky Mountain Institute's Green Development Services program to promote environmentally responsive real estate development. Recently he founded the consulting firm Browning + Bannon in Washington, D.C. He has co-authored several books on sustainable design and development, including *A Primer on Sustainable Building*, and *Buildings* magazine named him one of five people "making a difference." Browning has been intimately involved in USGBC, LEED, and AIA over time, and he hopes for "more good green buildings that are also really good architecture."

BURKE, Carrie Meinberg

Architect and industrial designer Carrie Burke feels design should be both accessible and intimate—"more about experience than form." Speaking of the need for an understanding of space that is less visual and more visceral, she discourages architects from relying too heavily on two-dimensional drawings. "Floor plans are given such archetypal importance by architects, but they don't convey the true experience of a place." Her own house, which she calls "an exploration of how a different awareness of time informs place and experience," has been featured in *Architectural Record, Dwell, Residential Architect, USA Today,* and *Plenty.*

BUTLER, Karen

After architecture school, Karen Butler spent some time working for firms, but by 1992 she found herself at the Environmental Protection Agency. Today, she manages New Building Design for the EPA's Energy Start program. She sees big shifts ahead. "I'm not preaching 'use better mechanical equipment,' " she says. "I want to get us off the grid, opening the windows, and using renewables."

CARROON, Jean

Jean Carroon leads Goody Clancy's preservation and renovation practice. She is an expert in the design of sustainability and accessibility solutions for historic buildings and directed the restoration of H.H. Richardson's Trinity Church in Boston, which included the installation of a 1,500-foot-deep geothermal well system. "I see buildings as a continuum," she says. "They go on. Perhaps this is why people in preservation tend to have a better long term view than others."

CARTER, Marjora

Fighting a waste facility in her childhood home of the South Bronx opened Majora Carter's mind to the possibilities of restoring that community. She founded Sustainable South Bronx in 2001. The organization's Smart Roof Demonstration Project opened in 2005 and several other projects are under way. Carter is a communicator and catalyst. "Getting the story out to the public is part of my job. Language is important."

CHAREST, Suzanne

Biologist Suzanne Charest is pursuing a master of architecture at the University of British Columbia and was a participant at the biomimicry workshop in Costa Rica in March 2006.

CHILDS, Kirsten

Interior designer Kirsten Childs was trained in Europe, and worked for several firms, including Richard Meier & Partners, before joining Randy Croxton at Croxton Collaborative Architects in 1985. Interior designer and writer Penny Bonda remembers meeting Childs and Croxton in the early 1990s. "They were saying, 'We don't do projects that are unhealthy for people.' It sounds overly simple now, but back then, it was setting a very high bar." *Metropolis* editor Susan Szenasy calls Kirsten Childs a "pathfinder." Childs is torn about focusing on the accomplishments of women. "Women have had a greater role in sustainable design than in 'high end design,'" she says. "And there is a very distinct line between being recognized as a great designer versus a great woman designer. I have avoided that, but I think the time has come to deal with it."

CLANTON, Nancy

Influential lighting engineer and designer Nancy Clanton runs her own firm in Boulder, Colorado, and teaches at the University of Colorado there. She is on the board of the International Association of Lighting Designers and the International Dark Sky Association, as well as the advisory committee of *Environmental Building News*. She says that sustainable design has been overly politicized. "We need to move sustainability out of the political realm so that it will make sense for everyone." She says that engineers, like other professionals, are struggling with sustainability, and even simple ideas about natural ventilation can be controversial. "I was invited to join a professional association committee," she recalls, "and the chair called me and said that two members had threatened to resign if I joined because I was a proponent of operable windows!"

CLOUD, Jaimie

Jaimie Cloud is the founder and president of the Cloud Institute for Sustainability Education, which focuses on elementary and secondary education in order to "prepare young people for the shift toward a sustainable future" and "ensure the viability of sustainable communities." Cloud believes that the mental models that most adults are currently using will need to change. "If you believe that the market and technology will take care of everything, you are not reading the right data. If you look at how life actually works on this planet, you draw different conclusions."

CONROYD, Danielle

Danielle Conroyd works as project manager for campus planning and projects for the Sisters, Servants of the Immaculate Heart of Mary in Monroe, Michigan. She serves on the board of Michigan Interfaith Power & Light, a coalition of faith communities promoting sustainability.

CORTESE, Anthony

Anthony Cortese has been active in sustainability education for years, as founder of Second Nature and a collaborator with Education for Sustainability Western Network. "The status of women in society is critical to creating a healthy, just, and sustainable world," he says. "Unless you have economic and social and educational equity for women, we'll never become a peaceful society that can be sustained by the earth. The male attitude is to dominate other people, the earth, and women. That's been the history of the human race and I don't think it is healthy."

COUSINS, Fiona

Mechanical engineer Fiona Cousins works with Arup. Her early interest in thermal performance of buildings led her to sustainable design. She says that diverse points of view are important in her field as in others, and suggests that perceptions of her field steer some women away. "The field is seen as dirty and aggressive, and while it's not very well paid, it requires a high level of intellectual engagement to do it well."

CRAMER, Jenifer Seal

Jenifer Seal Cramer helped to found NewCommons Group, a real estate investment management company that manages urban, high-performance, and land conservation-based funds. She earned architecture and environmental design degrees from Ball State University and a master's degree in Real Estate Development from MIT. She was a co-author of the Rocky Mountain Institute's *Green Development* and a contributing author to *Biophilic Design and Reforming Architectural Practice*.

CRANZ, Galen

Galen Cranz is a professor of architecture at the University of California-Berkeley and author of *The Chair: Rethinking Culture, Body and Design* and *The Politics of Park Design: A History of Urban Parks in America*. She is the currently principal investigator for the Latrobe Fellowship research collaboration between the Kaiser Permanente Hospitals, Gordon Chong Architects in San Francisco, and the UC-Berkeley's Department of Architecture to define and develop "evidence-based design" in the context of health care delivery. "Humans have increased the productivity of the earth—in a good way," she says. "It grows more than it would otherwise. How we do it is the problem. There's no such thing as waste—there's only material out of place."

DEL RANCE, Kim

Intern architect Kim Del Rance works for the Tampa office of the multidisciplinary design firm Gould Evans. She previously worked for City of Augustine, Florida, where she developed an intertwined philosophy of sustainable design and preservation. "We have so much to learn from the old buildings people love so much," she says.

DENWORTH, Joanne

Joanne Denworth is a land use and environmental lawyer, who began working in Pennsylvania Governor Ed Rendell's Office of Policy in 2003 with responsibility for policy issues in state agencies relating to land use. "We look at land use in the broadest sense," she says. "We wanted to empower municipalities to plan together and implement those plans. This was vital to reduce the crazy patterns that were really a recipe for sprawl."

DILLON-RIDGLEY, Dianne

"There are no women's issues. All issues are women's issues," says environmental and human rights activist Dianne Dillon-Ridgley. "Women are doing nothing less than redesigning society. We haven't been part of the structure, so we can see its flaws better. When we get a chance to make change, we can rush right in because we already know all the problems well." Dillon-Ridgley serves on the board of directors of Interface and Green Mountain Energy Co. She represents the Center for International Environmental Law and the YWCA at United Nations. She served on the U.S. delegation to the Earth Summit in Rio and others. Paul Hawken says of Dillon-Ridgley: "We have a conception of leadership in the world that is about charismatic male vertebrates and that's our template. Then we project that onto women, saying, 'she's great, but he's the leader.' Dianne does so much, yet one might not know her name. She doesn't have the hierarchical role, but she is a real leader."

DOUGLAS, Kristin Ralff

Christine Ervin calls Kristin Ralff Douglass "a ball of energy" and lauds her early role in the USGBC. Its founder, David Gottfried, who hired her, credits her with pulling off the first summit of that organization. "She has tremendous pluck and many skills. She is comfortable wearing many hats," he says. "She ran the group in the early years—she kept it alive." She served as editor/publisher of *Environmental Design + Construction* magazine and today works with the Public Utilities Commission in San Francisco.

EARLEY, Sandra Leibowitz

Architect Sandra Leibowitz Earley runs a green design consultancy. She finds the sustainable design community to be more open and collaborative than some others. "Sustainable design tends to attract people who naturally are open and like to share ideas. Greenbuild attracts 10,000 people because people are eager to share. It's a very connected community, compared to other professions. I'm sure our conferences are a lot more fun than accounting software conferences."

ENGLAND, Kim

Kim England studies industrial design at the Ontario College of Art & Design and was a participant at the biomimicry workshop in Costa Rica in March 2006.

ERVIN, Christine

Christine Ervin speaks and writes about clean energy and greening the built environment. She was the first president/CEO of the USGBC. She served as U.S. Assistant Secretary of Energy and before that as director of the innovative Oregon Department of Energy. Today, her consulting focuses on accelerating sustainable market transformation. Christine Ervin: "Early on, I never thought about differences between men and women. I thought that was immaterial—even resented the notion. I was one of the guys and that was perfectly fine. If you are competent, you will succeed. I didn't even pick up on the fact that I had developed more of the 'alpha male' persona that usually went along with the territory! But that changed as I came to appreciate how I was serving as a role model for some women looking to advance. That was eye-opening and humbling. It forced me to start thinking about role models in general—and about different contributions we need in the workplace."

EIZENBERG, Julie

Julie Eizenberg is a founding principal of Koning Eizenberg Architecture, which has won national competitions for the Chicago Public School Northside, and the Children's Museum of Pittsburgh, which opened in November 2004 and has won numerous awards. "Kids are really smart," Eizenberg says. "You don't design *down* to them. It's not about simplifying the world—it's about heightening the experience. This is often missing in institutional settings." She says they treated sustainable design and universal design elements as integral—not add-on features. "If it looks like you've done something because a code required it, then you've done it wrong."

EWING, Alison

Architect Allison Ewing is a principal with Hays + Ewing Studio in Charlottesville, VA. Previously she has worked with the Renzo Piano workshop in Italy, and she is a former design partner with William McDonough + Partners. She has appeared on the cover of *Residential Architect,* and the house she designed with husband and partner Christopher Hays was on the cover of both the *Washington Post* magazine and Jennifer Roberts' *Good Green Homes.* "I can't say whether this is true of other women," she remarks, "but I've always thought that the design of a house should consider the community of the family, especially the development of the child."

FEDRIZZI, Rick

Rick Fedrizzi, founding chair of the USGBC, became its president/CEO in 2004. He had worked at United Technologies Corp. for twenty-five years as an environmental marketing consultant. "The USGBC is the organization it is today because of a wide range of talented men and women. There are flamekeepers, warriors, and builders, and these include Gail Vittori, Penny Bonda, Lynn Simon, Vivian Loftness, and others. The women are a big part of our perspective. And the diversity is growing. The students and young practitioners are much more diverse than the older leaders in the field at this point, and that is very encouraging."

FLETCHER, Valerie

Valerie Fletcher is the executive director of Adaptive Environments, the internationally recognized nonprofit organization founded in 1978 by Elaine Ostroff. Fletcher oversees universal design projects at all scales and teaches, speaks, and writes extensively on human-centered design. "Knitting together issues—such as universal design and sustainability—is very powerful. It seems self-evident to those of us who are close to the issues, but connecting them yields a sense of wholeness and seems to generate energy."

FLORA, Rebecca

Executive Director of the Pittsburgh-based Green Building Alliance, Rebecca Flora says she is inspired by past leadership of women in the environment. "Rachel Carson, who stood her ground against powerful forces and scientifically proved her case, inspires me," she says. "Another inspiration is Teresa Heinz Kerry, a visionary and strong advocate for quality design of the built environment at all levels and for all people. I am driven by my desire to leave behind a cleaner and safer earth for my daughters to inherit—or at least know their mother tried to make a difference."

FLOYD, Elizabeth

Elizabeth Floyd is a project manager with Sustainable Design consulting in the Washington, D.C. area. A registered architect who as a consultant focuses on integrating multi-disciplinary teams. She feels that women generally seem more comfortable with multi-tasking, versatility, and communication, all of which she calls "essential qualities" for sustainable design.

FRANKLIN, Carol

Carol Franklin was a co-founder of Andropogon Associates, which has been a pioneer of ecological design in the landscape architecture field for thirty years. A finalist for a Cooper-Hewitt National Design Award in 2004, Andropogon has worked on many high-profile projects, including the Dallas Arboretum and Botanical Gardens and the Atlanta Botanical Garden. According to civil engineer Judy Nitsch, "Carol addresses this issue from 30,000 feet." According to consultant Bill Browning, Franklin and her colleagues "took Ian McHarg's work and made it real. They were the first to show that landscape architecture and planning could come from a basis of ecological restoration—and they do it with humor and grace." Franklin is working on a book called *Paradise Mislaid*, which documents the social, political, and ecological decisions that have shaped the Wissahickon Valley Corridor.

GANDY, Kim

Kim Gandy was re-elected to her second term as President of the National Organization for Women (NOW) in 2005. "I'd be happy to work myself out a job," she says. "We work on issues of women's equality and reproductive rights, but also economic justice and human rights. They are all connected." Gandy says that many of her colleagues in the women's movement have a long view that perhaps they share with people working in sustainability. "I want equality for me, but I'm really doing this for my daughters and my granddaughters. Some men also do this, but it is a particularly female focus in many walks of life."

GANG, Jeanne

Architect Jeanne Gang is a founding principal of Studio Gang, whose work has been featured in the Architectural League of New York's "Emerging Voices" series and in *Architectural Record* as one of nine design firms to watch. Gang's Aqua Tower, an eighty-story lakefront high-rise that architecture critic Blair Kamin calls "Chicago's most sensuous tower," is said to be the largest commission ever received by a female architect in North America. Kamin says of Gang, "Her work is important for green architects because it layers green into a broader aesthetic." Gang has said that her work is influenced by the feminist idea of fluid identity. "When we make form, we're thinking about how we can make the identity fluctuate; it doesn't have to be one thing all the time."

GARDNER, Jean

Jean Gardner is a professor of architecture in the Department of Architecture, Interior Design, and Lighting Design at Parsons School of Design, part of the New School. She is author of *Urban Wilderness: Nature in New York City*. She has been labeled "a living treasure," by *The Utne Reader*. She has developed the Whole Building Matrix using semiotics as a framework for investigating sustainability and architectural intention. Gardner believes that the secret to sustainability lies in our senses. "I think that the separation of touch from sight is one of the most basic reasons that we're not building sustainably." She says that sustainability is much broader than many people realize at this point. "To me, sustainable design is the signs that we are regenerating in the built environment. I love the link between the word 'design' and 'sign.' We need signs of change!"

GOODMAN, Ann

"Sustainability is an ideal that helps you get up in the morning," says Ann Goodman. "For me it brings together many intellectual pursuits and personal passions. I saw many businesswomen who wanted that, too, and that spurred the idea of the Women's Network for a Sustainable Future." She is executive director of the group in New York, which helps businesswomen exchange best practices on the convergent issues of corporate social responsibility and sustainable development.

GOTTFRIED, David

David Gottfried founded the USGBC and the World Green Building Council. "Women have a huge role to play—a much bigger role than they've played in the past," he says. "Men have screwed up this planet. Not just through design. Wars are a male thing. Most of the bad stuff is based on the male ego. There are gender differences. Women are more holistic, communicative, and nurturing. The women I've worked with bring to the table new modalities of work and new ways to think about integration."

GUENTHER, Robin

Robin Guenther is the founding principal of Guenther5 Architects, an expert in healthcare design, and a co-author of the influential *Green Guide for Healthcare Construction*. "Robin Guenther is an architect with very definite ideas about design, healthcare and sustainability," writes Penny Bonda, "Big picture thinking—looking beyond the conventions of standard healthcare facility planning—has established Guenther5 Architects as a different kind of design firm and has led to amazing achievements." Guenther was the first architect to receive the Center for Health Design's Changemaker award, and *Interiors & Sources* called her a "champion of the environment." Says Guenther, "Years ago, I felt that I knew how to design buildings, but not how to make change. Advocacy allowed me to make more change and enriches my mission as a designer. It's all about asking questions differently. For example, why wouldn't we vet materials against a human and environmental health standard?"

GUZOWSKI, Mary

University of Minnesota professor Mary Guzowski works with the Center for Sustainable Building Research to explore how sustainability and ecological literacy could change both the content and the methods of teaching and learning. About her 1999 book *Daylighting for Sustainable Design*, author/architect Malcolm Wells wrote: "Mary Guzowski is showing us the way back to an appropriate, balanced, and beautiful world." She says that "a love of seasons and place" drew her to architecture, but originally a senior professor discouraged her from focusing on "environmental stuff" because, he said, it would never get her tenure. "I decided not to follow his advice and listen to my instinct."

HAMMER, Chris
Chris Hammer is the principal of Sustainable Design Resources, a research and consulting firm in San Francisco. She publishes GreenClips, a web-based newsletter that distributes environmental information in the design industry. Formerly with HOK, she helped create its sustainable design research initiatives. "I want to share information," she says. "Maybe I was a librarian in another life."

HARDEN, Susan Jackson
Planner and urban designer Susan Jackson Harden works with RBF Consulting in California and is on the faculty of the Neighborworks Training Institute. She recently co-authored *Place-Making on a Budget.* Her work focuses on downtown and neighborhood revitalization efforts through innovative public participation.

HAWKEN, Paul
Paul Hawken is an environmentalist, entrepreneur, and author. His 1993 book, *The Ecology of Commerce,* steered many of today's leaders toward sustainability, and his *Natural Capitalism* (2000), written with Amory Lovins and Hunter Lovins, is one of the most influential books in the literature of sustainable design. His next book, tentatively entitled *Blessed Unrest,* considers the history of the environmental, social justice, and indigenous movements, which he labels collectively as "the movement that doesn't know it's a movement." He says that women have been instrumental in this field, though they have not always gotten the credit they deserve. "Women have been overlooked on many levels."

HAYDEN, Dolores
Dolores Hayden, an urban historian, architect, and professor at Yale University, is the author of several award-winning books, including *A Field Guide to Sprawl,* a "devil's dictionary" of bad building patterns. *The Power of Place: Urban Landscapes as Public History* offered a new kind of architectural history by exploring urban memory through public art and preservation in ethnic communities in downtown Los Angeles. An expert on the relationships between gender and architectural space, Hayden has authored many articles and books on the topic, including *Redesigning the American Dream: Gender, Housing, Work, and Family Life.* She explains simply, "I'm interested in how people occupy neighborhoods together."

HAZLETT, Maril

Environmental historian and artist Maril Hazlett runs the John Talleur Print Studio, the only community print shop in Kansas. Her dissertation, "River Arteries, Human Veins: *Silent Spring* and the Ecological Turn in American Health," included a look at reactions to *Silent Spring* and Rachel Carson at the time of its publication. One finding that surprised Hazlett was that not a lot had changed. "In 1962, public health warnings were that one in four people would have cancer in their lifetime. Now it is one in three. I would have expected that the alarm regarding the cancer case frequency would have produced significant policy changes regarding chemicals and human health."

HELGESEN, Sally

Influential business writer Sally Helgesen authored the bestselling *The Female Advantage: Women's Ways of Leadership,* the first book to focus on what women can contribute to organizations rather than on how they should adapt to business as usual. Among her other books is *The Web of Inclusion: A New Architecture for Building Great Organizations,* which the *Wall Street Journal* called one of the best books on leadership of all time. Articles about her work have been featured in *Fortune, Business Week,* and *Fast Company,* and she has appeared on hundreds of radio and television programs. "What can we learn from women?" she asks. "Today there is so much despair about what development can mean—that no development can not be horrible. We're desperate for new models. What we've seen as women become more involved in communities is alternative ways of relating to one another."

HERDT, Julee

Julee Herdt is a professor of architecture at the University of Colorado-Boulder and directed that school's entries into the 2002 and 2005 Solar Decathlon design/build competition in Washington, D.C.—both of which earned top honors. Her research is focused on bio-based materials and recycled products.

HEERWAGEN, Judith

Environmental psychologist Judith Heerwagen studies the human factors of design, biophilic design, and "workplace ecology" and currently runs a consulting and research firm in Seattle. Previously she was a staff scientist at the Pacific Northwest National Laboratory and a research faculty member at the University of Washington College of Architecture and Urban Planning. Looking to history, she notes, "Men and women had different subsistence roles. Men were the technology makers. Within sustainable design, there is an emphasis on technology, which is traditionally a male focus. But the very need for sustainable design has been caused by over-reliance on technology." She believes that too often anecdotal evidence and the emotional side of human response are left out of the equation. "We don't always need to quantify everything," she suggest. "We need to listen to our bodies and minds—we know when a building makes us feel uncomfortable or unwell."

HENDERSON, Holley

Holley Henderson runs H2 Ecodesign, a sustainable design consulting firm. Previously she was a director of creative design at Interface, and prior to that she practiced interior design with Atlanta firm TVS. She was the first LEED 2.0 Accredited Interior Designer in the state of Georgia, as well as managing LEED AP for the Interface Showroom and Offices—the first (and currently only) LEED–CI Platinum Level Project. Currently, she is the chair of the LEED-CI committee of the USGBC. "For me, sustainability is the ability to sleep at night," she says. "That's the bottom line." She says the key to change is raising awareness, and that requires clear illustrations of the impact of design. For example? "In a single year, the wasted carpet from one manufacturer—the stuff that doesn't get installed on floors—can fill four and half Empire State Buildings. The sheer magnitude of that was an epiphany for me."

HESCHONG, Lisa

Architect and researcher Lisa Heschong is a principal of Heschong Mahone Group, which has conducted groundbreaking studies on the effects of daylight on human performance. She wrote *Thermal Delight in Architecture* (1979), a book that many people in the field refer to as influential in their early understanding of human comfort and architecture. Calling herself an "ardent feminist," Heschong says, "It's important for girls to have women heroes, so the more we can make of them, the better." On the other hand, she is unsure about behavioral differences between the sexes. "Whether sustainability means something different for men versus women may be counterproductive to ask." In her firm's daylighting studies, they looked at the impact of many variables, including gender. "There were significant differences between the responses of boys and girls or men and women. Do I find that interesting? Not really. There's a population of humans. Some of them have dark hair, some of them have light hair, and we have to provide for all of them."

HOFFMAN, Leslie

Leslie Hoffman, executive director of the Earth Pledge Foundation, has an architecture degree. Before coming to the foundation, she worked as a carpenter and green builder. Since 1990, she has run a small organic coffee farm in Hawaii. "I function from a strategy of hope," she says.

JAMES, Janine

Janine James' firm, The Moderns, was one of the first graphic design companies to adopt sustainability. Chemist Michael Braungart calls James "one of the smartest in the field." She designed *Cradle to Cradle,* the book Braungart wrote with William McDonough, and she actually introduced them to Charlie Melcher of Melcher Media, which produced the book's innovative synthetic paper. On the cover, the word "to" looks exactly like a mirror of Venus, the traditional symbol for women. "I didn't realize that until a year and a half after finishing the book," she recalls. "It's ironic, but it was totally unconscious. Call it my own little Da Vinci code."

JOHANSON, Patricia

After training as an artist, Patricia Johanson went to architecture school, where her ideas about the everyday, inspired by Jane Jacobs, were unpopular. "Opting for the everyday takes you out of the aesthetic dialogue of design schools of all stripes," she says. "I switched over from worrying about my place in history to worrying about how to make the world a better place. We are all human beings first, before we are designers." For the past twenty years, Johanson has been creating large-scale public earth art projects, such as Fair Park in Dallas; she is currently working on a project for the water treatment facility in Petaluma, California.

KAROLIDES, Alexis

Architect Alexis Karolides is a research consultant with the Rocky Mountain Institute. She says she's torn about gender questions. "I'm very concerned about my own children— what food they eat, what air they breathe. But I was an environmentalist long before I was a mother. I don't know that the two are necessarily tied to each other."

KERR, Laurie

Architect Laurie Kerr works for the City of New York Department of Design and Construction, which is an ideal place for her to indulge her fascination in the intersection between urbanism, preservation, and sustainability. "I've really enjoyed getting to know these buildings," she says.

KIISK, Linda

Architect and educator Linda Kiisk has studied the influence of gender on design and construction and promoted the value of diversity to this industry. "The differences we are sensing between one another are actually signs of an ongoing transformation in consciousness," she writes. "Over time, men and women of all races will come to understand the value of establishing a diverse set of connections because the modern, more conscious human has the capacity to literally 'see' how to design integrative environments. The positive message for humankind is that these newly evolved visualization styles will naturally foster a more sustainable future for all inhabitants of the planet."

KOKO, Sigi

After working at HOK, Sigi Koko founded Down to Earth, a sustainable design consulting firm. She focuses on natural building and her projects have been featured on HGTV and in magazines. "I think natural building techniques can have the effect of evening the playing field," she says. "It is so easy to learn some of these ideas and apply them in construction. This simplicity takes away barriers. To me, this speaks to the social side of sustainability."

LAVALLE, Joyce

Joyce LaValle, senior vice president of human resources for Interface, is part of an oft-told story. Her daughter recommended that she read Paul Hawken's *The Ecology of Commerce* and pass it along to Interface CEO Ray Anderson. That began what LaValle recalls as an intense period of learning for many people at the company, and the beginning of its transformation toward sustainability. She helped Ann Goodman found the Women's Network for a Sustainable Future as a support to women in business. "We need more human thinking," LaValle says. "I think that many women recognize that the technology challenge is not the biggest challenge ahead—it's the human challenge."

LAZARUS, Mary Ann

Architect Mary Ann Lazarus is a senior vice president with HOK and acts as its firm-wide director of sustainable design. With Sandra Mendler and Bill Odell, she co-authored the second edition of the *HOK Guidebook to Sustainable Design*. Lazarus also currently serves as program chair for the USGBC's Greenbuild conference. She earned her undergraduate degree from Mount Holyoke, a woman's college. "This was the time of Vietnam and the ERA," she says. "We thought equal pay was really on the horizon for women within a few years!" Today, she feels lucky because, she says, "I get to do what I care about *every day*."

LEE, Joyce

Architect Joyce Lee is chief architect with the City of New York's Office of Management and Budget. The city has recently adopted a law spelling out sustainability requirements for city-funded projects. "The mainstreaming of sustainable design is gratifying," she says. "I hope my work has helped in that direction. In some sense, I think mainstreaming helps to allow professional women to be at their best without having to choose between missions of home and work."

LEE, Kaiulani

Actress Kaiulani Lee portrays Rachel Carson in a one-woman stage play she wrote after years of research and interviews with Carson's friends, family, and colleagues. The *Pittsburgh Post Gazette* calls Lee's performance "something rare and almost spiritual. She merges herself with Carson's spirit."

LESNIEWSKI, Laura

Architect Laura Lesniewski is a principal at BNIM Architects in Kansas City, where she has worked on some of the firm's most advanced sustainable design projects. She sees prosperity as the biggest hindrance to sustainability. "We have not figured out how to handle prosperity wisely," she says. As for gender balance in architecture, she says that 'the boys' club is still pervasive. I hope that is going away. I tend to rely on myself to go into a room knowing my stuff; then people will listen."

LINDSEY, Gail

Design Harmony founder Gail Lindsey is an architect whose work in recent years has focused more on consulting, training, and facilitation. She got her undergraduate architecture degree at Georgia Institute of Technology, one of few women in the program at the time. Her university studies were interrupted by a brain aneurism that required long hospital stays, giving her a lot of time to think about how she wanted to use her education. "Early on, I recognized that I have a different perspective," she says. Bob Berkebile of BNIM Architects first worked with Lindsey when she helped develop the AIA Committee on the Environment Top Ten program. "She comes at this from a spiritual point of view and delivers a lot of energy," he says. According to Nadav Malin of BuildingGreen, on whose board of advisors Lindsey serves, "Gail is an incredibly smart, integrated thinker. She never accepts that two things are not connected. Whenever there is an either/or choice, Gail finds ways to put everything together—with both ideas and people. She believes that everyone will achieve together and benefit mutually. Gail embodies the virtues of collaboration."

LOFTNESS, Vivian

Vivian Loftness is a researcher, author, and educator who focuses on environmental design and sustainability, advanced building systems and systems integration, climate and regionalism in architecture, as well as design for human comfort and performance. She was dean of the School of Architecture at Carnegie Mellon University for ten years and teaches there today. She is a key contributor to the development of the Intelligent Workplace, a laboratory of commercial building innovations for performance. She has served on National Academy of Science panels, as well as being a member of the Academy's Board on

Infrastructure and the Constructed Environment. She works on the board of directors of the USGBC, Turner Construction, DOE's Federal Energy Management Advisory Council (FEMAC), and was 2005 chair of the AIA Committee on the Environment. Rick Fedrizzi of the USGBC calls her "the professor we all wanted to have." Environmental psychologist Judith Heerwagen says that Loftness is "a bridger—she knows the technology, but she really knows the human side, too."

LOGAN, Corina

Corina Logan was a biology instructor for the Biomimicry Guild's workshop for designers in Costa Rica in 2005 and 2006.

LOVINS, L. Hunter

Attorney Hunter Lovins runs Natural Capitalism, Inc., a consulting company through which she advises cities and companies about sustainability. She founded the Rocky Mountain Institute (RMI) in 1982 with Amory Lovins. She served as a Commissioner in the State of the World Forum's Commission on Globalization, co-chaired by Mikhail Gorbachev and Jane Goodall. Lovins has co-authored nine books and dozens of papers and is currently Professor of Business at Presidio School of Management in the first accredited MBA program in Sustainable Management. According to consultant Bill Browning, Lovins brought the social perspective to RMI. "If you read Amory's writing before Hunter's involvement," he says, "it's very technical. Her contribution was to humanize it—she understands that there are social implications to technology." Bioneers founder Nina Simons says, "Hunter can translate from one side of the brain to the other. She can share complex theories and ideas in a way that anyone can follow." USGBC founder David Gottfried says of Lovins, "She understands the corporate mentality, and she's a great teacher. She's a powerhouse."

LYONS, Susan

In the early 1990s, Susan Lyons was the creative director at Designtex, the commercial textile manufacturer. "I had an intuitive sense that the company's footprint was less than ideal," she says. "We knew we could make a better product." With that goal in mind, she commissioned William McDonough and Michael Braungart to develop the Climatex Lifecycle series, the first-ever compostable fabric. "We didn't have a traditional business plan. If we had, we might not have succeeded. We weren't willing to compromise." She realizes now that her son was born around the same time she began thinking more about the environment. "When you become a mother, you begin reading labels. You become much more concerned about what your kid is ingesting."

MALONE, Nancy

Architect Nancy Malone works with Siegel & Strain Architects in Emeryville, California. She has noticed a great deal of change in the last few years. "There is still a lack of understanding about integrative design," she says. "Many firms know they've got to get on board, but they are not there yet in terms of understanding what can be achieved and the means to that."

MATHIESSEN, Lisa

Architect Lisa Mathiessen is director of sustainable design at Davis Langdon, a cost planning firm, where she has been studying the cost implications of sustainable design and the use of rating systems such as LEED. "Perhaps because sustainability is still somewhat of a 'margin' activity is why there are many women involved," she says. "Women are more likely to pursue 'alternative' professions; whereas men are more apt to be in and dominate mainstream professions."

MAXMAN, Susan

Architect Susan Maxman was the first female president of the AIA in 1993 and made sustainable design the focus of the convention that year. She has run Susan Maxman Partners since 1980. She is a nationally recognized expert on sustainable design, and her projects have earned recognition for design and sustainability from many organizations. Her work with the Girl Scouts and other organizations has been a model of inspired collaboration between architects and clients. According to the USGBC's Rick Fedrizzi, Maxman has motivated him and many in the field. "In the early 1990s, Susan was speaking a language that I wasn't hearing from my male peers at that point. Men talk about things in terms of bits and bytes, science and clinical awareness. Susan was making connections between the science and human factors. To me she represents the notion that women often have a much more global perspective through their work—they can see the future in a different way."

MAYTUM, Marsha

Architect Marsha Maytum is a principal with Leddy Maytum Stacy Architects in San Francisco. She learned design as linked to environmental issues while at the University of Oregon and has practiced in that way since the founding of her firm. Current work on the Ed Roberts Campus exemplifies the links between sustainability and universal design. "It is part of sustainability to be thinking about how to provide control and comfort for a range of people who will populate any given space," she says.

MCCLINTOCK, Maurya

Maurya McClintock leads the Façade Engineering group in Arup's San Francisco office and is assisting in the development of the Sustainability Consulting group focusing on buildings. With a combined background in structural engineering, mechanical engineering and architecture, she has a broad understanding of the impacts façade systems can have on energy use, natural ventilation, daylight penetration and thermal and visual comfort in buildings. "I think a lot of people are struggling with what sustainability is and how to document and show it," she says. "There is a real need to tell the story in a way that will capture people's imaginations."

MCCLINTOCK, Moira

Architect Moira McClintock founded Ford 3 Architects with two partners after working in New York and becoming the first female associate at a large firm there. She sees the profession's specialization as working against sustainability. "If you are doing hospitals all over the country, you may not be open to regional differences." She and her partners are dedicated to working in their region. "This is about knowing a place well. We think that's the best way to do the best work."

MCDONALD, Margot

Margot McDonald is a professor of architecture at Cal Poly-San Luis Obispo and co-director of the Renewable Energy Institute. She helped create Cal Poly's award-winning Sustainable Environments program and was a key author of the Sustainable Environmental Design Education (SEDE) project, which produced a groundbreaking model curriculum for sustainable design education. "It's not just design that needs to change," she says. "On a fundamental level, the way we think about design needs to change."

MCDONOUGH, William

William McDonough is the founding principal of William McDonough + Partners, Architecture and Community Design, and co-founder of McDonough Braungart Design Chemistry, a product design and consulting firm. With Michael Braungart, he is co-author of *Cradle to Cradle: Remaking the Way We Make Things* (2002), widely considered a landmark book on sustainable design. McDonough says that some of his most important clients, including Teresa Heinz Kerry and Susan Lyons, have been women. "There's a whole way of looking at the world that cannot be ignored."

MCENTEE, Christine

Christine McEntee became the executive vice president/CEO of the AIA in 2006; she is the first woman to hold the position in the AIA's 149-year history. She previously served as CEO of the American College of Cardiology, and before earning her MBA she trained and worked as a nurse.

MCINTIRE, Donna

Donna McIntire is the U.S. Department of State's point-of-contact for sustainability. Trained as an architect, she has worked with William McDonough + Partners and with the SmithGroup, where she played a significant role on the Chesapeake Bay Foundation, the first project ever certified with a LEED Platinum rating from the USGBC. "I'm a facilitator," she says of her nature. "Bringing in the right people is the most important thing. Get them talking to each other."

MENDLER, Sandy

Architect Sandra Mendler is a design principal with HOK and a leader of its sustainable design initiatives. She has served on the board of directors of the USGBC and as the chair for the AIA's Committee on the Environment. With Bill Odell, she co-authored the *HOK Guidebook to Sustainable Design*, now in its second edition. Consultant Bill Browning praises her for her role in HOK's work. "HOK has been a real leader and has shared information openly. The *Guidebook* was a huge body of research, organized with great clarity. At a time when the AIA had moved away from this kind of research, HOK stepped up, and Sandy was an important part of that." Odell offers, "fifteen years ago, you were likely to be laughed out of the room when you talked about sustainability, so it took a thick skin to persevere. Sandy is unflappable."

MURRAY, Martha Jane

Architect Martha Jane Murray has been active in USGBC efforts in the Arkansas region, including the Greenbuild charrettes for rebuilding New Orleans. "My epiphany came when I realized that professionally we have always been so anxious to have a job that we might not question the ethics behind a project. Suddenly, I couldn't live or work the old way anymore." She says that being a mother has made her "aggressive" about these issues. "Parents, and especially women, understand the potential impacts on their kids. The public health side of this compels me every day."

NEAL, Mary Helen

Mary Helen Neal studied architecture at Alabama's Auburn University and participated in the Biomimicry Workshop in Costa Rica in spring 2006.

NETTLETON, Sarah

Architect Sarah Nettleton spent childhood summers at a non-electrified house reachable by boat. "My father called it 'studied inconvenience,'" she says. "It made me appreciate the value and richness of being unplugged." She founded her own firm in 1997, after she tired of "chipping away and always hearing, 'there's no money in the budget for that.' Having my own firm allows me to be purer in the philosophy." For her, that philosophy describes "a circular, not linear path. It requires a longer time horizon than our culture is used to." She designed the Tofte Cabin, which won an AIA Committee on the Environment Top Ten Green Projects award in 2002.

OAKEY, David

Designer David Oakey of Pond Studios led the design team that created Entropy, one of Interface's best-selling lines. According to Interface's Joyce LaValle, Entropy has been a sensation. "It was David's intense personality and dedication to learning that really allowed this breakthrough," she says. Patterns and diversity in nature inspired it, he says: "There is no question in my mind that if you designed spaces with a non-monoculture framework, those would be more beautiful to us, and maybe better for us, too. This is the future."

PAGANI, Freda

Freda Pagani recently retired from the Campus Sustainability Office at the University of British Columbia. Earlier, Pagani was responsible for the campus's first green building, the C.K. Choi Building. Bob Berkebile facilitated a workshop for that project, and sings Pagani's praises. "Pagani took a totally different approach to hiring and working with architects and other consultants," he says. Pagani recalls that that team had women in many roles—architect, structural engineer, owner's representative. Her inspiration for the project came after a period of re-examination. "I realized that I could live my values in my job by making this project meaningful and as sustainable as I could."

PARK, Sharon

Sharon Park is the senior historical architect for the Heritage Preservation Services Division of the National Park Service. Her leadership has been critical to the success of green restoration projects at the Presidio in San Francisco.

PATKAU, Patricia

Patricia Patkau is a principal with the Vancouver-based Patkau Architects, the firm she founded in 1978 with husband John. The firm is known for its sensitive but ambitious place-based design. "I've always resisted the term 'green,'" she says, "whether it's in design or politics. Architects who call themselves 'green' define their practice under that single issue, and it's not sufficient. Architecture is broader and richer than that. It relates to sustainability, to politics, to art, to everything. It seems foolish to me to reduce it. While the discipline should take this on, it should also not diminish the discipline in doing so."

REED, Bill
Architect Bill Reed, of Natural Logic, is exploring regenerative design at a deep level, and he believes that design and human endeavor generally are evolving toward a deep unity and wholeness. This idea, he says, is something that many women understand more readily than men. "I consider it a compliment that someone suggests I'm drawing on feminine sensibilities," he says. "That suggests to me that maybe I'm getting a grasp of what it means to be whole. We need a new consciousness, spirit, and meaning in the design process."

REID, Nellie
Designer Nellie Reid is the regional leader of Gensler's sustainable design task force and the first LEED-accredited professional among the firm's nearly 3,000 employees worldwide. *Interiors and Sources* selected Reid as one of the "25 Environmental Champions for 2004." She says that her age affects her environmental views as much as her gender does. "The younger generation of architects and engineers, those under thirty-five, has been raised with this awareness—we talked about recycling in grade school. It's integral to everything we do. Older people seem more comfortable with business as usual."

RIDER, Traci Rose
Traci Rose Rider earned her master's degree from Cornell University in early 2006 and is currently a Ph.D. student and lecturer at North Carolina State University in Raleigh. Her work as past chair and founding member of the Emerging Green Builders (EGB) Committee of the USGBC has earned her a USGBC leadership award, prompted *Dwell* to tap her as a "Nice Modernist," and landed her in the pages of *Vanity Fair*. "EGB isn't just engineers, architects, and contractors talking to each other," she says. "We have MBAs, developers, biologists, chemists, and food people involved, too. Diversity is key."

ROSE, Patty
Patty Rose is the executive director of GreenHOME, a Washington-based non-profit that promotes environmentally responsible affordable housing. "Strong storytelling skills are essential to moving your audience to making at least one new choice," she says. "We need a new version of *The Fountainhead*—one that redefines a contemporary Howard Roark as part of an interdisciplinary, collaborative, design team that contributes to designing sustainably."

ROBERTS, Jennifer

Jennifer Roberts writes books and articles about sustainable design. Her most recent book is *Good Green Kitchens*. "With my work, I'm trying to make the links between health and design more real to a large audience. There is really important work going on, such as the studies of human comfort and performance by Lisa Heschong, that needs to be translated to the public."

ROBINOWITZ, Beth

Beth Robinowitz is pursuing an M.B.A. at Columbia University and does strategic consulting with the Biomimicry Guild in Montana.

RODGERSON, Susan

Susan Rodgerson is an artist, teacher, and the executive/artistic director of Artists for Humanity, a nonprofit organization in Boston that prepares young people for professions in the arts. The project is now a recognized leader in youth arts and operates from the EpiCenter, the city's first LEED Platinum-certified building. According to Damon Butler, who was fourteen when he became one of three founding members: "Artists for Humanity gave me a voice when no one else would give me a thought."

ROMERO, Rocio

Missouri-based architect Rocio Romero has gotten attention in recent years for her highly compact prefab houses. "I've always been fascinated by how you make something really affordable," she says. "A lot of designers in school sit in a room and fantasize without any constraints. I wanted to do something more based in reality."

ROSENTHAL, Joyce

Joyce Rosenthal fell in love with interdisciplinary research while studying for a joint degree in environmental health and urban planning at Columbia University; she's now pursuing a Ph.D. and researching urban environmental and health issues. Before going back to school, she worked for Greenpeace in the U.S. and Germany (she introduced the chemist Michael Braungart to architect William McDonough), with the influential biologist Barry Commoner, and in a variety of activist and advocacy roles.

ROWE, Mary

Mary Rowe is the senior urban fellow with the Blue Moon Fund, a charitable foundation based in Charlottesville, Virginia. She lives in Toronto, Ontario, where for eight years she coordinated Ideas That Matter, a convening and publishing organization based on the work of Jane Jacobs, whom she came to know well. The focus of her work with the Blue

Moon Fund is to identify and communicate holistic processes that support the creation of sustained communities and human settlements. "We use words like *nurturing*—feminine words imply an agrarian sensibility. There's the notion of *husbandry*. I sometimes talk about how you *midwife* an idea." Of this book's topic, she confesses, "I probably wouldn't pick up a book about women and sustainability. That being said, anecdotally, does Western culture somehow support a linear, controlled thinking that predominantly occurs in men?"

RUBIO, Elva
Architect Elva Rubio is a principal and design director at the Chicago office of Gensler, one of the world's largest architecture firms. She teaches at the Illinois Institute of Technology and the University of Illinois-Chicago and encourages her students and colleagues to draw inspiration from nature. "I was raised in the South and lived around nature. It is part of your life down there. I've always been an ocean girl; I love palm trees and tropical environments. But I was never a Patagonia kind of girl. I loved Pucci and Halston but appreciated nature."

RUDDICK, Margie
Landscape architect Margie Ruddick considers natural systems as the starting point for design. She worked with Judith Heintz before running her own firm and then joining WRT, where she works today. Asked to name a current favorite project by someone else, Ruddick mentions the Ecotrust parking lot in Portland, Oregon. "It is a beautiful garden. But what's best is that you don't notice it. I love projects that don't call out that they are *design*, but that are something you would really love to experience every day."

RYAN, Janet
Janet Ryan is a clinical pastoral educator and since 2000 has served on the leadership council of Sisters, Servants of the Immaculate Heart of Mary in Monroe, Michigan. "All will thrive," she says, "if we do it together. As citizens of the earth, we will be diminished, if we continue to act out of individualism."

SALISBURY, Jill
Interior designer Jill Salisbury founded el: Environmental Language to create products and furniture that are both beautiful and respectful of the environment. "To me, the essence of sustainability is respect. Respect for nature and the well-being of people. It's about being mindful of what you're doing and how that's going to impact everyone else around you."

SANGUINETTI, Jennifer

Jennifer Sanguinetti is a mechanical engineer with the consulting firm Stantec, which recently acquired KEEN Engineering, where Sanguinetti led the Concepts Group. She seeks low-tech solutions for her sustainable designs, preferring to keep the design simpler with more natural systems. She comes from a family of engineers and went to an all-girls school that stressed the opportunities for women in male-dominated careers. She was attracted to sustainability issues within engineering. "It really gave my work purpose. This has been a big driver for me, because it makes the buildings much more meaningful than a nifty system or widget. Buildings have an impact on the environment, but they are fundamentally about people."

SAUER, Leslie

Leslie Sauer, a founder emeritus of Andropogon Associates, is a pioneer in the field of restoring and managing native landscapes. She is an advocate for the use of native plants and has developed a number of innovative strategies for establishing native habitats. She is consulting on the Bowman's Hill Wildflower Preserve Plant Stewardship Index (PSI) to evaluate the Piedmont plant communities of the Delaware Valley region in Pennsylvania and New Jersey. The PSI is intended as an assessment tool to gauge the biological integrity of a site. The idea that has driven her work is not just to push native plants, but to look at what she calls "the whole site." This can be challenging for Americans, she says, because we generally do not feel native to our own land. "Andropogon has hired lots of foreigners," she says, "because people outside the U.S. have been thinking about this for years. Foreigners seem to view themselves as citizens of the world."

SCHOPF, Anne

Partner and director of design at Mahlum Architects, architect Anne Schopf has led teams on many award winning projects. She has taught at the University of Washington and frequently speaks at conferences about sustainable design. "We are in a very male business," she says. "Until recently, I kept my femaleness away from the workplace. But I'm coming to understand that bringing that side of myself to the work can be a strength. Focusing on spirit and joy can help motivate people, but it's still difficult to tiptoe into a 'feminine' way of talking."

SCHWENNSEN, Kate

Architect and educator Kate Schwennsen is dean of the School of Design at Iowa State University. She was President of the AIA in 2006—only the second woman to hold the post. "For years I refused to think of myself as a woman architect," she says. "But

I have come to believe that being a woman architect means I need to accept additional responsibilities. We may have a greater sense of a moral imperative and may be more willing to address that in our work. Maybe women are more concerned about future generations. That's what sustainability is."

SIEGAL, Jennifer
Architect Jennifer Siegal's prefab work was initially inspired by the sense of community she saw in trailer parks and in Bedouin communities in the Middle East. She founded Los Angeles-based Office of Mobile Design to focus on "portable, demountable, and relocatable structures." She strives for an aesthetic that is strong but not loud. "I think a building should have a quietness about it—it becomes the background of your life. Someone like Frank Gehry is important to my generation, but I don't want to emulate him. I want to create something more serene."

SIMON, Lynn
Lynn Simon has run her own consulting firm in San Francisco, Lynn Simon Associates, since 1994. "She was one of the first in the country to do green consulting," says USGBC founder David Gottfried, who had earlier hired Simon to help him in the USGBC's early years. Simon worked with architect Marsha Maytum's team on the Thoreau Center for Sustainability at the Presidio in the early 1990s, which was a benchmark project for materials research and sustainable design melding with preservation. "Lynn is a good spokesperson," Gottfried says. "I think she has influenced lots of people."

SIMONS, Nina
Nina Simons is co-executive director of Collective Heritage Institute and has been co-producer of the Bioneers Conference since 1990. Previously, she was director of regional marketing for Odwalla, Inc., where she implemented a community-based and mission-driven marketing plan. *Utne Reader* named her a visionary in 1996. In 2002, she produced a retreat for diverse women leaders called UnReasonable Women for the Earth, to consider the possibilities of a women's movement with environment at its center. She believes that many of the unsustainable aspects of contemporary society are rooted in unproductive patterns. "We have a tendency to factionalize—to create false separations between people and ideas. We need to get past this, and part of that involves working toward balance between the feminine and the masculine." Simons says humanity's challenged relationship with the natural world is a product of cultural bias. "There are some deep similarities between how we have treated the earth, women, and people of color."

SMITH, Sylvia

Architect Sylvia Smith directs FXFowle Architects' educational and cultural studio. She was the managing principal on the greening of the Lion House for the Wildlife Conservation Society at the Bronx Zoo, one of the zoo's original Beaux Arts buildings and a New York City landmark. "We are trying to start the conversation early," she says. "We are talking to our clients about right-sizing. This includes looking for ways to use time and space in new ways."

SNOONIAN, Deborah

Writer Deborah Snoonian was trained as an engineer and she brings that perspective to her work covering sustainable design and eco-friendly living. For five years she was a senior editor of *Architectural Record*, where she covered design, green building, and technology, and helped conceive *GreenSource*, McGraw-Hill's magazine for the sustainable design community. Snoonian says that most architecture magazines don't really understand green design or how to cover it. "The magazines are very image-driven. Photographs rule, and it's difficult to portray sustainability in a photograph. So it isn't seen as sexy. When you try to illustrate green strategies through charts and diagrams, people's eyes glaze over." Now managing editor at *Plenty*, a lifestyle magazine, she writes about eco-friendly homes and design and appears regularly on TV and radio to discuss environmental issues.

SNOW, Julie

Architect Julie Snow runs her own firm in Minneapolis and engages sustainability as a part of the design process. "An idea will evolve out of one system and create a dialogue with another," she says of that process, which can be complex. Light is a big driver in her work. "In a northern climate, you have to have a profound respect for light, especially since there can be so little of it in winter. That respect shapes the architecture."

SOLOMON, Nancy

Nancy Solomon is an architectural journalist. She has written on architectural technology and practice for many publications including *Architecture* and *Architectural Record*. She served as editor of the AIA's Environmental Resource Guide. She is now editing a book celebrating the AIA's 150th anniversary. She believes that sustainability really comes down to personal choices. "Ultimately, a more sustainable world will be achieved only by the participation of each and every individual at the most personal level of day-to-day living."

SOSNOWCHIK, Katie

Katie Sosnowchik worked at trade magazine publisher L.C. Clark in the 1980s, through which she started *Green@Work* magazine and the EnvironDesign conference. According to Penny Bonda, who recently co-authored *Sustainable Commercial Interiors* with Sosnowchik, "Katie is directly responsible for introducing and promoting green design to thousands of designers."

STELMACK, Annette

Annette Stelmack is the design director of Denver-based Associates III Interior Design in Denver, Colorado. With Kari Foster and Debbie Hindman, she is co-author of *Sustainable Residential Interior Design and Turning Green:* A Guide to Becoming a Green Design Firm.

STEINGRABER, Sandra

Ecologist, author, and cancer survivor, Sandra Steingraber is an expert on the environmental links to cancer and reproductive health. She is a distinguished visiting scholar at Ithaca College in Ithaca, New York. Her books include *Living Downstream* and *Having Faith: An Ecologist's Journey to Motherhood.* In the former, she writes: "Our bodies, too, are living scrolls of sorts. What is written there—inside the fibers of our cells and chromosomes—is a record of our exposure to environmental contaminants. Like the rings of trees, our tissues are historical documents that can be read by those who know how to decipher the code." In 1999, the Sierra Club heralded Steingraber as "the new Rachel Carson," an honor that Steingraber takes seriously. "From the right to know and the duty to inquire flows the obligation to act," she writes. Environmentalist and author Paul Hawken says that Steingraber's contribution is vast. "She brilliantly summarizes the research and makes the compelling case for action."

STEPHENS, Eileen

Eileen Stephens studied mechanical engineering at MIT before earning her MBA from Wharton School of Business. She attended the Biomimicry Guild's workshop in Costa Rica.

STEPHENSON, Karen

A self-professed "corporate anthropologist," Karen Stephenson is the president of New York-based NetForm International, which maps and measures social capital in organizations and businesses. She has taught at Harvard's Graduate School of Design and has worked closely with many designers and architects. "A designer sees the shape of space the same way I see the shape of culture. The challenge with either discipline is to render these things visible. The shape of culture interacts with the shape of space."

SUSANKA, Sarah

Architect Sarah Susanka is the bestselling author of the *Not So Big House* series, a guide to "building better, not bigger." In 2000, *Newsweek* selected her as a "top newsmaker" for that year, and in 2001, *Fast Company* named her in their debut list of "Fast 50" innovators. According to the *Washington Post*, Susanka "shows how to downsize the dream house without diminishing the dream." She says, "It's not just about sustainability—it's about making places that inspire people."

SZENASY, Susan

A recognized authority on design and sustainability, Susan Szenasy is editor-in-chief of *Metropolis*, where she recently started the magazine's "Next Generation Design Prize" program, which focuses on innovation among young designers. As professor of design ethics at New York's Parsons School of Design, she works to instill the values of responsible sustainability on the next generation. She is the force behind *Metropolis* events, such as the Tropical Green conference on sustainable building in tropical zones and the International Contemporary Furniture Fair. She says her participation in the women's movement in the 1960s has given her firm ideas about labeling and segregationist thinking that play into her views on sustainability. "I don't want to see environmentalism as something separate— that makes it easy for people to dismiss it, or leave it on the margins. Environmentalism is *so* important. We're talking about life!"

TALKINGTON, Jane

Jane Talkington is pursuing one of the first doctorate degrees in sustainability offered in the U.S.—through the Environmental Science Program at Oklahoma State University. After carrying a child at forty-two, she began to reflect on sustainability in a more personal way. "Once you sustain one life, you want to sustain it all. All life becomes sacred, and that philosophy permeates every action and decision. The opposite of sustaining life is extinction, so the stakes are rather high."

TALEN, Emily

As associate professor of urban and regional planning at the University of Illinois, Emily Talen studies the spatial patterns of American cities, investigating accessibility, spatial equity, sprawl and ideal urban form. She says the idea of a "sustainable" community relates to making places that feel like home, but what feels like home varies from person to person, especially by sex. "To my husband, home is refuge," she says. "To women, home is something else. It's the whole community."

TILT, Anni

Architect Anni Tilt runs Arkin/Tilt Architects with her husband, David Arkin. Their work has received design and sustainable design awards, including the AIA Committee on the Environment Top Ten Green Projects award.

TOCKE, Rose

The ebullient Rose Tocke is a biologist and serves as director of community dynamics with the Biomimicry Guild in Montana, focusing on expanding the research and product development capabilities of the organization.

TODD, Joel Ann

Joel Ann Todd is an environmental consultant and vice chair of the USGBC's Technical and Scientific Advisory Committee. She has written widely on materials assessment (for the AIA's *Environmental Resource Guide*), innovative concepts for environmental life cycle assessment (for the *Journal of Life Cycle Assessment* and the U.S. Environmental Protection Agency), and building performance measurement (for the Federal Energy Management Program and the National Renewable Energy Laboratory). She has worked with public sector clients such as the National Park Service and the U.S. Department of Energy, and she co-authored a handbook on charrette facilitation, published by the DOE. Todd says she's more interested in changing minds than she is one-off building projects. "I am really fascinated with how the developing and developed worlds look at this issue differently," she says. "I believe that we can learn a great deal from how the developing world is trying to fit the social into the overall picture."

TUCKER, Mary

Mary Tucker serves as the supervising environmental services specialist for the City of San Jose, California, and manages its green building program. She is a member of the board of directors of the USGBC and past chair of the American Solar Energy Society. She is the proud owner of a 2.6 kW photovoltaic system on her 1909 craftsman bungalow home, a net zero home.

UBBELOHDE, Susan

Susan Ubbelohde is a tenured faculty member of the architecture department at the University of California, Berkeley, and a founding partner of Loisos+Ubbelohde, a design, research and consulting firm in Oakland, CA. The firm focuses on daylighting, energy analysis, and evaluation of building performance and has collaborated with such architects as Herzog + De Meuron, the Renzo Piano Workshop, and William McDonough + Partners. Ubbelohde runs the artificial sky simulator at Berkeley's Building Science Laboratory and she has been director of the Regional Daylighting Center at the University of Minnesota. She has received the Progressive Architecture Research Award and the Council for International Exchange of Scholars/Fulbright Indo-American Fellowship to support research on buildings' thermal performance in India. "The hardest work in doing good consulting," she says, "is getting the team to ask the right questions. Once you ask the right questions, you can find the right tools to answer those questions."

VITTORI, Gail

Gail Vittori is co-director of the Center for Maximum Potential Building Systems (CMPBS) in Austin, TX. *Metropolis* magazine calls her and her husband, Pliny Fisk, "pioneers of the sustainability movement" who have dedicated their lives to "fostering a more symbiotic relationship between architecture and the natural environment." Vittori also co-authored the influential *Green Guide for Healthcare Construction.* "Women have always played the role of protecting community health and welfare," she says, claiming that this public role naturally expands on the private role of women in the family. "Men generally don't think about what their kids are doing between breakfast and returning home from school," she tells us. "Women do." A former colleague, Greg Jackson, says, "Pliny would shoot off into space if Gail didn't ground him." Alex Wilson of BuildingGreen's *Environmental Building News* concurs. "Pliny is brilliant," he offers, "but it is Gail who is able to give form to the ideas and make them into something that can be implemented." He calls her the Center's "salvation."

WERNER, Jane

Jane Werner is executive director of the Children's Museum of Pittsburgh. "Sometimes you can't afford to do all the right things," she says. "You do what you can do and hope to do more the next time."

WILLIAMS, Kath

Kath Williams, president of the World Green Building Council, consults and speaks widely on sustainability issues. She has been an integral part of the USGBC and has served as the program chair for the Greenbuild conference. Consultant David Gottfried says of Williams, "She has a very broad vision for how to create a really integrated project." Gottfried says her work on the global scale is significant, especially in the developing world. "She is like a goddess in India. No one can work a country like Kath." Says Williams, "Americans are always in a rush. We don't have a strong past. We're such a young country, so we don't have as much of a tradition in architecture to draw on, compared to a place like India. They have so much 'green design' in their history, and culturally they have a better attitude toward the environment. And they move at a slower pace. In the U.S., we expect immediate results. We need a longer time horizon."

WILLIAMS, Lisa

Poet Lisa Williams teaches writing and literature at Centre College in Kentucky and has won the Rome Prize for Literature. She worked closely with William McDonough and Michael Braungart on crafting the language of their book, *Cradle to Cradle* (2002), as well as their earlier *Atlantic Monthly* article, "The Next Industrial Revolution" (1998). The experience awakened her environmental awareness but also transformed her work, she recalls, "I stopped writing poems about myself and starting writing about pre-human phases of the earth's evolution—the struggle of the earth to create itself. It was an awakening to the creativity of the planet. I wanted readers to see their own connections to the earth." She thinks of her poetry as "giving voice to the earth."

WINTER, Catriona Campbell

Catriona Campbell Winter is a project engineer with Clark Construction and promotes the growth of that firm's high performance building group. She earned her master's degree in architecture at the University of Virginia and is serving as an adjunct advisory group member to AIA's Committee on the Environment.

WOODS, Medora

Medora Woods describes herself as a "roving, trouble-making grandmother." She has been a high school English teacher, a practicing attorney, a bank vice president, a Jungian analyst, and a writer. She spends time each month at her cabin on the North Shore of Lake Superior.

WRIGHT, Tammi

Tammi Wright recently graduated magna cum laude from the architecture program at Cal Poly San Luis Obispo, where she minored in the award-winning Sustainable Environments program.

YEN, Jeannette

Biologist Jeannette Yen is the director of Georgia Tech's new Center for Biologically Inspired Design. "The term sustainability is new to me. I study organisms; of course, I want them to live! If that is sustainability, then that works for me."

We are the women who
will transform the world.

ROBIN MORGAN, FROM *A WOMEN'S CREED*